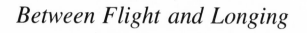

Between Flight and Longing

Señorita Ana Teresa Parra-Sanojo,
Teresa de la Parra, 1924

BETWEEN FLIGHT AND LONGING

The Journey of
Teresa de la Parra

BY LOUIS ANTOINE LEMAÎTRE

VANTAGE PRESS
New York / Washington / Altanta
Los Angeles / Chicago

Between Flight and Longing: The Journey of Teresa de la Parra *is
published on the fiftieth anniversary of Teresa de la Parra's death.*

FIRST EDITION

Copyright © 1986 by Louis Antoine Lemaître

Published by Vantage Press, Inc.
516 West 34th Street, New York, New York 10001

Manufactured in the United States of America
ISBN: 0-533-06649-2

Library of Congress Catalog Card No.: 85-90149

To Elena Mederos,
Henry J. Perkinson,
Norma H. Thompson, and
Stasia M. Ziobrowski

My deepest gratitude and appreciation
to Phyllis Taylor and Michael Friedman
for editing this book.

Contents

Preface:
An Aristocracy of the Spirit—
Portrait of Teresa de la Parra

Photographs show her as a woman of quite extraordinary beauty, but Teresa de la Parra's beauty went far beyond the purely physical. From her eyes shone what can only be described as an aristocracy of the spirit—a quiet assurance and elegance that Lydia Cabrera says made Parra "different from any other human being" she had known. Parra dressed with simple but exquisite refinement, in soft, colorful fabrics, her lovely face frequently crowned by a charming, floppy-brimmed hat. In her childhood, friends described her with lavish praise, using such descriptions as "adorable as a fairytale princess" and "marked with the fabled charm of royalty," and this youthful promise was more than fulfilled by her mature beauty. Perhaps the best comparison is to one of the exotic birds that Parra so admired, for she was all color and brilliant contrasts—her emerald-green eyes, dazzlingly clear complexion, white teeth, and black hair were complemented by a grace of movement that combined swiftness and softness. Clearly she was an arresting figure, and not surprisingly, her personality was as striking as her physical appearance.

On the one hand, Parra was a modest woman, never flaunting her exceptional beauty nor her obvious spiritual superiority and even referring, late in her life, to her biography as "nothing extraordinary." On the other hand, she had a quiet sense of her self-worth, emanating, Cabrera says, from the fact, that Parra considered her aristocracy a spiritual value, which came from her familial antecedents. Doubtless, her ability to deal with life's petty difficulties calmly and philosophically came from this same source, for Parra was a true diplomat. She never became upset with such annoyances as disrupted travel plans, difficult servants, or the inevitable frustrations attendant on dealing with publishers. In fact, she was a charming woman, who dealt with all people with openness and tolerance.

Given this tolerance of others, Parra's corresponding independence in her own life and actions is not surprising. She cared little about criticism of her personal life, describing herself as a woman of "independent thought." This independence of spirit, like her beauty, was evident early in her childhood when, as she said, she was "a person apart from the group," pursuing her own interests rather than those of the crowd. Yet there was one area where she could be hurt: her work. She was deeply distressed by the initial reaction to *Ifigenia* and worked diligently to disperse misconceptions about the book, finally becoming disgusted by the slurs on her that emanated from these misunderstandings of her work. After all, she pointed out to Rafael Carias, she was a woman who loved *"tout le monde,"* who judged others by personal experience rather than on hearsay, and she expected the same from others.

This "love of everyone" was, indeed, not an exaggeration. Parra took enormous pleasure in helping others, both on a personal and on a political level. She was a good listener, concerned with others rather than herself. However, though apparently at ease in large gatherings, she preferred small gatherings of family and friends, reserving her greatest love and loyalty for those closest to her.

Parra's intense involvement with family began early in her youth and continued throughout her life. As a solitary, strong-willed child, she developed her first powerful connection with her father, whom she clearly emulated, following him around the estate on horseback and determinedly shunning the "normal" pursuits of girls in favor of outdoor games. She later described herself as having "an ironic sensibility like her father," and because she felt all experiences deeply, the events of her childhood affected her profoundly. This can be clearly seen in her obsessive repetitive references to the experience of her father, who chased his daughters away because their outside play disturbed him so much. She refers to this event in *Memorias de Mama Blanca* together with the comment that "each time a girl was born, a curtain came down between him and his new daughter."

Obviously, Parra's involvement with her father was fraught with ambivalence, and such ambivalence was doubtless exacerbated even further by the tales told her by the female members of her family. Of these, her maternal grandmother was a powerful influence, constantly telling vivid stories of the trials and suffering that had befallen women in the family in the past. Again, it is the women of her family who ultimately had the strongest effect on Parra's development, both as a writer and a woman. Not only her grandmother, but her great-grand-aunt Teresa Soublette-Buroz exerted a tremendous spiritual and intellectual influence on Parra. These influences were strengthened by her friendship with the nun

Sister Maria Teresa del Corazon de Jesus and also, somewhat paradoxically, by Parra's powerful distaste for her early schooling. The strict rules, regulations, and pointless drills simply fostered her independent will and spirit. "I must follow my inner inclinations, for otherwise I am not displaying my own vitality," she said. Similarly, her early acceptance of Catholicism was soon to be tempered by her awareness of the ways in which the church contributed to the oppression of women.

Thus Parra's childhood experiences inevitably thrust her toward action, and her ability to instantly grasp and understand the essentials of a situation, together with a natural and exceptional talent for writing, provided an obvious forum for her protest. Of *Ifigenia*, she said it was "the only way she could protest without having to scream loudly from major street corners of Caracas," and her strong will in the face of opposition made her an excellent force for change. She had enormous integrity and her dedication to her work was absolute. As she put it, her work was "simply and without trancendental pretensions, a pure depiction of the female soul at this moment in history."

Such a powerful assessment of her own work indicates an admirable combination of self-esteem and integrity. In her perception of herself as a good, worthwhile person of strength and independence, she was the ideal example for women of her time, not only in her work, but in her life. We might compare her to a woman she herself deeply admired—Doña Manuelita—who lived her life exactly as she saw fit and had "her own code of morality to which she was true and faithful to her death."

Yet Parra, despite great strength, beauty, and intelligence, was also human, and a close look at her life presents some intriguing contradictions—contradictions that ultimately add to rather than detract from the fascination and appeal of this exceptional woman. Moreover, it is Parra's ability to prevail in the face of her flaws and weaknesses that, in the end, moves us the most. For example, she was a vibrant, strong-willed woman, whose brilliant mind must have frequently pushed her to disagree when with those with less perceptive opinions. In fact, there is some evidence that she had an argumentative streak and used her sharp tongue when debating. Cabrera describes her as someone who "found it difficult to become annoyed."

Another facet of Parra's personality is her physical sense of esthetics. This is evident in her love of comfort, her beauty and love of dress, and the charm of the decor with which she surrounded herself. Despite this Cabrera depicts her as being "unaware of her sexual drives." We can only speculate on this apparent paradox. Did Parra perhaps suppress her sexuality in the interests of presenting an example of strength and independence that was beyond criticism? Or perhaps those who knew her well are simply unwilling to reveal a private side of a very modest and proud woman. We shall never know—nor, perhaps, should we.

What we *can* surmise is that this sensuousness was sublimated in her love of the good life. She was certainly a spendthrift, as Cabrera can testify, and Cabrera is also known to have said that Parra was more interested in enjoying life than in peforming its duties, laughingly comparing her friend to the sloth Parra had once given her. Such an assessment of a woman who clearly never shirked from the demands of her calling is charming and infinitely appealing, particularly in view of Parra's own, apparently straightfaced, comment that she despised the work her craft demanded of her and preferred instead to travel.

Quite obviously none of these flaws, if we can even call them such, stood in the way of Parra's dedication to her work. In fact, she frequently turned them to her advantage. Her refusal to marry—not surprising, given what marriage meant to a woman of her time—and her apparent lack of involvement in any romantic attachments gave her the freedom to pursue her work without distraction. Thus her work was her life. Similarly, her exceptional diplomacy and self-control enabled her to deal effectively with the most difficult of people in the most adverse situations. Finally, her love of the good life can surely be seen as nothing more than a charming, harmless indulgence in a life of superior dedication to duty.

This dedication was never more apparent than after the discovery of Parra's illness. Her first response to her illness was absolutely characteristic: a calm resignation to God's will, together with a determined delight in the beautiful surroundings of Leysin—surroundings that clearly reminded her of happier times in the countryside of her homeland. Her second response was a desire to use her sharply inquiring mind both to find out more about her illness and to investigate the philosophy of mysticism. This tendency toward mysticism was not surprising, given her lifelong involvement with her interior life.

Her experiments with Coué during her illness—leading to "moral regeneration, interior happiness and goodwill toward others"—led this former lover of the good life to become more and more repelled by excessive comfort and luxury; her physical needs seemed less important, and she finally, though with a charmingly human regret, described herself as "a woman who did not need anything."

Yet, despite this involvement with mysticism and the stress of her illness, Parra's literary interest remained strong. "If I would start writing again, how happy I would be," she said at one point, longing to be well enough to write a book. Here again her longstanding concern for others was paramount, for the book was to be one that would give greater understanding of her illness, thus providing comfort to other patients. In fact, less than a year before her death, she published two articles; however, they were not on the subject of her illness, but rather on a topic closest to her heart—the oppression of women.

It must have been devastating for Lydia Cabrera to watch her beautiful, vibrant friend gradually debilitated by tuberculosis—particularly in the face of some highly questionable medical treatment. Yet clearly Cabrera's assessment of Parra holds true even, or perhaps particularly, in the face of extreme adversity. Parra seldom, if ever, complained or blamed others, maintaining a loving concern for others throughout her illness. This concern was evident both on the smallest personal level, in her going out of her way to spare the feelings of a fellow patient when it was clear that his translation of her work was inferior, as well as on the larger political scale, in her continuing and compassionate involvement in the rights of women.

Though Cabrera was helpless to save her friend, she spent much of Parra's last years with her and, in fact, was there at the time of her death. Parra's uncomplaining acceptance of the inevitable, coupled with a courage consistent with the bravery of her life, is nowhere more evident than in her quiet response to Cabrera's offer of food or drink shortly before she died: "I will soon eat a little earth." By then she must have been extremely tired of suffering, yet this suffering and her tragic defeat by illness at such an early age must be placed clearly in the context of a life of triumphant struggle to alleviate the suffering of others.

In the end, Parra is at her most potent as an example to other women—for words, no matter how powerful, are merely words if they are not backed up by action. And Teresa de la Parra's life was one of words in action. Like Doña Manuelita, she lived for convictions as surely as any of us can. This "true aristocrat" was capable both of brilliant intellectual debate with the finest minds of her time and, at the same time, displaying an earthy empathy with women of all classes, with the common suffering and oppression that knows no status, no wealth—only sex. This wise and strong-willed woman, beautiful as a "fairytale princess" yet strong as the revolutionary women she so admired, stands finally as a stunning, loving model for women of all races, of all classes, for all time.

Introduction

In writing of the relationships between the biography of a writer and his or her works, we are trying to give substance to shadows cast by each in the light of the other. Recently, the question of the nature of these relationships has become more acute as women's writings have been explored in terms of their complex awareness of and intimate connections to lived daily life. The object of much innovative critical attention, fiction by women seems often to differ most markedly from that by men in its openness to biographical interpretation.

Teresa de la Parra gave substance in her art to the shadowed lives of those South American women who were the unsung heroines of her country's foundation and growth. In creating from her own profound sense of conflict and paradox, she discovered a voice that spoke for all, recognized and confirmed as such by her immediate popularity, on the one hand, and notoriety, on the other.

The writing of women has often reflected the discontinuous and oppressed nature of their lives; their fiction seems more frequently to spring from the intimate and personal, the daily life rather than the large measures of men's history. The autobiographical tradition of women, as the examination of bibliographies from several countries will show, is usually expressed in diaries, journals, and notebooks rather than the solid, monumental volumes left by men. Parra's two novels—one a "diary," the other "memoirs"—attest to a tradition of discontinuity in women's writing; the form is analogous to the fragmented, interrupted, and enclosed nature of women's lives. These forms are not accidental: The lives of women are *structurally* different from those of men, and their expression accords with this difference.

Although she denied the correspondences between her own life and the story of her first heroine, Maria Eugenia, Parra came in her second novel to validate through the recreation in memory of her own past a cultural past with which she had often felt at odds. In accepting the autobiographical roots of *Mama Blanca*, Parra was not in any way authorizing a one-to-one correspondence between life and art, but accepting herself as the vehicle of a consciousness she had perceived as buried in her country's history. The play between the facts of a life, a fiction, and our reading leaves us on treacherous, shifting ground. Parra reconstructs not only the forms of her own life, but the life of her country and, more than that, elucidates, as Virginia Woolf did, the inner life of women in an overtly patriarchal world.

Like her contemporary Woolf, Parra was privileged and beautiful; unlike Woolf, she had no direct access to the modern sensibility sweeping across Europe, no milieu of intellectual equality and exchange of ideas with men. In her novels, Parra expressed the experience of the Latin-American woman of any class, oppressed by both church and state alike. That her distrust of the fixed, immutable reality handed down by the patriarchal system and Catholic dogma was tuned into the current of European modernism may explain her success in Paris, but it was secondary to her need to speak with the voice of her countrywomen.

As in so many artists' lives, there is a paradox at the heart of Parra that seems to be the dynamic of her art. Rich, aristocratic, and devoutly Catholic, she embodied perfectly that culture she found so stifling. That conflict of loyalties to country, family, and self may explain her disavowal of the inferences drawn by her readers from the verisimilitude of Maria Eugenia's story in *Ifigenia*. Indeed, Maria Eugenia's choice of a loveless marriage might be seen as the reverse image of the reality of her creator, whose life retained an enigmatic and solitary quality until her poetic and lonely death. In *Mama Blanca*, Venezuela's own mythology, summed up in the strange character of Cochocho, enabled Parra to come to a more secure resolution of the conflicts that divided her, uniting her deep religious sense with the firm conviction of the truths of female experience.

What is it, though, that causes an individual to develop sensibilities so at odds with her environment? In common with so many of her European counterparts, Teresa de la Parra was existentially homeless, a true representative of a modern sensibility that has become familiar in the North, but is perhaps surprising to discover with such similar contours in the South. In telling the story of herself, she returned an unspoken history to her country, weaving together a mythic consciousness with a religious sense that permitted her a perspective at once inside and without the culture she sought to depict. In those obscure lives Parra explored in her later years when she was searching for an ideal role model, she found, as Woolf did, a story buried by ages of male history. Like Joyce's

Daedalus, Parra set about forging the "uncreated conscience" of her country. Ultimately, she was expressing the rage of humanity's silent half, of women.

In obscure lives, the lives of mystics and visionaries—the outsiders' stories—might be found the seeds of a new conscience. The unwritten part of Parra's life is what we attempt to elucidate here, as she sought to write in the unwritten history of her people. In the interstices between biographical data and fiction, the imagination of the reader supplies substance for the shadows, a sense of the soul of the artist.

Teresa de la Parra wove together the deep contradictions of her own life—family, society, self—and in doing so created a fabric that transcends all three. She achieves, in speaking from her own experience, a universal voice that is the modern exploring consciousness; she uses the single life to illuminate a general truth, shining its light into murky corners to complete a picture left unfinished by "official" history.

In reading Parra, her life and art, we must follow her guide and eschew the complacency of "facts" and a fixed reality. Her life was fully a life of the imagination, of myth, and lived experience transmuted into art. To reconstruct from her glimmers and shadows the sense of the life of the writer, we must remain always conscious that the reality we create is provisional, a light shot into the darkness momentarily, a light that, while it illuminates, will produce further shadows, heretofore unnoticed.

Louis Antoine Lemaitre
Long Island City, N.Y.
April 1986

CHAPTER I

Parra and Venezuela
in Years of Innocence

Word, Deed, and War in Parra's Venezuela

Teresa de la Parra was born into a world of privilege. Her environment was like a sheltered garden; its tropical profusion of sense impressions, the passionate diversity of its denizens were the very flavor of Latin America. Her childhood was a landscape crowded with the colorful and heroic ghosts of her ancestry—Basque adventurers, Spanish generals, and blue-blooded duennas—and the struggles, sorrows, and accomplishments of three races whose collected histories constitute South America's grand clash of extremes. On the plantation land surrounding Caracas, Venezuela, behind the crumbling walls of the old colonial order, Teresa the child grew to adolescence. Oblivious to war and commerce and innocent of the Tree of Modern Knowledge, all in her midst, she became learned in the language of nature's balance and barter and beholden to its wisdom.

She was not born here, but rather in Paris, on October 5, 1889.[1] Baptized Ana Teresa del Rosario Parra-Sanojo, she was the first daughter and fourth child of Rafael Parra and Isabel Sanojo. Rafael, carrying out his duties as consul general to Berlin, Germany, in Paris that year, found himself suddenly without a job when insurgents toppled the military government of Venezuela sponsoring his post, and in 1890 he took his family back to his native Caracas, where he could manage the family sugar plantation.

Tazon was the name of the hacienda, and it has since been destroyed, along with most structures immanent and overtly no longer useful according to the aims of the industrial age. Like the colonial era itself, the

1

No 18

BAPTÊME

DE

Herman
Ana Teresa del Rosario

L'an mil huit cent quatre-vingt-dix le _premier février_ a été baptisé e
Ana Teresa del Rosario
née le _cinq Octobre dernier_
fille de _Rafael Parra Hernaiz_
et d _Isabel Sanojo de Parra_
demeurant _avenue Wagram 26 bis_
Le Parrain a été _Antonio Parra_
avenue Kléber 18
La Marraine a été _dela Heyy_
rue Chaillot 76

Lesquels ont signé avec nous

S. M. Parra   _Lola Reyes_   _Isabel J. de Parra_
Dolores Eche... _P. y A. R. Parra Hernaiz_   _Hernandez_

Teresa de la Parra

Teresa de la Parra's certificate of baptism

Parra plantation exists now only as dream, inviolate as the paradisiacal Caráquenian valley, rising 3,000 feet above the tropical heat that ravages both the Caribbean coast to the north and the coffee lands of Aragua to the south.

Lola Reyes, the godmother of Teresa de la Parra

Toward the end of the nineteenth century, when Teresa was born, the colonial heartbeat still powered the household, through the steady workings of the women, their lifetimes of labor in isolation, and their stories of warning and fanciful flight guiding generation after generation of girl children into adulthoods of maternity and marriage. Teresa guarded those stories as treasures. She retained in her memory the figure of her maternal grandmother, the grand storyteller Mercedes Ezpelosin, gate-keeper to her childhood past and even beyond, to the past in which the

Mercedes Ezpelosin-Tovar, the wife of Luis Sanojo and the grandmother of Teresa de la Parra.

4

family forebears saw their glory subside and their dispossession come to pass. "Without being guilty of conceit," Teresa wrote years later, "of all her grandchildren I was the favorite."[2] Rising to meet the attentions of her grandmother with riveted soul, Teresa the child received an abiding love of letters "accompanied by the sound of the beater in the bowl" and an indelible portrait of life in the aftermath of Venezuela's secession from Spain, which was a "sad, dark era" for Teresa's aristocratic ancestors, "without heroes, battles, statues, or historians other than the old homes with crude windows that are rapidly disappearing." It was full of the pain and sorrow of lost wealth and lost honor, the humiliation of servitude: like the Indian and African before him, the Spanish *hidalgo* also had lost a kingdom, adding his voice to the chorus of the dispossessed after independence. Humiliations suffered by a particular family would be told and retold, with the hope that the telling might one day inspire and secure the vengeance so necessary to the possession of honor.

The traditions of both the Spanish and the Indian had accorded ancestors an important role, although to differing extents and emphases. Where the Spaniards venerated their family's history and lived a code of honor inextricably linked thereto, the Indians worshipped their ancestors as deities, believing them to exert a tenacious influence on the living from beyond the grave. The tone of Indian tales had always been one full of pain and sorrow, only ringing with a more specifically oriented bitterness after the Spanish conquest. A sixteenth-century friar wrote that the Aztec songs were "so plaintive that the mere sound and the dance brought a feeling of sadness." The Quechua tribe provides another example: ". . . More reserved and bound by tradition than any other people, they possess the gift of tears and the cult of memory. Guardians of mysterious tombs and forever mourning among these cyclopean ruins, their favorite diversion and bitter consolation are to sing about the woes of their history and the poignant grief that lies in their hearts."[3]

Teresa de la Parra belonged to the most influential class of Creoles, or South-American–born Spanish descendants, in Venezuela, called the Mantuans. Socially they were as exclusive as a royal line; each marriage had to maintain, if not improve, the participants' financial standing, as well as preserve their children's racial purity. Like any privileged class, the Mantuans were exempt from many of the limitations the culture imposed on their less fortunate compatriots. Partly because of the exposure to the new ideas of the French and North American revolutions that their sophistication allowed them, they nourished in their ranks the chief instigators of discontent with Spanish rule, as well as those most loyal to it. Under the influence of theorists Francisco de Miranda and his disciple Simon Bolívar, some of the Mantuan men and women formed clandestine societies where they studied the taboo philosophical texts of human rights roaring out of England, France, and the United States. Bolívar's charisma was strong. He succeeded in magnetizing some Creoles around the idea of autonomy from Spain, but polarized others against himself, so that within the upper classes, as occurred elsewhere, two ideologies crystallized: liberal and conservative. Originally a liberal was simply for independence and a conservative against independence. After the war, the division within the upper class remained, but the ideology was more complex: the landed conservatives stressed their church affiliation and resisted change of any kind; the liberals, living mostly within the growing urban centers, placed their religious trust in materialism and industrial progress.

There were many contradictions at the root of the colonies' break from Mother Spain, which surfaced not only within Teresa de la Parra's family, but within other families as well. Sometimes political affiliations were felt strongly enough to drive a permanent wedge between relatives, as was the case in the United States during the Civil War. Each of Teresa's parents had an ancestor belonging to the most prominent Mantuan family of Caracas, de Tovar. From the 1600s, when the first de Tovar was sponsored by a Spanish bishop to travel to the colonies, until independence, members of the family consistently and conspicuously held the office of mayor of Caracas.[4] Through royal mandate, they were liberally granted land and political power, and by 1771, the King of Spain had bestowed the title of Count on Martin de Tovar y Blanco. Count de Tovar must have been grateful for such favor. During the first murmurings of Creole discontent, he authored a manifesto of Mantuan loyalty to Spain, but when all the chips of the war were down, his politically astute son, Don Manuel Felipe, recognized the sea change and declared himself pro-liberation and pro-Bolívar; Manuel's reward was to become the first president of Venezuela after the war ended. The family's wealth remained so great that even one hundred years later, the people of Caracas had a saying: "If it's a big house, it belongs to Tovar."[5]

Other Tovars were not so fortunate. One of the count's granddaughters was Doña Francisca de Tovar, the mother of Mercedes and protagonist of many of the sad tales Teresa heard at Tazon. "Mama Panchita," as she was known to her family, had remained to the end rabidly "godo"—this a liberal epithet directed at conservative Creoles, referring to the barbaric, backward Goth tribe of Northern Europe that had pillaged

6

the falling Roman Empire. She had begun her life in the shelter of her country's highest social and economic class: "She had slaves to fan and dress her, rich laces, cashmere shawls. . . . I think that Mama Panchita never opened a book except for her missal for 10 minutes at Sunday mass, and indolent, frivolous and graceful with her face framed by curls like that of her contemporary Josefina Beauharnais, she did not display any greater seriousness nor stricter circumspection than that displayed by a hummingbird in flight."[6]

Doña Francisca's trials began when political unrest came to revolution in Venezuela, and although her husband was "politically neutral," his enormous landholdings, Spanish-Basque lineage, and position as administrator for the notorious shipping monopoly Compañia Guipuzcoana hardly implied neutrality in the eyes of the new patriotic party, which promptly confiscated all of the family property and forced Don Francisco to flee the country. Mama Panchita remained to stage a one-woman battle against the new government, hoping thereby to regain her old colonial status. It was, after all, the only life she knew. Having no power in legal matters and suspected of loyalty to Spain, Doña Francisca Tovar was reduced to the life of a woman at the bottom of the social ladder, with its concomitant poverty and trouble.

There could have been no better example for Ana Teresa of the changeability of political seasons and the helplessness of a woman without male support. She learned frugality, but more important, she learned that a person born with all possible advantages could still lose everything. Though Mama Panchita was presumably not alone in being stripped of her wealth by the new regime, her misfortune at the hands of politicians seemed particularly cruel. Her aristocratic breeding and sense of personal dignity, neither trammeled nor touched by her enemies, inspired admiration in the eyes of her descendants and raised her sufferings to near-legend. A passage from one of Parra's 1930 lectures gives a remarkable portrait of the destitute but still proud Mama Panchita: she, ruined and alone, went to ask her first cousin Cristobal Mendoza, governor of Caracas, for mercy. He did not even look up from his work, but dismissed her, saying, "whoever is not with me, Panchita, is against me." Then came a trip on foot to La Guaira, a voyage by merchant vessel over a very rough sea, years of exile in Puerto Rico, sons dying in the flower of their youth, and finally, a return to Venezuela in complete ruin.[7]

Mama Panchita had been forewarned by her relatives not to marry a Spaniard, especially one of Basque origins and so deeply enmeshed in the web of the Compania Guipuzcoana. This shipping company had been installed by Charles II in 1728 as sole exporter of Venezuelan products to Europe. The growers of these products—valuable foodstuffs—were the families holding large parcels of land, and thus a most profitable alliance between producer and consumer cemented the power of the colonial economy over its dependent populations.

The Basque element in Parra's lineage offers a colorful backdrop against which that nomadic strain, driving her to love her travels and often lament her homelessness, takes on extra dimension; Parra herself would always place its origins within the restlessness of the modern era. Family shipping tales, usually told by her father, had been the first to impress on her imagination the power of the sea to create those states of spiritual longing she later experienced during her many ocean crossings. In her family's history, Basques sailed the ocean for financial gain, and at least twice, in the cases of Soublette and Ezpelosin, Basque was wedded to Mantuana for social gain.

The Compañia Guipuzcoana to which Ezpelosin belonged had its origin in the economic autonomy granted to Basques* in the sixteenth century, with which license the first recorded Parra ancestor, Zubileta (meaning, amazingly, "across the sea and under the bridge"), shuttled goods up and down the coast between France and Spain. Within succeeding generations, the name Zubileta evolved to Soublet, the list of ports open to Basque traders expanded to the South American colonies, and by 1756, a Martin Soublette was firmly established in the main Venezuelan port of La Guaira, with his family's mercantile interests enclosed within the wide embrace of Compañia Guipuzcoana. His son Antonio was to elevate the Soublette name to the pinnacle of Caraquenan society when, against great Mantuan objection, he succeeded in marrying beautiful Teresa Aristeguieta, one of the famous "Nine Muses of Caracas" and cousin of Bolívar. Antonio and Teresa's son was to become Gen. Carlos Soublette, who married a Tovar and was the maternal great-grandfather of Rafael Parra.[8]

The fortunes of a family rose and fell with the political tides. Only some members, for instance, of the large Tovar family flourished after

---

*The Basques are even to this day politically and socially unique, partly because of the mysterious origin of their race and language. It is supposed that neither are they descended from the Cro-Magnong race of *Homo sapiens*, as was the rest of Europe, nor is their language based in Sanskrit. The mountains of the Pyrenees have long been an obstacle to invasion from France and Spain, and in their dark heights, the Basque population still denies allegiance to either country, despite the enforced partition.

the war: the conservative Tovar-Ezpelosins were exiled for obvious reasons, but the prestige and finances of the liberal Tovar-Soublette branch also suffered when General Soublette was exiled, like his commander Bolívar, amidst the turmoil of postwar Venezuela. Soublette's daughter, Teresa, lived to tell Teresa de la Parra about the betrayal of her revolutionary hero father by the new Venezuelan government, a tragedy whose wounds, Parra felt, the ancient spinster nursed along with "some secret sorrow." Teresa believed that "behind those complaints she must have lamented some other injustice which was more personal and deeper, and

Gen. Carlos Valentin Soublette, great-great-grandfather of Teresa de la Parra.

9

which her lips did not let out.'' In those days, it was common for a woman betrayed in her first venture into love to remain inconsolable, and Teresa, ruminating over the past, discovered in her great-great aunt a prototype, like Mama Panchita, of the colonial woman who suffered in love and in war.

On the de la Parra side of Rafael's ancestry, also, the men threw in their lot with the liberal forces. Their military skill was recorded as far back as 1567, when Juan de la Parra participated in the conquest of Caracas.[9] Two hundred years later, a Miguel de la Parra joined the Spanish opposition to Napoleon after having been sent to study in Spain by his father, and upon his return to South America he continued his military calling, this time to fight in Bolívar's army. He was the last to carry the ''de la'' next to his name and the last military man as well. He was Rafael Parra's paternal grandfather.[10]

Barely three generations came between independence and Teresa's birth, comprising some seventy years that still foundered in the revolutionary aftermath of political skirmish and social change. For Bolívar's dream of a single united continent failed, partially through the disunity of his subordinates, the armies, and subsequently the people. In *Latin America, Yesterday and Today,* the revolution is described as being: ''. . . full of crossed signals, amateur armies, and makeshift warfare that for the first time acquired the name 'guerrilla'. . . . A typical example of a week in the war when nobody knew who his allies were, where supplies were coming from, or for whom he was fighting . . .''[11]

Bolívar, for whom the idea of independence was no more separable from personal glory than it was from the philosophical egalitarianism of the American and French revolution or from the ideas of such democratic thinkers as Locke, Rousseau, and Thomas Jeffferson, had nevertheless understood that democracy did not correspond to the hierarchically ordered Latin American sensibility.[12] He became embroiled with his opponents in a contest of ideals polluted beyond redemption by the taint of greed and tyranny, of which both sides stood accused. Whereas Bolívar, who had been the first caudillo, possessed a vision by which to structure his politics, the new breed of caudillo, riding horseback in his wake and wielding that pistol in revolutionary stance, had no other goal than to siphon off a reward from profits the landed aristocrats had formerly kept all to themselves. Bolívar ended up bitterest exile to say, ''We who have fought for independence have but plowed the sea.''[13]

Without pretending to possess the authority of sociologists or historians, we wish to note here some characteristics of both politics and social mores south of the Mexican border salient to Parra's life and work. She pondered long hours and wrote long letters on the subject of her heritage, trying to sort the good from the bad. Kaleidoscopically, it turned through colors of a bedazzled peasant mysticism and chronically seditious distrust, all among mixed races and upended classes and encircled by the strict dogmas of the Catholic religion. She, like the Latin American described below, appeared to be strung out between many polar opposites: ". . . between revolution and inertia, between the truth of the word and the truth of the deed, between the Virgin and the Prostitute. It is this vacillation, this trembling betweenness, that falls to the bottom of the Latin American soul, pushing him violently between extremes."[14]

In politics, because the liberals had been responsible for declaring obsolete the dogmas and spiritual guidance of the Catholic church, Parra resented their failure to provide inspired leadership in the new world of moral choices arising with the growth of the working class, the increased awareness of women, and the ethics of securing earthly rewards. Materialism had become the road to all heavens, and the liberal dictators were its self-proclaimed priests. Their philosophy, positivism, challenged the religious mysticism of the Spanish colonial era with its assurance of a future technical, secular utopia.[15] Parra's distrust of positivism was shared by a large-enough sector of the populace that revolution lurked on the horizon for each successive military regime; responsibility for this attitude was laid at the Indian's door. "Latin America's distrust of material progress, its reliance on God's will, and its resignation to hardship, are all traits inherited from the Indian soul," wrote John Rothchild.[16]

The relationship between Spaniard and Indian is central to every South American's sense of nationality, and its importance to Parra is evident in all of her written work. The Indians and Spaniards, so radically opposed in war, shared a complementary world view in that each confirmed by the behavior of the other his notion of the workings of God. Unlike the Protestant sense of "manifest destiny" that guided the North Americans in the conquest of their continent, the South American religions stressed with finality man's impotence before the forces of nature, an attitude that the environment itself did little to disprove. The Spaniard was more passive toward his environment than the Englishman was, and his aggression took a more individual, less predictable turn. Within the placid Inca character that had permitted 500 years of more-or-less peaceful civilization and the Aztec's belief that the Spaniard was a legendary returning god, the Spaniard himself harbored a guilt that festered in the inevitability and rightness thus granted his authority. For, in fact, greed for gold had been the motivation for having dispossessed a whole population, not conversion of souls for the glory of God as proclaimed. And though he could ease his conscience through the mere act of confessing, the roots of his insecurity were deep. Once again he sought the solution in an elaborate play between word and deed: "Ironically enough, while the real Indian is subjected to dire poverty, unflinching prejudice, and subjugation, the abstract Indian of literature and art is praised as the soul of the continent, the source of its virtues."[17]

The conservatism of the Indians blended well with that of the Catholic church, as did the sympathies of priests and nuns with the Indians' poverty and sorrow. Since the conquest, the colonial empire had tried to extend its Christian notion of respect for all human life to the Indians, but had come up against tremendous resistance from the feudal barons who depended on Indian labor. Consequently, the sole colonists to have ever proven their concern for Indians' rights were in the Catholic missions—especially the Jesuits, who conducted utopian experiments with Indians in Paraguay. For their efforts, they were expelled from the entire continent in the eighteenth century. The argument over human rights is a long-standing one between church and state in Latin America; this glaring Achilles heel of the entrenched powers there provides an easy target for communist ideology today, linking for the first time socialist ideals with those of organized religion.

If the strange mating of these philosophies cemented the contradictions of the Spanish Catholic mind to the embittered patience of the Indian, the ubiquitous physical mating of the races caused a special quandary in the assignment of loyalties. Mestizos, who now constitute most of Latin America's population, had to reconcile master and slave within their own persons; they had to thank the conquest for their existence and regret it for the rape involved; they had to deny the Indian blood to succeed in Spanish-dominated society and then live with the guilt of their own part in renewing their betrayal. Such confusion so close to the surface has doubtless contributed to the emphasis on governmentally imposed discipline. The nonaristocratic Creole was considered much wilder and harder to control than the more "civilized" Spaniard, and it is his character that dominates the character of Latin America in general. As on the northern continent, the expanse of an untamed countryside helped produce a more individualistic, iconoclastic person—one who, especially in Argentina, developed his own style of the cowboy. Thomas Pynchon has a vivid description of the Argentinean gaucho in his novel *Gravity's Rainbow,* where the pull between tyranny and anarchy that characterizes, in differing degrees, most of Spanish America can be seen:

In the days of the gauchos, my country was a blank piece of paper. The pampas stretched as far as men could imagine, inexhaustible, fenceless. Wherever the gaucho could ride, that place belonged to him. But Buenos Aires sought hegemony over the provinces. All the neuroses about property gathered strength and began to infect the countryside. Fences went up, and the gaucho became less free. It is our national tragedy. We are obsessed with building labyrinths, where before there was open plain and sky. To draw ever more complex patterns on the blank sheet. We cannot abide that openness; it is terror to us. Look at Borges. Look at the suburbs of Buenos Aires. The tyrant Rojas has been dead a century, but his cult flourishes. Beneath the city streets, the warrens of rooms and corridors, the fences and the networks of steel track, the Argentine heart, in its perversity and guilt, longs for a return to that first unscribbled serenity . . . that anarchic oneness of pampas and sky. . . .[18]

Domingo Sarmiento, in "Machos and Caudillos," tells us that during the period of Rojas's rule between 1835 and 1840, almost the whole population of Buenos Aires were sent to prison, for the simple purpose of exercising discipline.[19] The machinery of the universe is too large to comprehend, but its apparent chaos at human level is the incitement to all serious thought; in the labyrinth of the universe, we are both trapped and lost. Fear of openness or fear of jungles or fear of the mysteries of the mountains—it seems to be a fear of the natural state itself, the quaking of man before God and, mythologically speaking, the fear of the female principle.

Las Memorias de Mama Blanca:
Reading the Past through Lines and Lips

As the rest of the world is beginning to discover and appreciate the points of view unique to South America, so the various national cultures in South America are awakening to the clear, pure sounds of their own voices. It has taken some time for people of the South American continent to take pride in the artistic expression of their various national identities and to differentiate that expression from the Spanish. Up until the eighteenth century, the continent as a whole had remained remarkably unreceptive to the influx of new ideas from abroad, mainly due to the untiring efforts of the Spanish Inquisition, and after the Inquisition, new trends in thinking arrived—via the upper classes—solely from the Eu-

13

ropean shore. Just as we in North America have looked to Europe for cultural guidance, it was essential, especially around the early 1900s, for Latin Americans inclined to a life of letters to sail to France in order to get published, and this usually meant abandoning all things Latin American. It was not until after the turn of the century that the slow blending of Indian, black, and Spanish in the isolation of jungles, mountains, and plains had become sufficiently integrated for the new people to begin articulating a new awareness of their distinct and special heritage.

More than by any other characteristic, this contemporary literature is defined today by an ubiquity of hallucinations and an unquestioned expectancy of the miracle; in Parra's day the infant Creole genre was still weighted by political and sociological pedantry, the result of an unpracticed realism. For in the popular culture, the highest credibility was still given to perceptions and visions grounded on emotion and faith alone. Hazy distinctions in the Spanish language bear this out: the word for *proof*, for example, *prueba*, has the simultaneous meaning of "sign, indication, mark." Thus a mystical-emotional Venezuela discouraged its daughters, especially, from all intellectual, analytical activity, and a suppressed Parra wore the conflicting mentalities on her sleeve, seeking a compromise in her novels, which bridged, for the first time, the Creole and European cultures bordering opposites sides of the Atlantic Ocean.

Outside her novels, Parra had difficulty building a permanent bridge between her opposing self-images of ultramodern woman and Christian mystic. She would profess her belief in the achievements of logic in the fields of science and medicine, yet flirt shamelessly with various occult disciplines. There she would look for proofs of the otherworldly, knowing all the while that such proof is most desired by those somehow deficient in faith. Instinct and the senses functioned always as vital antennae to her, but they became muffled in the haven of empty talk and bustle that Paris provided her from Venezuelan opprobrium. Towards the end of her life, she would come to profess a need for faith in a fixed and external spiritual source, to which she could surrender total mind and body, like the mystics and saints in religious history she had studied. Her acceptance of the supernatural never was to find stronger expression, however, than in the theme of ancestor fear and worship; her ancestors' voices, calling her to heed their advice, follow their example, and study their wars, lured her—the modern sophisticate—back into the past. She was not so much reverent toward her heritage as analytical—with an ironic twist that in her first book, *Ifigenia,* was to cause a strain in her relations with the

Venezuelan establishment that engendered her. The preoccupation itself was typical; the reverence for ancestors in the context of a fierce attachment to national cultural heritage accounts in part for the particular way the South American mind conceives the world. For North Americans, whose sense of the past is tenuous at best, the Latin American immersion of the present in the turgid and turbulent waters of history might seem fearfully wasteful. For Parra, the past was instantly accessible by the simple act of looking ahead, as into a mirror; thus, this apparent backward motion, like that of the spokes in a rapidly spinning wheel, is only an illusion. Her feelings of nostalgia toward the inexorable ancestral voices alternated with feelings of resentment, bringing her to adopt, on the one hand, the pen name of Teresa de la Parra (". . . it is my real name, the old name of my family, which together with that of Teresa has a certain classical flavor, a certain resonance from the Century of Gold. You see: Sister Juana de la Cruz, Teresa de Cepeda, how great they are!"[20]) . . . and on the other hand to write *Ifigenia,* the modern woman's refutation of everything old-fashioned.

Parra's ancestral names—Soublette, de Tovar, Ezpelosin, Olmedo, Sanojo, and de la Parra—were all once synonymous with great wealth, military courage, and progressive social concern. Like Mercedes Ezpelosin, her progenitors were long-lived and their wartime experiences still fresh, and it was through eyewitness accounts of the women in the family that these experiences came to life in Parra's imagination. Often sorrowful, always obscure, these storytellers were wives, daughters, and mothers of illustrious men. Of all their tales of adominishment, of praise, or of lament, Parra took most to heart those limning the private struggles of the women, to which, in her lectures of 1930, she assigned the value of having formed the roots of her feminism. Rejecting the snobbery of many of the Spanish descendants that allowed them to live a life unchallenged by their own inner resources, Parra immersed herself in the emotional and intellectual worlds touched by and touching her forebears—men and women alike—with the intent of picking up threads that she felt should not have been lost, and weaving them into fuller design. If the stories of the lives of her female ancestors imparted a sense of social injustice, the brilliance of the men inspired her to feel a rightful heir to their more universal concerns.

The fact that so many history-makers of the Independence Era were related to Parra had more to do with the extreme stratification of society than with their successful competition within the broad population of

Venezuela. In the area called New Granada under colonial rule, and now covered by Panama, Ecuador, Colombia, and Venezuela, the new families holding power guarded the myth of their superiority with all the ritual trappings of bureaucracy, church, and arranged, often incestuous, marriage. Parra had learned that to study her own ancestry was to study the history of Venezuela and that to search the soul of Venezuela was to eventually face the historical person of Simon Bolívar. In a moment of international mass upheaval, it was he who had commandeered the forces of change on the continent; once stripped of that command, he died in exile, and change turned to chaos for a century thereafter. According to her lifelong friend, Lydia Cabrera, the conflicting attitudes within Teresa's family toward the Liberator and the moral questions raised by his idealistic campaign troubled Teresa all her life. Her sense of urgency toward the issue was boosted by his being a distantly related member of her selfsame family. In 1930 she would go so far as to seek a cure for Venezuela's current spiritual and social ills by writing a biography of the "real" Bolívar, after having sought, through her second book, *Las Memorias de Mama Blanca,* to cleanse herself of personal ills in the pool of childhood memories.

In Venezuela, *Mama Blanca* has attained the status of an esteemed folktale. With its scenes of plantation life, its delineations of the indian/black peasant and the upper-class Spanish descendants, Parra evoked a quality of turn-of-the-century Caracas experienced by many of her compatriots. She studied the character of her country not only from the cool vantage point of distant Europe and with the sympathy of a native, but with a decidedly unfearful stance toward its lurking chaos. With the candle of her maturity she lit up rooms full of varied tangibles, speaking with a gently cutting wit of compassion, of intense communication between the human, the animal, and even the vegetable. Her own sprouting personality taking hold in this time and ground peers through the eyes of Mama Blanca's childhood self, Blanca Nieves. "Blanca Nieves, the third of the girls in order of age and size, was five years old at the time, dark of skin, dark-eyed, black-haired, legs tanned to the color of saddle leather by the sun, arms darker still. I must blushingly confess that, wholly undeserving of such a name, Blanca Nieves was I''* (p. 15).

Parra tossed out her self-images with artistry of her writing craft like

*All quotations in this chapter from *Mama Blanca's Souveniers* are from the translation by Harriet de Onis, which was published by Pan American Union in 1959, and are reprinted by permission of the Organization of American States.

appearances mastered in the course of her everyday life. There is no existing commentary by her friends and no possible speculation by people, whom she continues even in death to beguile, that can do more than punctuate and synthesize these slippery, sometimes—through her carelessness—slipped descriptions of her inner and outer makeup. Because of her need for privacy, jealously and loyally guarded with the aid of the formidable ranks of her family and friends, there are available few anecdotes that might have illuminated the critical stages of her life from the outside. Toward those few we must be cautious and proceed with a love for mystery, allowing ourselves to be led by the suggestive power of empty spaces remaining as they do in the assemblage of an old, incomplete puzzle.

Parra's most vocal, if often reluctant, interpreters have been three women to whom she revealed vastly different faces: her youngest sister, Maria Parra-Bunimovitch; her inseparable companion, the enterprising Cuban Lydia Cabrera; and Nobel Prize–winning poet Gabriela Mistral. It was Maria who told us about Teresa's ingenuousness, her stunning simplicity, and her absentmindedness. Lydia was the person who knew Teresa best as an adult and artist and from whom we get a contrasting image of great emotional and intellectual complexity. Gabriela Mistral shared many aspects of Parra's life without the benefit of intimate friendship; they accompany one another now in books on South American literature as they did then in the exile circles of European intelligentsia, where their mutual loneliness and homesickness for their native land brought them together in person, in politics, and in poetic prose.

Teresa's favorite symbols were the mirror and the Greek statue. The one a truthteller and the other a frozen image of perfect grace, they both possessed the capacity to betray the trust they inspired—the former through subtle distortion and the latter by brutal theft of motion. With her famous green eyes, she was known to be shockingly observant and disgracefully absent, shifting to shape the reflection of others' hopes and dreams. It was in her power to both demystify and to mesmerize, for, as Mistral would come to describe her, she was "natural . . . and supernatural."[21]

Despite subservience to traditional biography, where strict adherence to chronology, from birth to death, is considered to render its subject most comprehensible, we find ourselves having to introduce two Teresa de la Parras: adult and child. For it was only at the age of thirty-eight that she came to study the significance of her childhood experiences and present them to us, and thus limited by a context of her mature concerns, a muted self-description shimmers from the pages of her book *Las Memorias de Mama Blanca.*

This is how she appeared in 1928, only months after the completion of *Mama Blanca*, to a Colombian writer known in the literary life of Bogota as Luis Eduardo Nieto-Caballero: "In 1928 I was in Paris with my wife, and Teresa came immediately to the hotel to meet us. She was an imperial woman with sleepy emerald eyes, the most beautiful and white teeth that God has ever placed in the mouth of a human being, an electrifying smile, a rhythm to her voice that drove me to madness. Extraordinarily elegant, she was completely wrapped in furs (it was February), and a discreet and evanescent perfume crowned the effect of her bewitchment."[22] Beneath this enchanting exterior, Parra, having only recently broken a five-year public silence, was just beginning to come to terms with her native heritage and the fruits of her impetuous nature. Single and childless and thus removed from the exigencies of survival brought on by family life, she felt she had reasoned herself into a corner of emotional and spiritual bankruptcy. Her contemporaries were no better off; it was in particular their excessive intellectual reductionism, born in the spirit of Europe's artistic and political enthnocentricity, from which she sought deliverance. This is how she referred to it in *Mama Blanca*'s introductory pages:

> In our days, the gifted spirits tend to produce in the shadows, employing disturbing forms, and with their backs turned to nature, brilliant but incomprehensible works. To penetrate their meaning one must struggle hard, trying the doors with seven golden keys. And when one finally reaches the inner sanctum, what one wearily finds is a veiled question mark suspended above an abyss. As for me, and I say it with the satisfaction of a duty observed, I have always carried to the expositions of the Cubists and the anthologies of the Dadaists a soul garbed in humility and thirsting after faith. Just as at spiritualist seances, I have never seen or heard anything but darkness and silence.
>
> (p. 13)

Teresa fled Paris for the solitude of Vevey, Switzerland to reenter the domain of her innocence and retrieve threads of a redeeming psychic reality, for the purpose of weaving into reunion the "pleasures of the spirit and the satisfaction of ideas." *Mama Blanca* is an episodic narrative: its namesake, an old woman of seventy, has upon her death entrusted her memoirs to a twelve-year-old girl who grows up to edit and prepare the manuscript for publication. These memoirs consist of a series of cinematic portraits and scenes from Mama Blanca's fifth year, when she was called Blanca Nieves (Snow White) and lived with her five sisters on Piedra Azul, a sugarcane plantation outside Caracas. Parra, writing in the alpine shadows cast by the literary colossi of the age—Joyce and Mann, Proust, Kafka, and Rilke—confronted her readers with the figure of Mama Blanca, who possessed a "disorderly pantheistic soul" and experienced her life as a "dream saturated with melancholy grace." Teresa placed on Mama Blanca's lips words that "harmonized with life," evoking images of people long gone who had taught the author the value of the childlike response to the world. Cochocho in particular, the plantation hand in *Mama Blanca* taken straight from life, is the embodiment of that natural linkage between the knowing self and the rest of the cosmos so keenly absent in the lives of European intellectuals and artists. Parra, stunned in her retreat from the abyss of unretrieved faith, sought the path toward redemption for her lost generation in that emotional and intellectual synesthesia reflected in Cochocho's magical ability to feel his thoughts and think his feelings.

We risk the reader's confusion in attempting to relate these fictional memoirs to Teresa's own life as a child, for we also wish to relate the fictional introduction to the memoirs, a structural component of the novel, to Teresa's mature state of mind with the purpose of introducing her, middle-aged and much the wiser, to our readers. The potential for confusion stems from Parra's manipulation of several first-person points of view through acrobatic leaps of time. (She pushes *Mama Blanca* backward from age seventy to age five, and the nameless author of the introduction forward from age seven to a young adult.) As Flaubert was Bovary, so Parra is all three characters, past, present, and future; the last—old Mama Blanca—was constructed from Parra's idealization of the typical Creole grandmother.

The novel begins with the voice of the young editor, who remains nameless and speaks only in the book's introduction. Describing to us the Mama Blanca she knew, she tells us how they met when she was only seven and the old woman lived nearby in an old, ramshackle cabin, to the embarrassment of her sophisticated relatives. One day, out of curiosity and a sense of adventure, the seven-year-old girl stuck her head through the cabin door. The old woman, far from proving dangerous, welcomed the girl instead as the miraculous answer to her lifelong prayer for a daughter. In return, the little stranger gained by her impulsiveness a friendship far more valuable than that of her uncomprehending peers, for Mama Blanca concealed, under her unsophisticated peasant exterior, "the temperament of a magnificent artist and a subtle, exquisite intelligence which, more than upon books, had fed upon nature and the daily savoring of life." To defend her apparently unwarranted devotion to such an eccentric old woman, the young editor states (p. 6): "Her friendship, like prayer on the lips of the mystics, opened up to me limitless horizons and satisfied mysterious anxieties of my spirit. I do not believe I exaggerate when I say that I not only liked her but I loved her, and as happens with every love worth the name, in the last analysis, what I was seeking was myself." Their bond lasted until Mama Blanca died. Her disciple, having reached the age of twelve, took into safekeeping the ream of handwritten pages entrusted to her, guarding it religiously until old enough to do it editorial justice and secure a publisher. Thus the background is filled in against which Mama Blanca can begin to invoke her still-vivid images of a colorful and instructive childhood. Parra admitted freely that the timeless lessons Mama Blanca derived from her experience of Piedra Azul as Blanca Nieves closely paralleled her own, when she was called Ana Teresa and lived at her family's plantation, Tazon.

The character of Mama Blanca was not based on an individual who lived in Parra's actual childhood, as were the sisters, parents, and other characters of the plantation. With all her contradictions, Mama Blanca was a fictional ideal, a composite of many memories. Seida de la Torre, sister of Teresa's Cuban friend, Lydia Cabrera, tells us that their mother, Elisa Bilbao-Marcaida, contributed to Parra's inspiration for Mama Blanca with her white hair, poise, and small house. Most clearly, however, Mama Blanca is recognizable as a member of that exquisite and feminine culture represented by Mercedes Ezpelosin; her gifts of expression and her eagerness to pass on her knowledge to a female heir stand out against the culture of her father, Juan Manuel, described in her memoirs as sardonic and insistent upon the speedy birth of a son.

Juan Manuel was a typical hacendado (plantation owner), based on Parra's memories of her own father, Rafael Parra. Emotionally distant, too congenial to be authoritarian, yet resting secure in his male prerogative as master of all, Juan Manuel was possessor of human beings, animals, and land alike: "poor Papa, without suspecting it or deserving it, took on in our eyes the thankless role of God. He never scolded us; and yet, out of religious instinct, we paid his supreme authority the tribute of a mysterious fear tinged with mysticism" (p. 18). Teresa's father, Rafael, was known to be gifted in the conversational skills of wit and irony, the

Isabel Sanjo-Ezpelosin, mother of Teresa de la Parra

same skills with which his daughter, recognizably similar in temperament to him, later galvanized her Parisian following. It was he who taught her how to ride a horse. But his premature death left her with only a fragmented image of who he was and could have become. His love of glamour, politics, and diplomacy, his devotion to the easy life of the plantation, might have eventually come to compare unfavorably with the deep commitments espoused by his own father, a physician, by his Parra and Soublette antecedents, and even by his wife, Isabel, a woman unflinchingly loyal to the tenets of the old world. As the reader will discover in the pages of *Ifigenia,* the adolescent Teresa wished to emulate his fickleness and his love of luxury, seeing in such behavior a refutation of the limiting conservatism and severity required of the respectable woman. But her curiosity about life would soon exceed the limits of frivolity and refinement, and with them, we imagine, the scope of her father's memory. For Juan Manuel is revealed as self-centered and indifferent. He represents the opposite of those qualities Teresa, and Blanca Nieves, most appreciated in others; humility, compassion, and personal integrity.

Isabel Sanojo-Ezpelosin, daughter of Mercedes, was a "charming, respectful lady, well-educated and socially prominent, prossessing a strict moral and religious integrity she had inherited from her forebears."[23] Because her father, Dr. Luis Sanojo, was a jurist and politician of controversial reputation, Isabel in her formative years suffered the vicissitudes of political favor or harassment that had plagued her mother Mercedes's life from beginning to end. At one point, the Sanojo family lost its entire home in the region of Guarico. Isabel had access to a large library, she loved to read, and being of artistic temperament, she played the piano well.

But Isabel did not seem to enjoy the play of ideas. Like Venezuela, she was emotional, romantic, fanatically conservative and religious, and therefore barely tolerant of her daughter's independent streak—manifested in the ambition to be a writer, the refusal to marry, and the choice of friends. Yet the colonial world that Isabel represented resided tenaciously inside her. Throughout Ana Teresa's peregrinations, Isabel kept her maternal guard, weathering finally and with unceremonious dignity her child's premature illness and death, to live on for another twelve years afterward.

It was Isabel's embodiment of the traditions and provincialism of Venezuela that provided Teresa with the essential focal point for her psychological positioning, which in *Ifigenia* can be seen in its protest, in Mama Blanca for its more understanding stage. Due to the influence of mother and country at the time when Teresa was most impressionable, she derived her creative force from their steady pull on the imagination to the extent that she would say in 1927 that she could not write of any but Creole subjects.

It is likely that Teresa's mother was more formidable than Blanca Nieves's soft-edged Mama, who was the object of her daughter's unrestrained love (p. 22). "Mama was a romantic without apologies and without knowing it. . . . I would say that the romantics were always imitating her. It is my opinion that like tobacco, pineapple, and sugarcane, Romanticism was an American product which grew, sweet, natural, and unknown, amidst colonial languor and tropical indolence until the end of the eighteenth century. . . ." Mama's poetic personality brought an arbitrary order to all the surfaces of her environment. Like Napoleon, who later "caught the disease of romanticism from Josephine Tascher" and seated his brothers on the "proudest thrones of Europe," Mama elevated her offspring to the "throne of creation" by giving them the unabashedly pompous and even comical names of Aurora, Violeta, Blanca Nieves, Estrella, Rosalinda, and Aura Flor.

Mama bothered obsessively over her daughters' perfect curly hair—all perfect and natural, in fact, except for that of poor Blanca Nieves, who, like Teresa, had to submit her stubbornly straight locks to daily curling by her mother's hands. These special sessions between the two allowed occasion for an unrestrained flow of charmingly confused fairy tales with which Mama manipulated her dreamy daughter's imagination. Spiced with religious metaphors and delivered with a musically hypnotic voice, these stories revealed Mama's very personal notion of reality. Teresa's cousin has confirmed that she also heard these stories from her grandmother and that Isabel's style was exactly like that of Blanca Nieves's mother.

After Ana Teresa, Isabel gave birth to four more children: three girls, Isabelita, Elia, and Maria, and one boy, Rafaelito, who became the second of her sons to die in infancy. Teresa remained very close to her three sisters, and they in turn exhibited a lifelong devotion and loyalty to her, although all of them, respectably married, chose to stress more zealously than Teresa their aristocratic, conservative upbringing. In the family hierarchy of their childhood, Teresa reigned over her three sisters and looked up to two older brothers. These brothers, Miguel and Luis, are noticeable in their absence from her books and letters, although Luis administered her financial affairs from Venezuela when she first went to Paris and before she replaced him with her friend Rafael Carias.

In *Mama Blanca,* Parra designed for her protagonist four younger sisters, whom she painted in the soft hues of meek femininity. One older sister, however, named Violeta just as inappropriately as Blanca Nieves had been named, became the recipient of distinctly male personality traits. It is she who engages with Blanca Nieves in significant dialogue, representing the only serious threat to her. Clearly the brothers, some combination of siblings, or even the voice of an inner opposite could have inspired this character. Uncivilized and uncensored in their childhood states, the two personalities of Violeta and Blanca Nieves stand in opposition, as do the qualities of unreflective self-confidence and daydreaming introversion. Their love-hate conflict is rooted in a context of major philosophical and temperamental incompatibility; Mama Blanca goes so far as to suggest, in retrospect, that Violeta is the male heir her father always wanted (p. 37). "I believe that Violeta's body lodged the spirit of Juan Manuel the Desired, and this was the reason he had never been born; for six years he had walked the earth disguised as Violeta. The disguise was so transparent that everyone recognized him, Papa first of all. For this reason from time to time he greeted him with hearty laughter. . . ." In this gender twist, Parra used the classic male and female principles to characterize the argument between sisters, describing at the same time and in an unorthodox manner the stereotypical battle between the sexes. Hearty laughter, one can imagine, will not continue to greet Violeta's too-active behavior as she matures. Under the strictures of convention, she is likely to become one of the flowers in the garden of repressed young ladies that her sister, as Mama Blanca, will nurture and contemplate in her backyard. This is the garden with which Mama Blanca, in the introduction, charms her curious disciple and editor-to-be:

. . . See, these daisies are vain, coquettish young ladies who like people to see them in their low-necked dance frocks. Those violets over there are always sad because they are poor and have no sweetheart or pretty dresses to show off, at the window. They only come out at Eastertime, barefooted, with their violet robe, like penitents in Holy Week. Those gardenias are great ladies who ride about in their fine carriages and know nothing of what goes on in the world except what the bees tell them, who flatter them because they get their living from them!

And in this way, my curiosity and hunger slaked with violets, daisies, cake, and ladyfingers, Mama Blanca and I walked hand in hand down the highway of our great friendship.

(pp. 5–6)

Violeta's real crime, as perceived by Blanca Nieves, was her intolerance; the tough older sister refused to concede any value at all to Blanca Nieves's "world of symbols and fictions," sentimental and pathetically naive was it may have seemed. Violeta even had a "positivistic" quality, which to a certain body of Spanish American intellectuals in the '20s, opposed to their various military governments, suggested great lack of imagination as well as vulgarity and evil. Although perhaps cruel, Violeta was also spontaneous and lively, and she exercised command over the material world; for these qualities she earned Blanca Nieves's begrudging admiration. Blanca Nieves, mouth perpetually agape in wonder at the world, nicknamed Flycatcher by Violeta, could not even relish her eventual—if only temporary—victory over her sister; rather, she wept with guilt and sypathy at the sight of Violeta suffering a punishment she herself had caused Mama to execute. The defiant and vengeful potential in Blanca Nieves's otherwise gentle nature had finally gained sway out of utter desperation and self-defense; usually it was directed to the more noble pursuit of changing the end of a fairy tale to suit her ideals. "Beauty and the Beast," for example, was one of the favorite legends her mother tailored to her daughter's romantic requirements. Her demand was that the Beast should remain Beast even after acceptance by Beauty; otherwise Beauty's love was neither a noble impulse nor a true love. Parra, too, distrusted any display of emotion motivated by the expectation of reward. Proving that Blanca Nieves was without question a girl of Teresa's own kind is the description by Maria Parra-Bunimovitch that her sister had been a "lively girl, without traces of genius . . . more inclined to ingenuousness. Mouth agape, she was called Flycatcher because of her constant distractability. . . ."[24] Such meekness, the only crime of Blanca Nieves and her younger sisters, stemmed from the original sin of having simply been born female. In the end, Parra's device of all-female offspring for Juan Manuel enabled her to make a simpler, less specifically autobiographical statement about the impact of patriarchy on both father and daughter (p. 20): "Definitely a latent misunderstanding existed between Papa and us which was to endure for a long time. The truth of the matter is that we never disobeyed but once in our life. But that single time sufficed to disunite us without scenes of violence for many years. This great act of disobedience took place at the hour of our birth. Even before he married, Papa had solemnly stated: 'I want a son who will be named for me, Juan Manuel.' ''

Parra's fusion of social message with telling anecdote, circumscribing the personalities clearly and simply as in a fairy tale, continues to extol the spontaneous and unadorned in the character of Cousin Juancho, another relative after Mama Blanca's own heart. Cousin Juancho is based on Rafael Parra's brother Antonio, out of whose attributes Parra could hardly have created a more obvious fictional metaphor for her vision of modern degeneracy encroaching on a poetic, schizophrenic South America. Word and deed, intention and action, are never successfully coordinated in Juancho, and Mama Blanca describes his tirades as eliciting no stronger reaction than the barking of the affectionate dog, Marquesa. ''I believe that this gift of the word was the origin of both his happiness and his misfortune. Even though in his conversation he was continually harping on politics, the tumult of this thoughts prevented him from bringing any story or thesis safe to port'' (p. 54). Juancho is driven to live out the chaos as a bird is driven by a storm. No amount of wit and extraordinary learning can keep him from joining the ranks of the chronically defeated in a world that demands direction for success in its terms. Mama Blanca compares him to an unbound Larousse, ''with all the pages loose, and upside down.'' Like Borges years later, she expresses a fascination with the absurdity of the dictionary (p. 50). ''He was like a moving train, or, better still, a dictionary. There was a kind of basic unity to the apparent disorder. . . . To go from cat to catechesis to cataclysm is a pleasant diversion. . . . The dictionary is the only book whose delightful incoherence—so like that of Mother Nature—is a relaxing change from logic, oratory, and literature.''

Mama Blanca's bemused appraisal of the futility of Cousin Juancho's existence gives way to the brilliant charm of his ''misadventures, his ire, his learning and eloquence.'' She considers herself greatly indebted to her cousin, whose gift to her was in ''the whole history of that life and the secret of that soul, in which continually and jovially, like two good friends, the sublime and the ridiculous met'' (p. 48). Mama Blanca has absorbed, through exposure to Juancho's oxymoronic personality, a wealth of principles to guide her: he paved the way for her instant and honest appreciation, quite separate from historical importance, of the exploits of Don Quixote; then, when she later visited Spain, she was able, because of Juancho's training, to see a ''deep, infinite beauty'' where others ''found only poor roads, cooking that reeked of olive oil, and an absence of baths." Above all he taught her to understand and love, even if by default, the "idealistic soul" of her race.

The quixotic Juancho was condemned—like Job, but less cruelly—to a life whose days "transpired beneath a modest drizzle of misfortune." Through the ingenuous fluctuation of his opinionated outbursts, Parra expressed her awareness of a kind of purity in not declaring just one set of conditions to be absolute truth. Indeed, it is typical of the overly analytical mind to suspect a kind of falsity lurking in the apparent arbitrariness of any extreme stance, all the while remaining painfully aware of society's praise of singlemindedness; it gets little consolation from knowing such tenacity can result from the courage of a thinking person just as it can from the prejudices of the merely selfish. But Juancho's dwelling in the land of illusion both sheltered his hope and kept his standards lifted high above the real world. Rothchild notes that "Latin America has always been a continent of illusions. . . . El Dorado was a flaky quest, but it still lingers: something in the gold myth is reflected in most Latin American enterprise, driving people to attempt the impossible and then to be destroyed by the impossible."[25]

The quixotic confusion seems contagious to Teresa when she defends delusions as if they were identical to ideals, yet she is clear on the elusiveness of reality. The question of commitment to an ideal, to an illusion, or to a reality was as unanswerable as the question of how to govern a country. Juancho's worldliness and love for debate applied themselves avidly to the field of politics. Typically, he could be heard ranting and raving about both conservatives, who on the one hand were "nincompoops, enemies of progress, completely unfit to govern; it's their fault we're in the state we're in," as well as his "coreligionists, the liberals" on the other, "barefaced thieves, who are leading us to complete ruin." Mama Blanca goes so far as to say:

> Between ourselves, and meaning no offense to these gentlemen, everyone knows that the one objective of delegates to all congresses and assemblies, from the times of Assyria and Babylon down to the League of Nations of our own days, is to skillfully conceal from the public the utter uselessness of such meetings, while at the same time assuming to themselves maximum importance. Cousin Juancho, always more upright, more honest than anyone, would have broken the conspiracy of silence. He, however, would have done something useful, for he would have amused his colleagues with his agile, unexpected, and unique leaps from the future unity of

27

Spanish America to the excellence of the soap of Marseilles or the properties of sesame seeds.

(p. 56)

Cousin Juancho was the embodiment of what Mama Blanca perceived as the natural state of chaos, hounded but never successfully tamed by society's compulsion to order. Because he idolized England and everything English, his lifelong dream was to be sent on a diplomatic mission there. For years he stood poised to accept the appointment that somehow, always at the last minute, was thwarted by the death of his political sponsor or by some change in the political wind, thus sparing him the cruel experience of having to limit himself once and for all to one cause, at the great cost of his spontaneity. In Juancho's example can be seen the relentless contradictions of that natural state and the fate awaiting those who, preferring to give full vent to their "natural" grace and wit, hurl those contradictions right in the face of an amused but unpersuaded world.

Blanca Nieves had to grow up in order to "... understand why you [Juancho] lived in a state of constant indignation, and why you attired yourself in your black funeral coat each morning. You knew that all were leagued in a plot to assassinate the simple, joyous grace of life, and as she was being buried bit by bit each day, each day you faithfully attended her piecemeal burial. . . ." As Mama Blanca, she sheds tears for "the infinite sorrow it gives me to know that above the cherished ashes, always triumphant, always terrible, like an angel of vengeance with a flaming sword, barring the gates of all that is pleasant, instead of grace and wit stands emphasis."

Parra had come to associate grace and wit with the colonial era, and emphasis, order, and vengeance with positivism. One of those angels of vengeance was doubtless General Guzman-Blanco, whose deed of closing the convents in 1874 symbolized to her the end of protection for the female intellectual. He came to power in 1869, after the country had experienced fourteen years of war and forty-five years thereafter of the changing dictatorships that so victimized Cousin Juancho. After independence, the strong resentment toward the clergy that had arisen culminated in the radical expulsion of the church from its central position in Latin American society, in Diaz's Mexico reaching the high pitch of religious persecution. In Caracus, nuns of the Dominican convent were ordered to leave their buildings without any preparation. The otherwise homeless women prayed in vain. When the governor of Caracas arrived

28

with his soldiers to "urge them to leave," some were fortunate enough to find shelter with Caracas's more pious families. Parra made special note of this event in her second lecture about the influence of women on Latin America during colonial times. Up to this point, we have been discussing Latin American history with a "he" as protagonist; it was Parra's belief that her people, and especially members of her own sex, had neglected to recognize the part women played in forming Latin American culture, relinquishing with this neglect the possibility of any future improvement in their status. History was a text of male prowess and therefore only a partial truth, the missing pieces of which were capturable in the lives of those women themselves. The influence of the closing of the convents within Parra's childhood landscape was strong enough to last until that time when she was questioning her religion in the context of her country's political shift away from mysticism:

> I was able to meet one of those expelled nuns during my childhood. Her memory has taught me to discern many obscure things. I have seen in that memory not the quiet idealism of the women who as mothers, shut in their houses, made our society into what it is, but rather of the others who had great authority in the Colony; those who, cornered by the surrounding prejudices and vulgarity, turned, without being devout, towards mysticism and went to the convents: they were the lovers of silence, the eternally thirsty for a spiritual life, and although it may seem contradictory, the forerunners of the modern feminist ideal.
>
> That nun, a recollection of my early childhood, a symbol of colonial and feminine idealism, was called Mother Teresa. She was one of the last survivors of that cruel dispersion. She lived in the ancient house of a widow who had taken her in and who was as old as the house. My sisters and I frequently went to visit them because we were neighbors and, although we were only five and seven years of age, we were already infected with that compulsion to roam that characterizes our times.[26]

Parra's compassion went beyond her own blood; she expanded it to include all heroines unsung in triumph or tragedy—including Indians—of Latin America's past. Perhaps the "unsung" was for her to become above all the mark of true quality, a debt of gratitude she took upon herself to pay. Mama Blanca was a "celebrity only to my admiring soul," and Juancho, "shattered with thunderbolts," yet invested with grace and nobility the defects of human nature with the mere example of his own person. But by far the most interesting character to Parra's Venezuelan readers has been Cochocho, who dominates *Mama Blanca* with all the mythical force of "Beauty and the Beast." To his memory, Mama Blanca speaks: "Remember that your art and your greatest glory was that of having made the ugly beautiful."

The Life and Passing of Cochocho

In the world of Piedra Azul, nothing is as it seems. The kernel of contradiction is bared through irony, and irony's face wears a lean, knowing smile rather than a mask of ill will. Cochocho, nicknamed Louse, turned ugliness to beauty, his dirt no more a fault than that of the ferns "laved by the stream or kissed by the dust," his shabby clothing a proof of his commitment to his far more important inner life; in his servitude and humility, he achieved an indispensability that turned the apparent power structure upside down. Cochocho the louse, with the "flat, cordial head in which Indian and Negro had humbly come together," lived by his own rules entirely and as such was king of a country whose personal law of integrity, whose unbesmirchable dignity, lent validity to his submission and thus to the plantation's existence as a whole. He was the plantation's front-line man in every way, standing as magician and medium on the border between the hopelessly out-of-touch Spanish household and the earth that fed its members, involving himself with every season of the land, agricultural or political (p. 69). "It was Vicente who ruled the water like Neptune and, with feet firmly planted on either side of the sluice raised the gate, releasing the tumultuous stream like a keeper letting a wild animal out of a cage. . . ."

Mama Blanca deems Vicente's contribution invaluable to her understanding of being human. In such an unlikely body as Cochocho's, "one barely four fingers taller than Aurora", all the attributes of a superior man were housed: "In addition to teacher of philosophy and natural sciences, player of the maracas, cleaner of ditches, cane feeder, and weeder, Vincente was the doctor, druggist, and undertaker of Piedra Azul. He was also, as will be seen, a soldier when the occasion arose, and a military genius." Because others were blind to what could not be seen with the eyes, they considered him less than human. Cochocho allowed himself to be whipping boy of the plantation, because "belonging as one might say, to the vegetable kingdom, he accepted without protest the iniquities of man and the injustices of nature." That very saintliness

30

earned him no friends among the vicious and vain, as the baring of truth earns recrimination from its natural enemies regardless of the originator's motivation. But he was so insignificant to white society that there was no danger in Parra's Venezuelan readers' recognizing, down to the name Cochocho, the real man behind the myth. Maria confirmed in 1947 that: "Vicente was our servant, fashioned out of the earth's clay, just as Teresa described him. Papa used to say upon seeing him: 'To him his feet seem loud as heels.' And in his house, crammed with dozens of people, Papa questioned him: 'Vincente, who are the people at your house?' 'I don't know, señor, I only give them sustenance.' "[27]

Maria did not comment, however, on the fictional Cochocho's military activity. It is possible that this aspect of his life was an idealization on the part of Teresa, an attempt to delineate what she would consider an honestly motivated activism. Which party he chose to fight for is not specified in the novel—perhaps it doesn't matter, or perhaps she was being cautious, since at the time she was receiving a stipend from the Gomez dictatorship and knew the repercussions of even a slight offense against its sensibilities. What is significant is that he was always on the side of the revolution, not the government, and that, further, Parra chose to emphasize chiefly his natural talent for soliliery rather than any political acumen. It calls forth a response Teresa once made to a Cuban interviewer in 1928, when questioned about her feeling towards women's activism. She answered, "I am not qualified." About Cochocho she says (p. 77): "In the field of military strategy Vincente's genius exceeded his vocation; in that of medicine, his vocation exceeded his genius."

Vicente's central position on Mama Blanca's canvas was in itself unique and original in South American literature. Out of the reality of his existence Parra forged a paradigm for a Latin American ideal as unlikely as it was unexpected. From 1888, when Ruben Dario formulated what became the modern trend in poetry, up until the writing of *Mama Blanca* in 1927, Venezuelan literature gave expression to a single major trend—one away from imitation of Spanish writers and toward definition of the "criollo" voice. But the criollo style was still that of the Spanish male, formerly unquestioned heir to the land, who was suffering the slow erosion of his power by the forces of a variety of policies, both social and economic, conceived by a succession of governments. Dillwyn Ratcliffe speaks, in his introduction to *Mama Blanca,* of a change occuring in the general tone of criolla writers around 1916, when the book *En Este Pais . . . !*, by Luis Manuel Urbaneja-Achelpohl, was the first to signal an optimistic trend, replacing the self-pitying tracts of "satire and pessimism'' gone before. Romulo Gallegos and Jose Rafael Pocaterra were the most representative of that group of regional writers: "By 1925, Gallegos also had abandoned the defeatism of his *Reinaldo Solar* and had shown his whole-hearted acceptance of the new democracy with all its social consequences. In *La Trepadora* (Climbing Vine), the old plot still survives, but the enterprising upstart who gains possesion of his former employer's plantation is now the hero instead of the villain.''

According to her own testimony, Parra developed her literary voice wholly under the influence of nineteenth-century French writers and up to the writing of *Ifigenia* managed to remain ignorant of her Venezuelan contemporaries' work: ''. . . Anatole France, Alphonse Daudet, Catulle Mendez, Maupassan [*sic*], and Valle Inclan. I say they are my masters because I believe them to have influenced me most. At the time I had not read Jorge Isaacs. . . .''[28] At that time there were no women novelists to follow. The poetess Luisa del Valle Silva and historian Lucila Perez Diaz had influenced Parra by the fact of their achievement in male-dominated fields rather than by their work itself. Due to her cultural adhesion to France and her insistence of the universality of her feminine point of view, Parra was not considered a true native writer in the criollo genre. As Ratcliffe writes, she avoided the ''well-worn muddy jungle trail of criollismo—that is, of rustic Venezuelan regionalism.'' Still, she communicated successfully, in international terms, all the larger themes of racism, sexism, and Catholicism within the regional framework of Venezuela's ethical preoccupation. Her attitude toward that central issue of Venezuela's industrial and political awakening did not fall within the neat lines that divided criollo literature historically, at least not as evidenced in *Mama Blanca*. Neither for nor against anything, without exception, Parra always was the one to say, with disarming effortlessness, that the emperor, handsome though he was, was not really wearing any clothes. Or she would say that the emperor was disgracefully naked, yes, but he certainly was handsome!

In a letter to her friend Rafael Carias in 1927, Teresa attempted to define her notion of irony; it did not by any means have the bad connotation her countrymen claimed—they were much too quick to take offense. Far from being motivated by the desire to insult, she defended herself: "True irony is like a good law . . . It is that which arising from itself (?) comprehends equally the notion of charity, that which must always maintain a smile of benevolence and a perfume of indulgence. But not everyone in the world can smell this perfume, nor can everyone see the smile. Irony is very distinct from cruel laughter of the vulgar.''[29]

Teresa considered her expression of the truth to be rendered completely palatable and inoffensive by her ironic style, but her truth often lay too far from convention for the small consolation present in that style to ease its bite, as was the case with *Ifigenia*. Her balking at convention fit in with the tenor of her more general challenge to the obvious and the visible as sole arbiters of what is real. Though based in the solid precepts of antiquity, convention comprises the rules of etiquette, of dogma, that rarely are infused with the same conviction personal experience brings. Throughout the course of *Mama Blanca,* Parra enunciates her own moral code; with each human example she demonstrates that the basic tenets of Catholicism are not always interpreted in good faith, that in fact the true ones are often obscured by an unsightly pile of dust in the corner. Within the confines of the plantation, conventional morality had an especially rough row to hoe. The beleaguered agent of its discipline at Piedra Azul was the children's governess, Evelyn. At Tazon a French-woman, in the novel she is a quadroon from Trinidad who "reprimanded us in Spanish devoid of articles" and whose chief qualifications for her job are sternness and a "positivistic" lack of imagination. When the children unabashedly seek Cochocho's companionship, Evelyn tries to stifle their fascination while invalidating his world of knowledge. But the sensuality of the tropical landscape, straining relentlessly against the boundaries of formality, carries a much different message from Evelyn's. Her explanations are not convincing and therefore have an inverse effect than that intended: "It goes without saying that our devotion to Vicente Cochocho, fanned by persecution and fed by being forbidden, grew by the hour" (p. 71). Because Mama Blanca has the willpower to transmute harm into benefit, she draws the conclusion that "by forbidding us things and places, Evelyn imbued them with life," and the glow of the forbidden imprinted itself that much more sharply in her memory, saving it thereby from oblivion. The truth of Evelyn's inner landscape was not apparent until later, however (p. 71). "At bottom—I understand it now—the war to the death which Evelyn carried on against our beloved Cochocho had its origin in a complex, personal race hatred. For that reason it was relentless and without quarter. Evelyn's three-quarters of white blood cursed her quarter of Negro blood. As she was unable to bedevil the Negro in herself, she took it out on Vincente."

Besides being guilty of African blood, Cochocho also committed one very serious affront to plantation society: he lived with two women, neither of whom was his wife. To Evelyn and Mama this behavior was "depraved," but of the fact that "basically the customs of Piedra Azul were worthy of a brilliant court'' they seemed to be naively unaware. Rather than directing their energies toward self-improvement, the two women persisted in their blunted assessment of Vicente's morals. Mama Blanca reports that, in fact, free love was widely accepted at Piedra Azul—"the men, once the knot had been tied, gave themselves over to infidelity with remarkable dedication and plurality.'' Thus no one paused to note the harmony and mutual support among the three people under Vicente's roof—rather they heaped scorn and threats upon his head with vengeful relish, lest he not conform to their propriety. Mama Blanca's perception of Vicente's apparently self-awarded license is, needless to say, quite the opposite. "Vicente was refractory to the marriage bond. Not because of that hardness of heart to which the Scriptures allude, but out of a deep-rooted unshakeable sense of fidelity.'' His relationship to the two women, springing from no different source than that of his own humility, is as empty of the selfhatred of Evelyn as it is full of an understanding of human need within the life process. Only an ugly little half-breed to some, to Parra he is not only more competent than his "superiors,'' but a better Christian as well. She closes the chapter with the certain feeling that Vicente is one of God's chosen ones, that in his last testament "He set down your obscure name, Vicente Cochocho, for you were meek, you were pure of heart, you were merciful, you suffered persecution for the sake of justice'' (p. 92).

Along with understanding, as with knowledge, comes power over the understood. From that point on, the intention of a man is the moral issue. Cochocho's oneness with the vegetable kingdom does not cause him to pick the poisonous plants to use on his white masters; he does not direct his military cunning toward destroying the plantation. Use of control is the central moral issue in governing a people, not the control itself. Without exception, Parra used voice quality and language to betray the intention of a character. Notably sensitive to the expressive power of the human voice herself, she is said to have studied voice improvement upon her first year in Paris. In *Mama Blanca,* the little girls are moved by voices, like puppets are by strings. Their mother's melodious voice is what seduces and charms Blanca Nieves into submission for the hair-curling sessions; Juancho's only power lies in his mesmerizing use of language and voice modulation; Cochocho has a deep current of rhythmic pulses driving his every expression. His Spanish is the antiquated language of the conquistadors—from the Age of Gold (p. 75): "As many times as I have attempted to explain to you how Vicente talked and how Mama talked, those two opposed poles, one the essence of rusticity and the other of refinement or preciosity, one in which the rhythm predominated, the other, the melody, I have sadly realized the uselessness of my endeavor. The written word, I repeat, is a corpse.''

Daniel the cowherd supersedes them all in the voice department, however: he not only woos his cows into letting down their milk with his talking, he actually sings to them. His is the same poetic impulse as Mama's; with no thought of dishonoring the girls, he has given all the cows in his stable long, flowery names according to their dispositions and coloring. Blanca Nieves and her sisters are proud to be thus associated; they are intrigued by Daniel's willingness to have learned the animals' language so skillfully. In his barn they enter a different world from that of the plantation (p. 102): ''The order which existed was perfect: the order of the ideal future city. In the open air, under the sky and sun, each cow was happy and in its house, that is to say, tied to a tree or post. There were those who had a tree—even a tree in bloom; others had only a short, bare post. Nobody complained and nobody was resentful, there was no class warfare. To each according to her needs, from each according to her ability. All was peace and all was light.'' Daniel came from another part of the country, from the plains, or llanos, of Venezuela, and so his habits were strange. As his ''voice swayed with every syllable like a palm tree in the breeze,'' he was consciously exercising a ''Machiavellian statecraft'' to achieve the proper apportionment of everything to everyone. Even the dairy's balance sheets did not escape his manipulation (p. 106): ''. . . in addition to being an excellent cowman and an excellent epigrammic poet, Daniel was crafty and covetous. Always conciliatory, always pleasant, his every act formed a part of a finespun web whose threads are invisible even to the sharpest eye.''

Juan Manuel had his hands tied. Less clever than Daniel, he could not prove any cheating in the dairy's treasury. And what's more, Daniel had trained the cows in such a way that no other cowherd could replace him; like any good paternalistic dictator, he had made sure the cows were completely dependent on him alone. Daniel's system exceeded Papa's in form as well as content, never despoiling anyone ''without smiles, courtesy, and good manners . . . all flattery and good advice.'' Whereas he was not free of that congenital disease of all politicians—dishonesty and greed—he did respect the individual needs and feelings of his cows. He understood the need of all living things for happiness.

Juan Manuel, ruler of the plantation, was not so skilled. He governed by hit-or-miss indifference, laziness, and a brittle egotism. Although the plantation was owned by two brothers besides himself and eventually had to be sold due to the larger economic climate, one cannot help taking these moral lessons to their logical conclusions and suggesting that Mama Blanca, remembering the sinking hearts of herself and her sisters every time their father offended or misunderstood one of the people who kept his plantation running, blamed the disintegration of Piedra Azul on him. The dichotomy had been staged: On the one hand are a group of small, powerless people—girl children and peasants—who all seem to possess a sharpened Disney-style awareness of their surroundings. Far from being sentimentally anthropomorphic, their attitude stems instead from a respect for the existence of all creatures like themselves. On the other hand stands Juan Manuel, who has never forgiven his daughters for not being male, who introduces modern medicine to the plantation but still cringes under the only partially successful challenge of Cochocho's folk medicine, who is embarrassed by Juancho's clothes, who tries to fire Daniel for his clever stealing, and who, with one misspoken word to Cochocho, punctures the protective bubble of good luck surrounding Piedra Azul.

Vicente Cochocho has not just dared to compete with Papa in medicine, but has insisted on his right to participate in the periodic revolutions staged against whatever government is in power. For his skill as a guide and ambush soldier he has earned fame throughout the countryside, and he is considered indispensable to any skirmish. Papa only tolerates these temporary leaves because the safety of his cattle and plantation depends on Vicente's protective influence with the army. Juan Manuel rises to the challenge to his intelligence and magnanimity that Cochocho might have presented a better man, and his resentment grows with each reminder of the tenuous nature of his control over the plantation. In one final scene, Vicente has come to take his leave and Juan Manuel is ready. He first tries to persuade Cochocho not to go, but Cochocho says he cannot break his promise. Juan Manuel refuses to respect this reason and to the horror of his daughters standing nearby, lets out all his contempt for his ranch hand in this bitter, sarcastic retort: ''I had forgotten. I stand in the presence of the illustrious Captain Don Vicente Aguilar. Your humble servant! Go off, go off to the war, Sir Captain. . . .'' This is the worst insult Papa could have ever spoken. The twist in his face and scorn in his voice are devastating; they are the ultimate expression of Papa's persecution of Cochocho, which Mama Blanca has even before this incident compared to the persecution of the early Christians by Diocletian or Nero. Vicente hangs his head, ''beaten like a dog with his own name,'' and from that moment never sets foot on Piedra Azul again.

The waning of Juan Manuel's influence marks the beginning of the end for Piedra Azul. For Teresa and her own family, father Rafael's death also signaled the end of the plantation, neatly encapsulating this carefree time as a phenomenon in Teresa's life. From within the heart of the plantation, the sugarcane mill, Mama Blanca remembers with the sharpness calling forth a once-forbidden pleasure the ambience of unhurried busyness "so varied, so full of life and color," of tremendous freedom of movement and thought, wonderful smells and melodious voices. And "the thirty or forty mill hands took part in the sugar making as though it were a birth: a little help, lots of patience, talk and nothing more."

> I can assure that there in the mill, awaiting the moment for the water to be released, sucking stalks of cane with hands sticky and rivulets of juice running down my neck and arms, I spent the pleasantest hours of my life.
>
> (p. 97)

The sheltered garden of the tropics provided an education unavailable in any school. Its wisdom echoed the conclusions Teresa had reached about modern life, the restrictions and aesthetic poverty of which were to cause a cruel awakening in the "backwoods" girls of the plantation. The subtle anarchy of the book lies in its insistence on personal experience as the means of interpreting life's lessons. As each character seems to draw a double-edged sword, so does the patriarchal structure itself, managing to lash out at Mother Nature while at the same time offering up the protective shelter under which Parra's Rousseau-like vision of innocence could grow. Mama Blanca declared that her childhood was happy because:

> . . . it transpired in the arms of nature, and because, though channeled, it flowed as freely as a river between its banks. My sisters and I were never shut up within four walls, sated with candy, dolls, wagons, rocking horses, all those gloomy toys which, like the cares of adult life, bow down the shoulders of childhood. . . . We made our favorite toys ourselves out under the trees of leaves, stones, water, green fruit, mud, old bottles and tin cans. Like artists, we were possessed by the divine fire of creation, and like poets, we discovered secret affinities and mysterious relations between the most diverse objects.
>
> (p. 100)

Notes

1. Parra's birthdate, once contended, is now validated by documentary evidence obtained from Paris. Services d'Archives, on November 13, 1978, by the author.
2. Teresa de la Parra, "Dos Juicios de Teresa de la Parra," *Obras Completas* (Caracas: Editorial Arte, 1965), p. 509.
3. John Rothchild, *Latin America, Yesterday and Today* (New York: Bantam Pathfinder Editions, 1973), pp. 56–57.
4. Luis Alberto Sucre, *Gobernadores y Capitanes Generales de Venezuela* (Caracas: Lit. Tip. de Comercio, 1928), pp. 154–55.
5. Thomas Ybarra, *Young Man of Caracas* (New York: Yves Washburn, Inc,. 1941), p. 111.
6. De la Parra, "Dos Juicios de Teresa de la Parra," p. 511.
7. Teresa de la Parra, "Conferencias," in *Obras Completas*, pp. 734–35.
8. Pedro Jose Vargas, *Carlos Soublette, Biografia de un Politico Ejemplar* (Caracas: Tipografia Garrido, 1946), p. 8.
9. El Fundador de Caracas, *El Universal*, Caracas, October 28, 1909, n.p.
10. Vicente Davila, *Proceres Trujillanos* (Caracas: Imprenta Bolívar, 1921), p. 261.
11. Rothchild, *Latin America* pp. 119–20.
12. Ibid., p. 146.
13. Ibid., p. 121.
14. Ibid., p. 144.
15. Ibid., p. 227.
16. Ibid., p. 52.
17. Ibid., p. 33.
18. *Gravity's Rainbow* (New York: The Viking Press, 1973), p. 264.
19. Rothchild, *Latin America*, p. 158.
20. Clara Isabel Gonzalez, "Teresa de la Parra," *Revista del Instituto Pedagogico Nacional*, April-June 1945, p. 231.
21. Gabriela Mistral, "Dos Recados sobre Teresa de la Parra," *Repertorio Americano*, San Jose, Costa Rica, September 26, 1936, p. 162.
22. "Teresa de la Parra," *El Espectador*, Bogota, martes 27 de mayo de 1930. n.p.
23. As told to author by Maria Josefa Aristeguieta.
24. "La Vida Intima de Teresa de la Parra," interview with Maria Parra-Bunimovitch in *El Nacional*, Caracas, December 7, 1947.
25. *Latin America*, pp. 7–8.
26. De la Parra, "Conferencias," pp. 716–17.
27. Parra-Bunimovitch, "La Vida Intima de Teresa de la Parra."
28. Gonzalez, p. 230.
29. Letter to Rafael Carias, *Obras Completas*, pp. 851–52.

CHAPTER TWO

Marriage: *Ifigenia* Cries Out

Lessons of the Convent

The true story of Rafael Parra's illness before his death was never related to his children. That he had suffered secretly of tuberculosis would otherwise have surfaced as a factor in his daughter's extended analysis of her own tubercular condition years later. Isabel probably expected his early demise, but the simultaneous wave of destruction upon other members of the Parra family arrived suddenly and unforeseen. Briefly, the official story went thus.[1]

Dr. Miguel Parra, one of Rafael's brothers, was living on the next block to the Parra household in Caracas over Christmas of 1898. After having lunch at Isabel's house on December 22, he said to his sister-in-law that he was tired and wished to take a nap; he ascended the stairs to the house's garret bedroom. Because he remained there an unusually long while, Isabel began to feel uneasy. She sent someone up to knock on the door of his room; there was no answer. When they finally opened the door, they discovered the source of her fears: Miguel was dead. In little more than twenty-four hours on Christmas Day in the same house, Rafael succumbed to tuberculosis, a disease that as yet had no cure and whose mysterious progression sowed fear and superstitition in the hearts of its victims' loved ones. It is interesting to note that in Rafael Parra's death certificate it shows that he died of chronic enteritis but some members of his family knew it was TB. When Isabel's youngest child, Rafaelito, no more than 3 years old, died of unknown causes after Rafael Parra's disappearance her grief was trebled. Every Christmastime thereafter was to herald the memory of her loss and her exclusion from the rites of joy forever reserved for others more fortunate than she.

Teresa was nine years old when her family plunged into deep mourning. Isabel, concerned for her children's education and financial security, gathered together her surviving family, including Mercedes Ezpelosin and sister Maria Luisa de Guerola, to embark on the long journey to Spain. Other relatives would welcome them there: another of Isabel's sisters, Mercedes de Llano, lived a prosperous life in the town of Valencia, lying midway down the Mediterranean coast, and under the aegis of her husband Juan de Llano's position as exporter of raisins, the Parras could function more comfortably among the elite than they could in Caracas without such protection. Soon after their arrival, Aunt Maria Luisa bought a house outside the Valencia city limits, and this became the residence of the Parra family for the next ten years. This house is still their property and the last descendants preserve and live in this house.

Teresa's world changed from the sheltered garden of the tropics to the cloistered halls of a Spanish convent, specifically designed to instill moral discipline in the young of the upper classes. The formal education available to her back in Venezuela, although equally infused with religious urgency, would have emphasized domestic skills to a greater degree than did the Spanish institution, where Teresa was able at least to receive solid, if hardly rigorous, training in the Greek and Latin classics. Caracas's best school for women, Saint Joseph de Tarbas, was not even accredited by the Venezuelan Ministry of Education until 1919.[2]

Teresa remained in the academy until 1907. She received numerous awards and commendations, including the distinction of a "green stripe," a traditional honor, in 1904.[3] The contrast she experienced between the viselike discipline of the convent and the fecundity of people and earth she had left behind was for her the first in a series of dualisms—geographical, theological, and philosophical—that would echo throughout the course of her life. These contrasts can be witnessed on the South American continent itself, where over against the harsh, granitelike beauty of the interior Andean mountain chain is cast the sensual wealth of the surrounding ring of coast; and they can be furthermore felt in the contradictions that inhabit Spanish culture, itself nailed end to end by the hammers of Catholic and Platonic theory.

Impressions from *Ifigenia,* in conjunction with statements by Parra, confirm that her Spanish experience had had "a severe Catholic atmosphere: the only excitement were the big church festivals, and an occasional trip to the country."[4] The Sisters of the Sacred Heart, with their strict, unsmiling admonitions, did their utmost to quell Teresa's thirst for worldly experience and tame her reactions thereto. Teresa, however, suffering the twin hardships of adolescence and the death of her father, was nurturing within her resistance to authoritarian dogma a curiosity toward the mysteries of the world that that dogma, even more myseriously, tried to occlude.

Maria Nolla remembers her old classmate as one who was happiest in school when she studied alone; other students would tend to spoil her concentration and put her wandering mind in distress.[5] There did not appear to be much about formal education that suited her temperament: the tasks of drilling and memorizing aroused an apprehension—visible throughout her life—about what she considered tampering with her inner inclinations, her capacity for independent thought, and her emotional vitality. The whole learning process itself, inflicted by rule and by rote, alienated Teresa in this early period of the practice of discipline. Just like an older Blanca Nieves, she still wished to discover the Beast for herself in his unaltered beastliness, yet where before the old romantic fervor had spoken in the disorderly language of her mother's free-spirited storytelling, it now found expression, in spite of herself, in the vocabulary of the Christian saints and the method of the Greek philosophers.

There is much in *Ifigenia* to shed light on this period of Parra's life,

Colegio del S. C. de Jésus godella -- Vue du Parc

Ana Teresa at the Convent School of the Sacred Heart in Godella, Valencia, Spain.

despite her own initial protests to the contrary. After the novel's partial issue in Caracas in 1922 and completed publication in France in 1924, it seemed as difficult for Parra herself as for her gossip-hungry public to judge where her own ideas diverged from those of her heroine, whose story, from the public's point of view, seemed taken from life. As it was, there existed sufficient matching of physical and emotional facts between character and author to warrant this public misapprehension; only Parra herself, however, was ever to know the precise measure of fiction in her plot. She left it to her devoted friend Rafael Carias to disclose: ". . . the occasion when Teresa confessed to us all the puppets of her novel, with the exception of Maria Eugenia, were derived from real persons, living beings, of course baptized with different names and much altered, because there were some personalities resembling real ones so closely that she was frightened. She said, 'And I feel they could compromise me. There is someone who was in on the secret,' she added, 'but don't tell.' and she looked at Doña Emilia, bathing her with a smile."[6] Doña Emilia was Emilia Ibarra, Teresa's good friend and mentor, and the phrase "with the exception of Maria Eugenia" has become testimony liable to amendment by Teresa's own mature, more illuminating remarks on the dispute. We can only assert that she and Maria Eugenia, her heroine, were linked more vulnerably to one another than she and the three selves of *Mama Blanca*. Carias continues with another anecdote revealing Teresa in the throes of her relationship to Maria Eugenia, full of psychological musings about what would always remain a major subtext in her life: the eternal battle between opposing selves and their so-necessary truce of recognition, about which she, at this early date, kept coyly mum:

> One time our conversation came to childhood memories, to the tales of fairies and elves; and we were delighted by Teresa's knowledge of the world of the imagination. The subject of the alter ego also came up (this mysterious being that sometimes treats us kindly, other times cruelly). Someone recalled how J. Barbey D'Aurevilly would take leave of his double every morning as he shut the door: "Goodbye, Barbey," as if it were the most natural thing in the world. With an exploratory smile Teresa asked me then with what name would I choose to distinguish my "other self," and I immediately answered: "I'll take a short name: Angel Ruiz." I ventured then to tell her that hers could be no other than Maria Eugenia.[7]

Dodge the question though she may have done, Parra the young author can be detected flickering in and out of Maria Eugenia's impulsive eyes, lamplike, haunting her unpredictably like the ancestral ghosts who vie for possession of the young woman's soul.

In the beginning chapter of *Ifigenia,* titled "A Very Long Letter Where Things Happen as They Do in Novels," we find Maria Eugenia in the act of writing an impassioned letter to her schoolmate Christina Iturbe. Valuable flashbacks fill in the stage set and introduce the characters; let the readers decide for themselves if this excerpt does not detail the portrait of a young lady very much like the one we imagine Teresa to have been while at the Spanish convent school:

> As you already know, I've always been fond of novels. . . . You and I were, for the most part, two intellectual and romantic girls, but we were also on the other hand excessively timid. Sometimes I reflect upon this feeling of timidity and I believe today that we must have acquired it from the sheer fright of seeing our own broad foreheads, bare and outlined by that black semi-circle formed by our poor straight, tightly-bound hair, reflected in the crystal of the windows and doors of the college. As you remember, this was an indispensable prerequisite, according to the opinion of the Mothers, towards the good name of the girls, who in addition to being well-behaved, were intelligent and studious like ourselves. I arrived at the conviction that tightly pulled back hair really constituted a great moral superiority, yet I always looked with much admiration upon those other girls, called "empty-headed" by the Mothers, who against all regulation retained the pleasant appearance of their curls and waves.
>
> In spite of our intellectual superiority, I remember that I always felt fundamentally inferior to the girls with flowing hair. I placed the novelistic heroines also in this group of the "curl-fringed temples," a group that clearly represented what the Mothers called with plenty of disdain "the world." We, together with the Mothers, the Chaplain of the College, the twelve daughters of Maria, the Saints of the Christian year, the incense, the confessional, the pews, all belonged to the other group. In reality I was never very enthusiastic about my membership therein. That wicked "world," held in such contempt and abhorrence by the Mothers, appeared dazzling to my eyes, and full of prestige in spite of its vile inferiority. Our moral superiority created a kind of burden inside me, which I remember carrying with constant resignation and sad thoughts that thanks to

43

it, I would not play out any but the most obscure and secondary roles [in life]. . . .[8]

Teresa hints again at the dishonesty she felt underlying the nuns' training at the Colegio in a biographical statement published after her death: ". . . there I learned many things, which, had I adapted myself to them, would perhaps . . . perhaps have brought me fame and fortune; but I have never been seduced by hypocrisy."[9] As to just how adaptation to the nuns' strict antisecular lessons could have brought her fortune and fame, the answer lies in an insinuation that those dogmatic lessons taught, more than anything else, a capacity for hypocrisy that was equally essential to the pursuit of more worldly prizes. Compare Maria Eugenia's outburst in *Ifigenia*: "Three years of philosophy I followed in college, and I tell you, the professors who corrected my work used to fill the margins with praise! For this reason order and method reign in my intellect, and naturally, to protect myself from premises as false and contradictory as those predicted by prudence, modesty, and decency, I could never bring myself to attach myself to them. . . . The Nuns of the college appreciated innocence and eulogized modesty for the sole reason that they themselves were virgins—one and all!"[10]

In 1904 Ana Teresa was doing her lessons well: she won first prize for a poem she submitted in competition with the students and alumni of all the Sacred Heart schools of Spain. Although her first cousin Luis de Llano states the acclaim encouraged her to continue writing, she later considered the poem so bad that her sister Maria could not be convinced to reveal more than the first line—"In whose brow is not serenity raised, before the glory of the beloved fatherland"—for fear Teresa, already dead eleven years, "would never forgive her" were it to be published.[11] Teresa's characteristic distaste for openness was to discourage any further attempts at poetry. Such naked passion of the soul, the "immodesty of the soul,"[12] in her own words, upon which lyrical poetry is based, required greater artistry than she possessed to elevate its nakedness above the danger zone of reproach and ridicule. It required "great purity of form," and the two or three poems that she claimed to have written up to this statement in 1925 achieved—in her judgment—only an embarrassing mediocrity.

By the time she was twenty years old, Teresa was filling her days with familial commitments to society and other feminine pursuits, usually pertaining to the household. If her formal education had ended prematurely at the age of seventeen or if she skipped a year in between the transfer and quit the Colegio closer to age eighteen, she would have received comparable tutoring in Valencia to fill the gaps. The family retained Señor Ramón Arroyo as a tutor, whom Teresa referred to as Don Ramon in the first dedication to *Ifigenia* and who accompanied her two older brothers back to Venezuela before her own return in 1910.[13] Until that time, there were occasional trips to Paris, according to Luis de Llano, which were common for the Spanish of the day. Direct railroad links provided convenient transportation up the French coast, and it was not considered excessive to visit the cultural hub of the Western world on a regular basis. The legend of Paris had so capitivated South Americans at the turn of the century that diplomats to all of Europe and exiles alike

Ana Teresa and her sister Isabelita out on vacation from the Academy of Sacred Heart (1908).

considered it the only place worth leaving home for. A diplomat assigned to London, for example, "would interpret his duty to mean he must live in Paris 11 months of the year and one month, if absolutely necessary, in London."[14] That Parra's birthplace was Paris and not Berlin, where her father was assigned as consul, is due to this stylish tradition. (Additionally, the family wished to be near Rafael's brother Antonio, whose entertaining personality was to inspire both Uncle Juancho of *Mama Blanca* and Pancho of *Ifigenia* and who was enjoying his brief mission as consul general to Paris in the year of his niece's birth.)

In 1909 Teresa's presence was reported at the Valencia fair for agricultural products, and it was the following year that she returned to Caracas with her sister Isabelita. The two young women stayed with Teresa's godmother, Lola Reyes de Sucre, until their mother and two younger sisters Elia and Maria returned in 1911, to reestablish the family home at the square Plaza del Valle, also in Caracas. A few years later, Isabel sold the plantation.[15] Luis de Llano hints at a "strangeness" surrounding the sale, inevitable though it was given the new industrialization. His comment harks back to an important device of *Ifigenia*'s plot—the thievery by Maria Eugenia's Uncle Eduardo of plantation shares belonging rightfully to her. Perhaps Tazon, also managed by one of the Parra relatives, met a similar fate and Isabel, like Maria Eugenia, returned to find that "the ration of those who are absent is always that on which the cat dines," as Uncle Pancho, ever too honest, was wont to say.[16]

Caracas of 1911: a victim of the "Second Conquest," just beginning to betray the spiritual vapidity of industrial boom in the aesthetic blight that frayed its environs. After 1905 General Gomez had emerged as the United States oil companies' man in Venezuela. The price for oil development was a scarcely controlled influx of foreign businessmen and foreign ideas: this was the now-familiar Americanization, since then infamous for its tendency throughout the world to debase and devalue indigenous culture. At the turn of the century there had been only a "thin surface of modernity," through which peeped the Caracas of the Spaniards; "of Simon Bolívar, Spain's nemesis in South America; of his successors, the rough generals of unnumbered Venezuelan civil wars."[17] To one critic of Parra's work, the Caracas of her time still adhered internally to old formulas. Despite an incipient middle class of bureaucrats and militarists, it was a city of proletarians and elite: milkmen, street-sweepers, coke vendors, coal merchants, and peddlers on the one hand and members of the regime—Parra's characters—with their class interests on the other.[18]

In the beginning of *Ifigenia*, Parra evokes a Caracas much changed from the idyllic image of it she had cultivated in her memory since leaving it in 1903. As Maria Eugenia, she is returning from school in Spain and a three-month sojourn in Paris to arrive at Venezuela's main port of La Guaira. Displaying her newfound talent for expressing herself, she describes the area as it looked then, poised in limbo, with the spirit of modernization encircling the spirit of the Age of Gold. La Guaira was only a small harbor then, run by sweating mulatto longshoremen and backed by a great "yellow, barren mountain upon which little houses of all colors bloomed, appearing to be climbing up between the rocks with the pastoral audacity of a flock of goats."[19] The palm trees signaled welcome to the tropics, and the road to Caracas led through that imposing mountain "whose peaks dominate the city and separate it from the sea. From the city one can see the mountain peaks change color several times a day; condensation from the surrounding atmosphere. The capricious fluctuations have given it a character all its own, copied with devotion by every painter, sung with more devotion by many a poet to the memory of the conquistador who took it from the Indians—I don't know when—it is named after him: 'El Avila.' "[20] The city itself lies down in the valley, and it appears to Maria Eugenia in the colors of her own unhappy mood, oppressed by the mountain and entangled in a web of telegraph lines: "Ah! Caracas of the delicious climate, the intimate yet distant city, ended up being this squat place. . . . It has an Andalusian melancholy but lacks Spanish guitars, flowers in the gates. . . . It is an Andalusian dreaming, fallen asleep in the sultry tropics."[21]

Utterly chagrined at the lifelessness of her new home, Maria Eugenia searches the streets of Caracas for something to uplift her. A sudden ray of light strikes from above, shining from inside one of the houses. As she looks up into the opened window frame, all the familiar welcoming signs of home—people, portraits, mirrors, flowers—that have given themselves over to the sad desertion of the streets lend her senses a reassurance. She does not feel the true thrill of arrival, however, until she is ushered into the extravagantly blooming tropical garden of her aunt Clara.

It took around thirty years for modernity to dig its roots into Caraquenian soil; for Parra, "modernity" always remained itself the root of confusion, a one-way door to greed and superficiality. For others, it simply ruined the city's special charm, creating the "city without distinction" described below:

. . . I cannot help thinking that my Caracas, the Caracas of the end of the 19th century, was more attractive than the Caracas of today (1941), despite the turbulence of the former and the sedateness of the letter.

. . . There may be beauty in the new Caracas. It has modern suburbs. It has modern highways reaching out to all points of the compass—to La Guaira, to Aragua and the Tuy, to the broad Venezuelan llanos—that would fill the soul of Macadam, Scottish god of pavements, with the cold Caledonian substitute for bliss. It has a couple of country clubs that would fit, without alterations, into Pasadena. It has many spic and span, brightly painted villas, which doubtless warm the cockles of the hearts of American oil men and oil women and oil children. But to me, its architecture—and its nature—reek of gingerbread. And, if that be treason, make the most of it, Dutch Shell! Make the most of it, Standard Oil![22]

By 1913 Isabel's sisters and their respective families had left Spain and bought houses in Caracas. Teresa's family had moved again to Mercedes a Salas. She was now twenty-four years old, having spent some six years carrying out—dutifully—the various chores expected of her and contemplating—warily—the inevitable next step of marriage. No doubt her mother had this in mind when, in 1913, she began to escort her beautiful, marriageable daughters to every significant social occasion the family's prestige in Caracas permitted. This was the turning point in Teresa's life. Her introduction to society in that year was an introduction to the world of Emilia Ibarra, the glamorous lady who defined for a much younger Ana Teresa a role to play in life, neither secondary to a husband nor shut out from the mysteries of the everyday world.

Emilia Ibarra belonged to a branch of the great Ibarra clan that was as liberal as Parra's de Tovar ancestors were "godo." But Teresa did not allow the prejudices of her maternal ancestors to discourage their friendship; rather, she allowed Emilia to illuminate that side of national history so maligned by those ancestors. It was through Emilia that Teresa came to embrace the Bolívar loyalists whose representation in her own family had vanished, all except for Teresa Soublette. In her most publicized letter of self-defense, written in 1926 to Ignacio Vetancourt-Aristeguieta, a poison-pen critic of *Ifigenia,* Teresa describes Emilia's contribution to her knowledge of history with ill-concealed pride and devotion:

. . . A third history of Venezuela, that of the progressive and liberal period, I saw reflected like in a mirror in the brilliantly clear soul of my great friend and second mother, Emilia Ibarra de Barrios Parejo. Sister-in-law of President Guzman-Blanco, she was the daughter of General Andres Ibarra, that young aide-de-camp of Bolívar who after saving his life in the assassination attempt of September 14, accompanied him loyally during the beautiful twilight of Santa Marta, saw him expire in his arms, dressed in his own clothes the remains of the martyr, and . . .

Brilliant princess of that brilliant court of the government of General Guzman-Blanco for 20 years, Emilia Ibarra, who was familiar since infancy with all the privileges of power, of beauty and luxury, was much later crossed by ill fortune but traversed it with the discreet hauteur and elegance of a queen. She was also an heir of the severe Mantuanas, the liberalism of her relatives taught her to smile in the face of the present, and from this fountain she drank in love that was always alive with gaiety. She drank in also that rarest science which is to [forgive by comprehending] everything, and reserving only for herself the austerity of her race, she distributed to all who surrounded her the white roses of generosity and of holy indulgence.[23]

Emilia was the youngest child of seven. Her sister Ana Teresa, whose Grecian beauty won President Guzman-Blanco's attention in 1870, was the oldest, born in 1847. Sometime between 1865 and 1870, Emilia would have been born, making her a good twenty years Parra's senior.

One Thomas R. Ibarra, cousin to Emilia, published an autobiography, *Young Man of Caracas*, in 1941. It is a collection of memories from his childhood in turn-of-the-century Caracas—memories that recount the individual stories of his many eccentric and stately relatives. Unfortunately for us, he never mentions Emilia, but within a description of his aunt Ines we can recognize a clear picture of the special Ibarra brand of femininity that so captivated Teresa's imagination. Aunt Ines was regal, a vision of "glorious Spanish loveliness"; she was without prejudices and struck straight to the core of this genuine friendship that lasted through life; she was sweet without being overpliant or wishy-washy, had a rippling laugh and an irresistible desire to be friendly, and above all, she wanted to like everybody and wanted everybody to like her.[24]

One window to the secrets of a personality is located in the identification of its heroes. Parra, perhaps in lieu of those intimate confessions for which the public hungered, made a point of identifying her own—for herself and for us—in a list whose names spanned the centuries. That list culminated in the name of Emilia Ibarra. The Ana Teresa Parra whom Emilia met in 1913 was shy and naive, eager to learn the ways of the world and quick to subject that world to her idealistic scrutiny. The image Emilia presented, in contrast, was one of a maternal spirit; she seemed the personification of feminine virtue, a kind of dark queen whose enigmatic source Teresa, her disciple, wished to learn and drink from herself. Maria Eugenia also had a tendency to seek guidance from a certain kind of woman—her young friend Christina Iturbe, for example, dignified and serious about her studies, transmits that seriousness to Maria Eugenia, who before had been unable and unwilling to find any value in studying. Then there is Mercedes Galindo, the most faithfully rendered from reality of any character in *Ifigenia,* in the opinion of Rafael Carias, who is none other than the mirror image of Emilia Ibarra. Compare this description of Mercedes to the former two of Emilia and Aunt Ines Ibarra: ". . . I contemplated the figure of Mercedes as I hid in the shadows—she was genteel, radiant like a queen, and I found myself petrified with admiration. . . . From under the half-light of her hat surged one of the most beautiful, silvery voices I've ever heard in my life."[25] And then:

> Mercedes sought to Orientalize her Creole indolence, and in place of stirring it up in a hammock under breezy palms, she cultivated it in her low and immense Turkish divan, huge and white cushions, where she read, dreamt, reflected, took tea, was at times disturbed, and also cried. Seated in her undulating and lovely cushions, Mercedes had a prestige that to me seemed exotic and suggestive. I always thought, when looking at her, that this must be what those famous Oriental queens were like, and as all of her house seemed like a garden, and I did not find it in good taste to call her Cleopatra, it was better to say Semiramis, of the hanging gardens.[26]

But Mercedes was also a tragic queen, the wife of an unappreciative husband. Even the problems of Emilia's marriage to Francisco Barrios-Parejo were easily recognizable in the relationship between Mercedes and her husband, Alberto Palacios, a complex figure who is described as ". . . very likeable, and like her, very sophisticated and gifted with people. I noted nevertheless, in spite of his gallantry and external amiability, that he spoke to her several times in a brusque tone of voice, making me think there was some truth in Abuelita and Aunt Clara's talk that he treats her badly. How could he mistreat a creature so full of every enchantment, of every attraction?''[27] It is an obsessive, unhappy affair, beset by signs of a deep dissatisfaction with self on his part, not the least of which is the classic preoccupation with power and other women. Mercedes has no desire for a divorce: "I prefer pain to deformity,''[28] she says, and to neutralize the bitterness in her heart, to fill the silence that answers to her sacrifices, she dedicates her days to the attainment of satisfactions awarded her by playing matchmaker with her friends, by entertaining them at gatherings tinged with the flavor of the occult and the pleasures her wealth can provide by trying to make them—at least—happy.

Palacios, like Barrios-Parejo, nurses ambition for one of the coveted diplomatic posts that in those earlier days crowned the career of many an aspirant to the highest circles of power and nobility. Diplomacy then had little to do with the delicate and complex tasks facing today's diplomats. That glamorous world inhabiting certain corners in Parra's work constituted in her adult social life a major arena, expanded by the careers of both her father and her uncle Antonio, her sister Maria's Russian husband, Marc Bunimovitch, and her good friends Gonzalo Zaldumbide and Gabriela Mistral. These posts were assigned on the basis of two qualifications: connections—through political maneuvering—to the current government in power and/or some outstanding literary or social achievement. Such plums could be awarded or withdrawn with startling fickleness in accord with the political climate. In those days, South America followed the custom, common to North America as well as to Europe before the Second World War, of sending her most cultured citizens to represent her abroad. Artists, poets, and intellectuals qualified along with the merely rich and aristocratic as vessels of national culture, and their governments displayed them proudly to foreigners. There were South Americans who attached these artistic titles unabashedly to their names, summoning images of the Renaissance men, or better, a more modern likeness of Benjamin Franklin. Many a "poet/historian/ intellectual/aristocrat" graced the diplomatic circles, with an occasional sprinkling of simple poets and novelists.

Emilia, since 1920 a widow, was to die in 1924 in Paris,[29] only a couple of months before *Ifigenia*'s publication and only eight months after Teresa had arrived in Paris also, innocent and trembling in anticipation of the next stage of her overnight success. There is a hint of disease in Teresa's phrase "she was crossed by ill-fortune"—possibly some horrible cancer leading up to the death.[30] Emilia's death certificate, made out most curiously with the first name of Mercedes (was this Emilia's name for her alter ego or her true second first name?), nevertheless confirms the approximate time we place the death according to the related events in Teresa's mournful letter to Carias, falsely dated 1927 by her editors. Emilia's patronage proved far-reaching financially as well as morally. Teresa in turn dedicated her novel to: ". . . the sweet absent one, beneath whose shade this book flowered bit by bit. To that most bright light of your eyes that always lit up the path of writing with hope, and also to the white and cold peace of your two crossed hands, that will never again turn the pages."[31]

During the decade of the nineteen-teens, Teresa, like Maria Eugenia, was immersing herself in the vicarious world of books considered so dangerous and corruptive by her elders. When the family vacationed in the country, she was known to shut herself up in her room for days on end to read, even to pursue studies in Latin.[32] "I tried to read as much as I could," begins her autobiographical statement to Carlos Garcia Prada in 1930, and in the following years of inactivity in Caracas.

> . . . I observed the continuous conflict existing between the new outlook of young women awakened to modernism by travel and reading and the life they really led, chained by prejudices and traditions of another era. Without believing in such prejudices they nevertheless allowed themselves to be dominated by them at all times, sighing, but only in their desires, for independence in their lives and their ideas, until marriage would come and cause them to surrender and submit, and finally convert them to the old ideas, thanks to motherhood, This continual female conflict that ends in renunciation gave me the inspiration for my first novel, "Ifigenia."[33]

Besides delving into the classics and refining her knowledge of Latin, Teresa discovered a love for French literature. It was this rich and progressive world of writers, from Anatole France to Proust, that opened her imagination more than any other to the literary potential of her own experience. Although her literary point of view is often ascribed to the influence of Romain Rolland, she did not appear to have been affected by him at this early stage in her career, beyond reading familiarity with *Jean Christophe*.[34] Out of all the books she was reading in Caracas, the one that suggests itself most strongly as inspiration for *Ifigenia*'s confessional style is a book Parra never mentioned. Indeed, if she did not know of it until after *Ifigenia* was written, the similarities present a startling coincidence. The details of the novel, very popular in turn-of-the-century Paris, were unearthed by Professor Nelida Norris in her 1970 dissertation. The novel was titled "The Diary of Maria Bashkirtseff" and represented the actual diary of a Russian aristocrat by that name, raised in Nice and Paris, who had begun writing it at the age of twelve and continued until her untimely death at twenty-three, of none other disease than tuberculosis. Six years afterwards, in 1890, her published diary created a sensation in Paris, especially with young readers delighting in its precocious adolescent fancy. Professor Norris speculated that Parra, who prided herself at that time on her modernity, as did Maria Eugenia, would have been familiar with the book. She questioned Lydia Cabrera, receiving confirmation that, yes, Teresa "knew the book very well." The frank and introspective diary revealed a Marie Bashkirtseff with many qualities similar to Parra's Maria Eugenia, including the "obvious sensual awakening, intellectual impatience, mystical reveling."[35] Norris does not point out the one occasion, however, of Parra's own allusion to the author of that Parisian novel. In her second lecture in Bogota in 1930, Parra referred to the Russian aristocrat's meteoric career as a counterpoint to the fate of her maiden aunt Teresa Soublette, "an old spinster who, like Amarilis, well could have been the silent lover of a Lope de Vega. I never knew her story—the love stories of the unmarried women who did not die young and in glory as did Marie Bashkirtseva are of no interest to anyone. The family doesn't even remember."[36]

Unlike Maria Bashkirtseva, or Maria Eugenia for that matter, Teresa never alluded to a diary written either in her teenage years or in her twenties. Considering her secretiveness, it is impossible to imagine her admitting to one, especially if she had woven its less personal parts and general tone into *Ifigenia*. But diary or no diary, it should be remembered that the bulk of a writer's work is done inside the head, in contemplation. Teresa was, if anything, an underachiever. She had given no indication at all of the virtuosity she would later call upon to write *Ifigenia*'s five hundred pages in less than a year, and the much shorter *Mama Blanca* in three months with minimal editing. Even Maria had been caught unawares by the fruit her sister produced out of those some ten years' incubation: "There was nothing to indicate the great writer pulsating inside her. A spirited girl, singleminded, surrounded by admirers, but without a trace of coquetry, she lived her life as a society woman. Pretty and interesting, green eyes, very white skin, black hair."[37] Adding to that some key details of Teresa's personality, she continued: ". . . simple. Profoundly simple; naive since childhood, it was easy to fool her.

She detested lies and protested, horrifed: 'But what if I've been told a lie!' . . . as if it were a crime.''[38]

Vulnerability to deception and capacity for deception can become linked as prey to predator; Teresa's preoccupation with the many faces of truth brought her into a game where her own "seduction by hypocrisy" was at stake. From the public's point of view, her elusive image, accompanied as it was by a wardrobe of stunning Parisian costumes, enticed them to pursue the person dwelling underneath. From Parra's point of view, it effectively distracted from her true self, throwing up a shell of illusions protecting a small territory "in the solitude of the soul, where the words can run freely without the imposition of wanting to be brilliant or the inhibition of fearing indiscretion.'' But she admits that there is danger in the game of appearances, played as it is in the mirror that multiplies self-image to infinity, dividing it thereby into pieces so insignificant that we might never find them again. The truth plays an even more dangerous hand, though. In Parra's opinion (as well as that of Maria Eugenia at her more "mature" stage), truth is, to strike a different metaphor, like a bundle of dynamite and can create wounds as painful as those suffered in the explosions of war. For peace-lovers it must sometimes yield to the worthy white lie of indulgence and tolerance.[39]

The strength of Maria Eugenia's personality proves insufficient to defend the integrity of such a fragile barricade. Her other personal qualities, failing to come to her assistance in the end, ring loud and clear in the beginning with tones reminding us of *Mama Blanca*. They are the qualities that Parra loves—spontaneity, unity with Mother Nature, and a distrust of logic's sterility. The light show projecting from the peaks of Mount Avila onto the amphitheater of Caracas provides a perfect metaphor for the changeability Maria Eugenia nurtures in herself. Riding across that mountain into Caracas, feeling oppressed by the absurd pronouncements of her relatives, and looking down at the town of La Guaira, diminishing behind her to the size of a child's toy, she imagines suddenly being free as a bird, soaring and ecstatic, a bird who "never would feel again what I feel—the sterility of final definitive repose.''[40]

But Ana Teresa was an oft-seen character in Caracas, and her family's activities were submitted for public inspection in the society columns on a regular basis. It was not only she who was bored during those eyears. Maria said, "We were all bored there in Caracas, where nothing hardly ever happened.''[41] One by one, Teresa's siblings were finding mates: her brother Miguel married in 1914; sometime later so did her second-youngest sister, Elia, who was considered the prettiest Parra daughter by Caracas's young bachelors. She had been chosen by the Venezuelan painter Tito Salas to model for his mural of the wedding scene of Bolívar and Teresa Toro, and eventually she married that painter's brother. Even Maria, the youngest, was married after 1915.

As marriage levitated her sisters out of boredom, Teresa fought resignation to the social sterility of spinsterhood with a halfhearted ambition for a literary career and the full-blown fantasy world into which she ventured through her books. Her known "admirers," one of whom was the minister of education of Venezuela himself, Luis Felipe Guevara-Rojas, were received with nothing more than tolerant disdain. On the other hand, the secret existence of an unnamed admirer has been neither admitted nor denied, presenting a ghostly Pandora's box that no biographer has succeeded in opening. Teresa's feminine charms and romantic nature were indisputable, and the reticence of family and friends alike to discuss even the absence of love in her life has been pronounced. Those people wishing only to aid their comprehension of her decisions in life have been left the sole option of seeking the answer in the pages of *Ifigenia,* where so much fiction embellished real life and diverged from it. Who, in short, was Gabriel Olmedo, Maria Eugenia's true love?

He was a man with tastes like Maria Eugenia's own, who appreciated the feel of silk on his neck, who was intelligent but overly ambitious, and who loved and understood her better than she did herself. But their romance was barely off the ground before he married a society woman who he did not love, for her money. In all fairness, it must be said that his desertion resulted from a confluence of two factors other than greed: Maria Eugenia's own skittish gamesmanship and the lying interference of her aunt Maria Antonia. Gabriel does not wake up to his mistake until a full two years later, when his misery has reached a breaking point. Able neither to continue to live the lie nor to obtain a divorce, he returns to Maria Eugenia to confess his love on the occasion of her uncle Pancho's mortal illness. Her senses in the meantime have been benumbed by forced incarceration and imagined betrayal; rekindled, they awaken with the fire of mutual attraction. Her hope for the future gains strength with Gabriel's assurance that once they elope to Europe, their love will surmount the social stigma of not being married.

There exist both the possibility that Gabriel Olmedo was a complete figment of Parra's versatile imagination and the possibility that he was a romantic figure in the life of one of her sisters. If we reject these notions, however, out of the known contenders for Parra's hand, only one man emerges as a potentially successful contender: Gonzalo Zal-

dumbide. He was a diplomat, poet, and respected intellectual from Ecuador, stationed in Paris as ambassador during the first years of Teresa's
residence there. From 1924 to late 1925, Parisian society viewed them
as a romantic pair. Inevitable whisperings about love and marriage circulated in the wake of their shared beauty and vibrant intelligence. But

Señor Don Gonzalo Zaldumbide, former minister of Ecuador in the United States
and member of the governing board of the Pan American Union, also appointed
minister of foreign affairs of his government.

he married the Ecuadorian Isabel Rosales, in May 1926, in a ceremony that Teresa suggestively did not attend. That same spring, she visited her sister Maria in Switzerland, having written to her friend Carias late in the previous year: ". . . nothing of settling down, nor of marriage; but to run, to go astray, until weariness overcomes me and perhaps I begin to write again."[42] The question in the public's mind is the following: was Zaldumbide present in Caracas around the period of Teresa's rise to social prominence there, before he moved on to his next post in Paris? Being a diplomat, had he ever graced Emilia Ibarra's salon? On August 13, 1920, *El Universal* had reported his marriage in Paris to a Margot de la Sota, complete with photographs, in a front-page article. Clearly a beauty, she was also known to be the daughter of a wealthy, well-connected Venezuelan. Just two and a half years later, when Parra joined Zaldumbide on the European Blue Coast Shore, he was suddenly unaccompanied by his new wife, and by 1926 he was calling himself a bachelor. This latter detail was confirmed by the priest who married him in that year to Isabel Rosales.[43] Both of these wives seemed blessed with wealth as well as beauty, compared to Teresa, who was blessed with every attraction except wealth. Rosales was, in addition, a pianist of sufficient reknown to play in a New York concert hall after she accompanied her husband to the United States in 1928.

Zaldumbide had been among the first to assist Parra once she arrived in Paris in 1923. When her novel finally achieved print in 1924, he sent a critique to *El Nuevo Diario* from Paris in honor of its publication[44]; as he was a respected man of letters and an enthusiastic participant in Parisian literary circles, his commentaries were accepted as stemming from a natural interest in the career of a fellow Latin America. His remarks on women writers, however—"Women know how to confess much better than to tell a story, and there is no disguise that will not betray them" and "How like a woman it is to fail at creating a heroine of entirely unrelated body and soul, who does not represent to her a sister"[45]—imply his own suspicion of Teresa's close relationship to Maria Eugenia.

Other observations on the nature of the couple's association are conflicting. Maria claims that Gonzalo simply did "not disgust" her sister, "that it was not he whom she loved. . . ."[46] One of his self-proclaimed intimates and longtime friends, Francisco Guarderas, published a biography titled *Pages of Gonzalo Zaldumbide,* in which one chapter broaches the disputed rumor; in it Guarderas insinuates heavily that the Ecuadorian poet wrote a sonnet under the pseudonym of S. de la Torre-Abolida wherein he exposes a desperately self-abandoned heart—a heart that still, "a few years" after the publication of *Mama Blanca* (the dates in this essay are often inaccurate), cannot forget someone with green eyes and a vagabond sweetness who dared him to go to the bottom of his own depths. Perhaps, the poet continues, although he hid in cowardice behind the love of another, though he indulged in the cheap pleasures of money and other women, perhaps she still awaits him from the grave. Guarderas underlines the "green eyes" and remarks on the distinctive poetic style that is so reminiscent of Zaldumbide's own poetry in "Eglógicia Tragica," but in the same breath he denies having any knowledge or proof of a love affair. The couple met, he insists, at a dinner party given by the minister of Venezuela in Paris, where they instantly became friends. Moreover, he is certain Zaldumbide had known neither the name Teresa de la Parra nor of the existence of her novel before she came to Paris.[47]

Whether Zaldumbide inspired the character of Gabriel Olmedo or not is an unanswerable question, but there is evidence that Zaldumbide visited Caracas before 1920, as shown in a Venezuelan newspaper. As to whether he loved her or not, he confessed to it very late in life: "I will add to that [praise] what you want to hear. I loved her, as I have loved no one!"[48] According to a rare family disclosure, Teresa received a phone call from Zaldumbide on the morning of his wedding day. It was a last-chance offer to halt the marriage, if she would only say the word.[49] Both Lydia Cabrera and Maria deny that Teresa ever loved the Ecuadorian, yet her final rejection of him could have risen from a far less specific compendium of factors: an earlier marriage that might have rankled in her heart; an "unshakeable sense of fidelity that made her refractory to the marriage bond," like Cochocho; and finally, a deep, generalized distrust of men.

Teresa, says Lydia, "often complained of male superiority and dominance in love"; her novels reflect this feeling of cultural injury, to which the double standard of marital behavior flagrantly evident in her social circle piled on insult. Not one marriage in *Ifigenia* escapes hypocrisy: if the man is not behaving like a tyrant or a child, he betrays his wife (or fiancée) either by his preference for other women or for money. In *Mama Blanca,* the plantation morals are those of a "brilliant court," but the honest, loyal bond between Cochocho and his two mistresses attests to a higher moral code. Further evidence appears in a letter written much later in life, wherein Parra told the story of two fellow tuberculars, a prince of Asturias and his girl friend, who had decided to marry despite the threat of the prince's father to disinherit him. In open defiance of his father and royal relatives, the prince, cheered on by students from Lausanne, went ahead with the wedding. Even after such a sacrifice, Parra doubted the prince's ability to sustain his love and hoped that he would not be dissuaded by his "ambition."[50] Thomas Ibarra's mother also had a bit to say about the state of marriage just before Parra's time:

> The women in Caracas could do much to stop the behavior in public of the men. But while they continue to accept them socially, to talk about their amours and talk before young girls of all these things, just so long will men go on misbehaving themselves. The tone of the women in Caracas is very much lowered too. . . . I remember when X. was shut out of society because he lived with a Frenchwoman he had brought from Paris. The whole tone is corrupt, and the young girls can tell you things, innocent old militar that you are, that would make your hair stand on end. And it's so all over the world.[51]

Teresa, in her midtwenties, must have been well aware of this situation, if only through Emilia Ibarra's example, and was weighing her alternatives. Higher education at that time would have been out of the question for a woman of her social standing and nonacademic temperament—it was attainable only by women dedicated enough to risk social ostracization and years of struggle with university administrations. In Venezuela, there had been a well-documented case in 1905 of the young woman Virginia Pereira-Alvarez who tried to break through the social barrier separating women from the field of medicine.

A few courageous women up to that time had succeeded in the literary and social fields, such as the "first woman journalist" of Venezuela, Concepcion de Taylhardt; the poet Mercedes de Perez-Freites; and Lucila de Perez-Diaz, the historian. The arts and humanities have always touched on woman's domain. Science and women, however, existed in the popular mind as natural enemies. The following is an extreme example of what any woman seeking entry into the male professional world had to expect. When Virginia Pereira-Alvarez arrogated to herself the right to apply for admission to the school of medicine, she was turned away for lack of a female precedent and the president of the institution had to authorize an exception to the unwritten rule on her behalf.[52] But even then her trials were not over. After passing the entrance exams she suffered such harrassment by her fellow students, all male, that she became disheartened and resolved to seek her degree elsewhere.

Fifteen years passed before her determination won out, far away from Venezuela, in the United States, where she received her medical degree at the University of Pennsylvania in Philadelphia.[53]

Ana Teresa Parra, serious student of life, made her first timid reach into the professional writing world in 1915 with some articles she signed with the pen name Fru-Fru. These beginnings, according to Maria, were purely the product of Teresa's boredom, and they earned the charge of lacking substance in a newspaper critique titled "La Señorita Frivolidad." By 1919, however, she was thirty years old and motivated by the implications of such maturity. Her friendship with Emilia Ibarra had expanded to include a third friend, Rafael Carias, a businessman and writer whom she met in that same year while fulfilling her obligations at a charity club event. Carias fell immediately under the spell of Teresa's personality; to Emilia's encouragement of Teresa's literary aspirations, he was able to add his practical advice. This was a loyal and unselfish role that he sustained during the course of her career.

Teresa never failed to credit to his faithful influence her first novel's ultimate succes. That his had been the very first eyes to scrutinize *Ifigenia*'s pages when it was still a rough manuscript was evidence of the trust she extended to him; and later, when Teresa moved her home base to distant Europe, it was Carias, rather than a relative, to whom she gave the mandate to administrate her Venezuelan financial affairs. Angel-Ruiz, as he was known in their games of imaginative fancy during the summer of *Ifigenia*'s writing, remained the object of Teresa's gratitude until the end. In a letter written one year before her death, Parra said to her friend that she had been revising her "archives," which formed a concrete past for her. In her "archives" were letters from 1922 in Macuto. Included was a letter from Angel Ruiz, which had moved her greatly when she received it. It was a very sweet evocation of the past—of Emilia Barrios, the Guzman house, the ruins Parra hid in so she could write, the sounds of the ocean, the tepid air, and the fragrances that carried hopeful messages from distant lands, and Angel Ruiz, who had arrived to inform her of what she at first thought was a hallucination: literary success! Twelve years later, with much of the same feeling and great sadness, Parra thought of the friend who had disappeared in the multitude and whom she could not thank for bringing the splendid news to her. And despite the forgetfulness, despite of having written twice without getting any answer, she determined to write a third time, not now to Rafael Carias, but to the first friend, the older one—that Angel Ruiz for whom she felt such an innocent and honest friendship.[54]

In 1919 Teresa was summoning the courage, under the shelter of this three-way friendship, to rise to the demands of her talent, and the opportunity to do so soon arose. Maria had just married a Russian diplomat, Marc Bunimovitch. In 1919 the newlyweds embarked on a long journey to the Far East via the United States and the Pacific Ocean. As Maria's letters began to arrive back home, fragrant with the spice of adventure in exotic lands, Teresa was inspired. She assembled the letters and reworked them into a travelogue titled "Diary of a Caraquena," which was published in two parts by one of Caracas's literary magazines in December of the same year.[55] The piece, unsigned, was considered a product of both sisters, although stylistically it is consistent with Parra's later work.

Before these events in 1919, no trace of Teresa's fascination with the Orient had surfaced. After the inundation of Oriental culture she experienced vicariously through Maria's trip, however, Teresa wrote two very short pieces of fiction—supposedly her first and certainly the first to be published. *Lotus Flower, a Japanese Legend* was published under the Fru-Fru psuedonym in Caracas. Teresa always remembered with affection "its gentle exposition of the interesting symbols of that immaculate flower."[56] The second, *Buddha and the Leper,* came out first in 1920, then was republished in 1926. It is an Indian legend, but its tale of a rich man discovering an overwhelming Christ-like compassion in himself for a wretched leprous woman echoes Saint Mark's Gospel, 10:20, in that the protagonist renounces his wealth and comfort to fast in the desert.

Both books, more than mere expression of her love of the exotic, were imbued with a religiosity reflective of the spiritual air saturating the literary atmosphere of Paris and Switzerland in the twenties, through the influence of such gurus as Jung and the more esoteric Gurdjieff. Former Catholics had become captivated by eastern religious disciplines—techniques for the attainment of the self-knowledge and peace of mind they sought in their fundamentally Christian pursuit of selfless love. Parra's vital receptivity to this most fashionable trend could have been predicted.

Though at *Ifigenia*'s writing she was at a stage in her religious journey bordering on heresy, Parra told her tale of longing all in the mystical language and imagery of the Christian Bible, determining and defining as they did the contradictions of her adolescent experience so extravagantly. Blended throughout, however, are passages signalling the pantheistic core of her personal cosmogeny and the aesthetic focus of her being: Maria Eugenia, bathing in the tropical pool of a river bordering her uncle's plantation, has sculpted a fallen twig into a small floating structure, which she sends sailing down the stream like "an Indian funeral barque floating solitary down the sacred current of the Ganges." Contemplating love and morality, she declares, "I possess a love that is elevated and at the same time pantheistic. . . . My system of spiritual fidelity is many times more pure and meritorious than that exterior and moveable fidelity which men and conventions and the laws seek to impose."[57] Once middle-aged, Parra would appraise her mystical affinity to the East as natural birthright: "I do not cease to think that the tropics, like the Far East, are lands where mysticism grows spontaneously."[58]

The year 1921 saw Parra in the limelight of Caracas's two most dramatic social occasions in years. The first was the one-hundredth anniversary celebration of the battle that decided Venezuela's independence from Spain: the Battle of Carabobo. Ana Teresa was chosen to provide a narrative of the battle that would appear in print throughout Caracas as background for the spectacular festivities. She sharpened her historical perspective, out of which a chronicle emerged, propelling her into the much more glamorous second event: the visit, in 1921, of Prince Fernando de Bavaria y Borbon, nephew of King Alfonso XII, and the son of his sister, Infanta Paz de Borbon of Spain, and arrived bearing a greeting to Chile and Venezuela from his mother. *El Nuevo Diaro* selected Ana Teresa, by now the obvious candidate, with her combined pedigree and writing talent, to respond to him in the name of all Venezuelan women and to appear at the royal residence along with ladies from the highest ranks of Caraquenian society. Her delivery loosed a torrent of praise—the audience was by all accounts enchanted. In the press accolade, she was now referred to as a "distinguished Venezuelan writer," and the text of her greeting was distributed as far as Spain. Titled "La Madre Espana," the composition of some thirteen paragraphs bore out her clear, incantatory sense of style, and its message betrayed her very poetic sense of patriotism.[59]

Public exposure of this kind excited Teresa tremendously; its timing was opportune. With her adolescence behind her, she now had both distance and self-confidence enough to write about its lessons without regard to any public or professional approval. As Maria was to stress, however, Teresa was unsure of herself in the writing of *Ifigenia*—enough that her literary ambition still felt like a schoolgirl's dream.

Teresa's life during the writing of *Diary of a Young Lady Who Writes Because She Is Bored* was, after the fact, unreservedly happy and serene. As she told her friend Elena Maderos Gonzales in 1928, the need for "screaming from every major streetcorner" of Caracas disappeared once she began to put her protest to paper instead.[60] Sometime in the year 1922, together with her friends Emilia Barrios, Rafael Carias, and Carmen Helena de las Casas, she began to vacation at Macuto. There she would make a daily habit of separating herself from the others, for the purpose of writing, in a beachside house provided for her by Emilia, who had inherited its use as part of the family estate originally purchased by Guzman-Blanco. Once the day was done, Teresa would rejoin her friends for tea, discussing the latest development in Maria Eugenia's tragedy. Parra described in later years the physical scenario of her inspiration:

> I have many good memories of Macuto. There I wrote almost all of my novel *Ifigenia*. I shut myself up to write in a small house in ruins that belonged to the Guzmans and that had a roof over only the living room. I swept it up and placed a pine table and an extended chair next to the window. I heard the conversations of the people on the street, who sometimes would stop in front of my open window without suspecting I was on the other side. They were intrigued at my motivation to stay enclosed in such a house they considered horrible, and that I found enchanting; the weeds grew up into the room; I saw on all sides rats and lizards running; the tree was full of woodpeckers and at times . . . the immense branches shielded me from the sky. In the evening I would leave my hiding place and sometimes go to bathe in the river: what a unique event—unforgettable!—to take a river bath in a hot country! One cannot have a more intimate contact with nature, one feels enjoined with her, one lives in the universal soul, in full pantheism![61]

Teresa's mother, Isabel, was by all accounts not pleased with the story of Maria Eugenia; she, like the character of Abuelita, was said to have called her a girl with a "head full of *cucarachas*," much to the amusement of Teresa and her sisters. This is not surprising, given Maria's claim that Abuelita, who appears in many unflattering scenes, accurately represented the combined maternal force of the Parra family's Tovar, Ezpelosin, and Sanojo antecedents.[62] Teresa took care to communicate to her mother the innocence of her intention in a dedicatory paragraph preceding the one to her "second mother," Emilia. Turning toward Isabel with the sentiment of a daughter chronically misunderstood, she assures her fervently of the strength of her filial gratitude. It is the same oblique angle along whose lines Maria Eugenia, an orphan, relates to her grandmother Abuelita.

Mama,

I dedicate this book to you, it pertains to you in that from you I learned to admire over all other things the spirit of sacrifice. In its pages you will see yourself, Grandmother, your Vieja, Don Ramon, along with the complete cortege of discussions against the rebels of the word.

Learn from it the great distance that goes between the word and the deed, so that you will never fear revolutionaries who debate, raising thereby in their souls the mirror of example and the root of traditions.

Turn also your eyes towards quite a bit of nakedness: assure yourself that all of us were born of you with only the smallest piece of cloth; you were the one to clothe us. See also these pages with the white wrinkles of indulgence. I embrace you with all my soul.

Ana Teresa
Paris, July 1925

Ifigenia: "The Best Is That Which Is Unwritten"

Teresa de la Parra thought—naively—that nothing of the truth of her own personality would be evident as she so excitedly wrote her five hundred pages in 1922. Her pose was a public one; not only did she perform her writing task under the encouraging eyes of her two confidantes, Emilia Ibarra Barrios and Rafael Carias, but all of Caracas knew of her enterprise. Upon the request of José Pocaterra, editor of the leading literary magazine *La Lectura Semanal* and well-known author of Creole modernism, Teresa had sent him a finished chapter of her book for publication.[63]

Two different words contended for a place in the title of that first chapter. *Ifigenia* was part of the originally intended title, but the subtitle—*Diary of a Young Lady Who Writes Because She Is Bored*—underwent an accidental change before the chapter went to press. Parra's first choice, the original word that she enunciated to Pocaterra, was *aburre* (from aburrir, meaning "bored, annoyed, disgusted, full of loathing"). Somehow he misunderstood her transmission, and the word *fastidia* took its place before Teresa could correct it. She explained that she allowed the substitution to rest because *fastidia,* which is a more general term for boredom in Castilian and lacks the connotation of disgust and loathing, lends a flavor in the Venezuelan colloquial that she considered more natural or spontaneous and, since she never expected her book to reach readers outside the country, it was not worth the trouble to withdraw the already printed issues.[64]

When all 6,000 copies of that magazine issue sold out the first day they reached the stands, Teresa went out into the streets to convince herself that success had truly arrived at her door. Asking nonchalantly for the issue containing her story, she was told, "The novel written by a lady? That's sold out! Would you like anything else?" and "upon hearing that I felt happy, because the vendor's words announced my glory and fame."[65]

In the midst of such applause, Teresa played to her new audience, not yet aware of the voyeurism motivating the public's love of confessionals, which she later considered the only reason behind the books's success. Her novel, the extraordinary diary of Maria Eugenia Alonso, told the story of a young woman's psychological conditioning by the greater forces of society to submit to an arranged marriage. The tone of the diary is Maria Eugenia's own melodramatic rhetoric, alternately self-mocking and self-dramatizing. It is the voice of a character who can hardly be called noble in the Greek sense. She was ingenuous and capricious, and Maria Eugenia's more worthy qualities—her intelligence and desire to be happy—are the ones she betrays and through which she becomes undone.

The link between Maria Eugenia's commonplace fate and Greek tragedy seemed farfetched and insufficiently earned to many of *Ifigenia*'s critics, the heroine's self-sacrifice merely the result of her selfish, dishonest, and weak nature. But Parra's unwritten message did not consist in proving or disproving the above. Through invocation of that classic tragedy, she demanded recognition for the seriousness of the unfortunate social realities depicted in her tale. The genuine similarities between the two heroines are mainly superficial: their names have the last five letters in common; Ifigenia, like Maria Eugenia, also suffers a kind of spiritual death by joint command of God and family that, in its absence, she would not have suffered; Ifigenia, like her modern Caraquenian cousin, was chained to a life spent in a sacred temple (Maria Eugenia's marriage), forever mated to sorrow (Leal). Maria Eugenia's marriage to a respectable man was an everyday event created by everyday forces—internal as well as external. But her independent spirit, a barrier to the marriage, had to be removed for the wedding to take place. These forces did so relentlessly, all in the name of virtue, by spinning a web of terror around Maria Eugenia's struggling spirit. Sheer normalcy attended this suffocation of a feminine spirit, and the smug monster of prejudice approved it.

In Teresa's "Letter to An Unknown," she analyzed the product and motivation of her much younger self. She could see how strained she was when writing, always seeking that musical quality that at the time most criticized as untrue and artificial. She felt *Ifigenia* would have profited by deleting unnecessary lyricism, but it was in this lyricism that Parra exhibited her true self, at least at that time. She saw excessive romanticism as something easily fallen into tropical climates and blamed the exuberance of nature and imported European influences. Therein, she felt, was her true autobiography, not in the narrative, as almost everyone thought. Parra stated that she made Maria Eugenia Alonso her antithesis in order to speak in a frank and uninhibited voice. But the writer insists that she placed defects and qualities in her that she did not have, in order to ensure that no one would confuse the character with the novelist. But Parra did not realize that the mask would serve only those who knew her intimately. She continued to say that, in reality, Maria Eugenia Alonso was a synthesis, a live copy of various kinds of women Parra had known intimately. These women suffer, in silence, and Parra was fascinated with them and wished to give them a voice as a protest against the pressure of their environment. If Maria Eugenia had actually been a disguised Parra, she would never have risked the exposure, due to a very natural concern with privacy. The sense of security Parra felt in not believing she was referring to herself is what made her exaggerate the unabashed tone of Maria Eugenia Alonso, and that tone appeared to be more real than reality itself. Nobody sensed the transferral, Parra complained, but all believed they were reading her authentic autobiography. The author believed it was here that the secret of *Ifigenia*'s success was discerned, as the public adored confessions. At first, when Parra noticed this, she was mortified and resented *Ifigenia,* published two years later when she was residing in Paris. By the time she wrote "Letter to an Unknown," the misunderstanding pleased her. It revealed to her the completely ingenuous steps of first youth, and she found that she identified with the personality of Maria Eugenia Alonso at that time. Parra stated in her letter that she would have been indignant to learn this while writing. At that time, she wanted her novel to be a *"disinterested revolutionary protest."*[66]

Teresa, trying to maintain her "disinterestedness" above the passion and turmoil of her subject matter, ended up injecting her protest with an irony that did not succeed in mitigating its disruptive message; the mere idea of a woman thinking independently sent shivers of outrage down the spines of her compatriots. In her much-publicized letter of March 5, 1927, to Rafael Carias, where she defines her notion of irony, she criticizes them for their excessive readiness to take offense: "It seems to me that another thing working against *Ifigenia* is this: that of not comprehending, over there, the true intention of irony. In our South American environment, and as a general rule with all those who speak Spanish, literature is opulent; in a torrent of bombastic words they praise or insult; it's always the ditiramb or the diatribe, both things grow on the same stalk and are equally facile and in bad taste!"[67]

Parra's irony became almost runaway in Maria Eugenia's diary; injecting her protest with level upon level, it culminated in the protest of wit against those who take themselves too seriously. By investing her heroine with merely the pretensions to tragedy, Parra—consciously or unconsciously—mocked her identification with the Greek tragedienne as an in-itself-unfulfilled aspiration, yet another manifestion of her delusion.

Within the complex workings of a young single woman's mind, Parra documented the combat of Old World versus New over the red-hot issues of sex and marriage. Maria Eugenia's diary, far from being a wholesale assault against men and Catholic morals, is rather a diatribe against the hypocrisy that mocks the concepts of duty, honor, and the family. It posits a discourse on the tension between individual and group morality, discovering new threats to the integrity of women entering a formerly all-male world and revealing the slipperiness of truth in the dynamic between oppressor and oppressed. The war of the sexes as drawn in this book is fought with ignorance, fear, and coercion on both sides, but the fighters are mere markers in a larger game played by the prejudices of society, sifted down through centuries to produce and reproduce nothing but influence itself.

Parra has stated "the best part of my book lies in that which is unwritten."[68] Maria Eugenia's diary, she claimed, is "simply and without transcendental pretensions, a pure depiction of the female soul at this point in history."[69] It is a soul powered by two conflicting drives: one the rational desire for complete personal independence and the other the ancient and pervading struggle for social survival.[70] The "unwritten" subtext conveys Parra's own perception of Nature under constant siege by Man, these opposing forces taking on the figurative attributes of their literal gender. Maria Eugenia, modern, spontaneous, communing with rivers and trees, is defeated and deflowered by Leal, who is barren, logical, and rational, and her relatives, who are lifeless and outdated. It conveys further the torment of suppressed, inexpressible sexual desire and the interference of church and society between a woman and her body to regulate its productivity, finally warping and perverting her natural, conspiratorial relationship to it.

At this time, an ordinary, respectable woman, who cared about her reputation and found herself in Maria Eugenia's position, had but one available course of action: to take a husband. From that given, she could choose only how she would resolve her submission to husband and how the reverberations from that resolution would affect her children. By the 1920s, the ribbon given for such self-abnegation in Victorian times was revealed as both undesired and undeserved by many women. Maria Eugenia is, in the final analysis, neither the impervious Greek statue she aspires to be nor the religious statue she dreads becoming—she is only human and mortal, with hopes and desires that she can stifle only at risk of crippling herself deeply. *"Ifigenia,"* Parra wrote, "is above all things a defense of a certain kind of modern girl, a girl ordinarily encountered in cities like Caracas.[71] What Maria Eugenia Alonso thinks, plans, achieves, and suffers has been thought, planned, suffered, and achieved by many a girl in Bogata, Lima, as well as in Mexico City or Santiago, Chile. It is as Maria Alonso that most of the girls in Latin America face life."[72]

Following is a short, moving picture of the world of Maria Eugenia at eighteen, spliced into scenes that attempt to cover the range of what we imagine Teresa de la Parra's own myriad reflections to have been. For lack of our readers' access to an English translation of *Ifigenia,* we strive herewith to illustrate the environment Maria Eugenia lived in and to vocalize those "first ingenuous steps of youth" that projected above and beyond the pages of the novel into her maturity.

Maria Eugenia's World—Adolescent Dreams

***

"A Very Long Letter in Which Things Happen as They Do in Novels"

From the locked privacy of her bedroom, Maria Eugenia Alonso pours out her soul in a letter to her old friend Christina Iturbe, peering out the window as she writes to the orange trees and bright patch of blue sky that embellish Aunt Clara's blooming patio below. In this first section of *Ifigenia,* the fully detailed thoughts and impressions of Maria Eugenia's eighteen-year-old mind are given us as if in slow motion: each thought has a counterthought; each impression brings with it a reminiscence. They run like a canyon river, looping from one bend to the other, the high and barren banks above echoing her self-imposed alienation. Even though Maria Eugenia has been hesistant to write Christina the new reality of her situation in Caracas, her loneliness and boredom, aggravated by a greater share of suffering than her due, since both parents have died, brings her to a new plateau where she feels free to speak her mind. Christina was, after all, her soul mate and only consolation at the strict college governed by the nuns. The excessive timidity Maria Eugenia spoke of earlier also has released its grip (pp. 34–35). "Now I absolutely do not consider myself a second-rate personality, I am plenty satisfied with myself, I have declared a strike against timidity and humility, and I even have gained, moreover, the pretension of believing that I am worth a million times more than all the heroines in the novels we used to read during the summer. You and I are heroes and heroines in the novel of our lives, which is much more beautiful and many times better than any novel already written. . . .* And most of all, Maria Eugenia is no longer embarrassed to tell the truth. The truth that used to be humiliating and degrading, that used to keep her silent, now seems even "picturesque, interesting, and somewhat medieval." But this truth still belongs only in writing, she declares. She has always been able to lie when she talks, but never when she writes. In dealing with her grandmother Abuelita and Aunt Clara, she represses her true feelings for the sake of delicacy and tact, maintaining the haughty superiority that she feels her greater intelligence and sensibility give her (p. 34): "Naturally, Abuelita and Aunt Clara, who can distinguish very easily the woven threads of stitching and trimming but who see nothing of those things which are hidden by appearances, do not perceive in the least the cruel and stoic magnitude of my alienation."

Maria Eugenia longs to be ushered into the world that beckons with silk dresses and red lipstick from the house of Guerlain. With a soul only partially exposed and thoroughly underdeveloped, she harbors an amorphous fantasy of the grandeur that life promises. Best defined by the shape of the city of Paris, it is the kind of fantasy that tinges many an adolescence with wistful pain. "Ah Paris! the sepulchre of our greatest fortunes," sighs Abuelita (p. 101). Traveling up there from Biarritz, having recently waved goodbye to Christina with a small, white hand-

*All *Ifigenia* quotes in this chapter are from *Obras Completas* (Caracas: Editorial Arte, 1965).

kerchief, Maria Eugenia had controlled her tears, as her pride had always dictated her to do. On the train, a strange and beautiful lady, surely an actress or artist of some kind, maybe even a woman who wrote under a pseudonym, lifted her from her melancholy and guided her into the glittering city with deep-voiced comments on the cruel ironies of life. This encounter prepared the stage for Maria Eugenia to shed every trace of the stuffy convent: the unflattering religious frocks turned Cinderella-like into a full wardrobe of Parisian elegance, paid for by Maria Eugenia's own modest inheritance, whose limited funds—left to her by her recently deceased Papa—she exhausted with the understanding that the proceeds from shares in her father's plantation, San Nicolas, yet awaited her in Caracas.

The three-month venture alone into this world of glamour and sophistication served her with the ecstatic taste of first independence; the many compliments she received brought to life a buried narcissism and concomitantly a new sense of self. Equipped with a short haircut and enough clothes to impress Caracas with her chic modernity, she boarded the vessel for La Guaira regretfully. Once on board, she began wielding her newly found elegance, much to the admiration of the other passengers, especially one ill-fated Colombian poet. His was the misfortune of attempting to give the fatuous young lady her first kiss; Maria Eugenia, apparently as uninitiated in this procedure as she was unaccustomed to the attentions of men, was suddenly shocked out of the narcissism into which his flattering serenades had seduced her. Taking no responsibility for the passive encouragement his attempt to kiss her might have rested on, she rejected him with a sharp, frightened motion of her head that sent his eyeglasses right off his "excessively long" nose. From the cool distance of her ruffled dignity, the specter of his humiliation elicited no greater response than if she had just heard a mousetrap snap its spring:

> From that time, Cristina, I have deduced that men, in general, know nothing, although they appear to know a lot, because, unaware of the reflection offered to them in the mirror of other spirits, they ignore themselves totally. When Abuelita, at the table, speaks indignantly of men today and cautions me against them, calling them boastful slanderers, I, distantly analyzing her indignation, remember my friend the poet in the moment of searching for his glasses, and I smile. Yes, Christina, more so than Abuelita says, I believe that men slander out of good faith, that they are boastful because they honestly are ignorant of themselves and they go through life happy

and surrounded by the most merciful aura of delusion, all the while escorted silently, like a faithful and invisible dog, by ridicule.

(p. 50)

Maria Eugenia had no idea what to expect from the new surroundings of her native land; she was no longer familiar with the many relatives who from now on were to be entrusted with her care. One by one, as they presented themselves to her, a picture began to crystallize of their many preoccupations as well as of their trustworthiness. Amidst their fashionably heated and vapid discussions on modern morality, the evils of Negroes, foreign influence, hygiene, and modern medicine, Maria Eugenia listened, developing an automatic antipathy toward her dark, crafty maternal uncle Eduardo, his persnickety mestizo wife, Maria Antonia, and their three meek children children who bray in unison like donkeys. Uncle Pancho, however, immediately attracted her with his frank wit and his similarity to his brother, her own dear Papa.

Abuelita's house is Maria Eugenia's new home. Together with the spinster Aunt Clara, they make up three generations of the maternal side of the family, living amidst the pungent aromas of jasmine oil, humid earth, wax candles, and Elliman's Embrocation, Abuelita's rheumatic medicine: ". . . The odor of wax comes from the two candles that Aunt Clara keeps permanently lit in front of a Christ statue dressed in a purple robe, and displayed since the time of my great grandmother in a glass case. The smell of jasmine and humid soil come up from the patio where roses, palm trees, ferns, gardenias, and white lilies grow." (p. 32.)

Under the "gentle pressure" of Abuelita's arm, of the langorous sights and smells, a vision of Maria Eugenia's future unfolds to reveal boredom, the cruel and loathsome monster. But a monster yet more odious is gathering shape on that same horizon: Abuelita, Aunt Clara, and Maria Eugenia, seated in their customary places, sewing and talking, turn their conversation to the family plantation of San Nicolas, Uncle Eduardo, and Abuelita's own means of survival. Uncle Eduardo, according to his mother, Abuelita, has out of the goodness of his heart managed the family affairs so that she and Aunt Clara have a small but steady income and so that the plantation, whose profits Maria Eugenia's own father totally squandered in Paris before he died, just barely supports his own family. Maria Eugenia has absolutely no claim on San Nicolas anymore—news beneath which the foundation of her hopes and dreams crumbles (p. 83): "Poverty! Do you understand what that means, Christina? It is complete dependency with its cortege of humiliation and pain. It means definite goodbye to traveling, to well-being, to success, to luxury, to elegance, to all the enchantments of that life I experienced during my latest stay in Paris, and to which I aspired with vehemence. It is also definite goodbye to you and to all the other things and people I will never know, which represent the glories of the world—the world, you know? Happiness, liberty, success—they will never be mine!'' The world of certain dependence closing in on her comes, as if it weren't enough to be thus limited, with more chains attached: Maria Eugenia must sit, dress, speak, and behave exactly as her relatives demand. Her lipstick is too red, they complain; she sits like a girl of the streets; her every action undergoes the scrutiny of those old women, who see in her a challenge to their self-denial as well as the threatening degeneracy of her own father. What a change from the freedom of Paris!

Much to Aunt Clara's further dismay, all these restrictions drive Maria Eugenia to seek companionship in Gregoria, the black laundress. Together with Uncle Pancho, Gregoria guards the gates of truth throughout the book—their most eloquent voices are wasted on ears deafened by the self-serving prejudice abounding within Abuelita's household. Knowing neither how to read nor write, much less how old she is, Gregoria is nevertheless one of "the most intelligent, wise people I have ever known in my life, with a generous, indulgent, and immoral soul. Her disdain for convention protects her from all knowledge that does not stem from the same naturalness" (p. 76).

Maria Eugenia now finds herself in a predicament in which her delicacy and tact have ceased to be effective. They give way to open defiance of Abuelita's criticism that the blame for Maria Eugenia's sudden poverty lies with her own immoral conduct. She should have saved her money instead of squandering it on clothes in Paris, Abuelita says. As Maria Eugenia's haughty dignity begins to disintegrate in the open warfare, Uncle Pancho comes to her defense. Abuelita is enraged at the double challenge to her authority—an authority, Maria Eugenia observes, that she takes for granted, never having gone "out into the street, always surrounded thus by the ancient-noble ambience of this house, encased in her notions of honor; surrounded with the aura of her years and her austere virtue" (p. 92). Letting loose her worst fears, Abuelita attacks Pancho as well (p. 90): "Why don't you council her also to drink, or take morphine or cocaine now that she has no money left to spend?" and finishes with a healthy dose of her ethics (p. 94): "We women were born for mercy. The treasure of our indulgence must agitate no one, not even amidst the most cruel thorns of sacrifice. With even more reason if this treasure is lavished on beings as dear as our fathers!"

Abuelita feels, however, that the future does hold hope for Maria Eugenia, if she only will let her clear intelligence and righteous heart judge without hate or rancor. In spite of her poverty, in spite of the encroaching degeneracy in society, men still worship the virtuous woman: "It is only important to be pretty ànd above all, virtuous!" she contends. "You must make a good marriage" (p. 101). Following this advice, Maria Eugenia reports to Christina the full implications of Abuelita's words, which were grounded in

> . . . the sorrowful history of all these criollo descendents of the conquistadores who called themselves Mantuanas in the colonial times, who founded and governed the cities, who won with their blood the independence of half of America; who since then decayed, oppressed under the persecution and hatred of the federation and whose children and grandchildren today are obscure and poverty-stricken like myself, without ever feeling shame for their poverty, awaiting with resignation the hour of marriage or the house of death, making sweets for the dances or weaving crowns of flowers for the graves . . . and as the tone and the names and the stories came into accord with my state of mind, listening to the voice of Abuelita, I allowed myself to be led gently into the winds of conformity; my nerves began to . . . the irritating ideas. . . . One after the other, the maternal tone like a song permeated my spirit and the monotone words remained resonant in my ears without meaning. Contemplating the many green flowers of the patio made me think of the eternal greening of the plants under the light of the sun—yes—life holds a mysterious force that overwhelms everything. Each time I would be able to return to happiness nevertheless—as Abuelita said so well. Marriage—that is, love that from the distance of one's youth still awaited me in life—perhaps would arrive with the realization of all the impossible dreams that tortured my existence now. My soul, like those small roses in the patio, had not yet bloomed. (pp. 102–3)

Hushed admiration for the whole idea of love and happiness fills Maria Eugenia's mind. Introduced by Abuelita to the only door by which to enter life, Maria Eugenia begins to realize that Abuelita's own definition of love and happiness is something very sad, very weary, something that—like the house—smelled of jasmine, wax candles, and Elliman's Embrocation, and moreover she realizes that these words have entered her soul through the back door, through that unnamed guest inhabiting her unconscious, to lull her for the first time into unfamiliar feelings of resignation.

It takes several hours for Maria Eugenia's resilience to rescue her. Aftere dinner, the influence of Abuelita's intonations has waned and the old Maria Eugenia wakes up to thoughts pitched defiantly against such a dreadful fate. "I will turn myself over to art!" she exclaims. "I will study piano eight and nine hours a day!" (p. 106), like her compatriot, the famous Teresa Carreno; and full of determination to bring this glory about as soon as possible, Maria Eugenia draws up her Japanese kimono and marches to the piano to begin practicing. But this time it is Aunt Clara who has something to say: how can she play piano with her dead father barely in his grave? And what will the neighbors think! Maria Eugenia is now beside herself with frustration and anger. Sparking her imagination into greater profligacy than ever, she puffs up into a stance of "Napoleonic arrogance," hurling the words: "In the morning you take away my fortune, in the evening you seize my glory!" (p. 109) at Abuelita and Aunt Clara; then powdering her nose and applying lipstick with great deliberation, she stomps out of the house, accompanied by Uncle Pancho, to assuage her poor thwarted ego.

> The sun went searching after a hilltop in the distance. The marvelous valley extended below, surrounding the city; the valley, whitewashed brick walls, red tile roofs, meanwhile presiding behind me, the majesty of the Avila, the great mountain, rose maternal and pensive.

> (p. 117)

Conversation flows between Uncle Pancho and Maria Eugenia—he the bemused cynic given to playing devil's advocate in his ultimate service to the truth, she spouting the classic cry of ambitious young womanhood: "If only I were born a man!" (p. 129.)

Maria Eugenia had insisted on seeing the poor side of town populated by those children of greatest misfortune, the mulattos. Beautiful, refined expressions of longing shone through the crudeness of their physical presence; as Maria Eugenia faced them eye to eye, she reflected back her own widening horizon of alienation and oppression. Riding in the horse-drawn carriage through the lanes of shanties winding up the hill, Uncle Pancho and Maria Eugenia contemplated the mestizo's unique status as crucible of all society's mistakes. They arrived at the top of the hill. Maria Eugenia, questioning Uncle Pancho about her new state of poverty, found her worse suspicions confirmed: not only did her Papa not squander his total fortune in Paris, but Eduardo had appropriated to himself what was rightfully hers. The sustenance that Abuelita is so grateful for is, moreover, a pittance compared to her honest due. Now, on the hilltop overlooking the twinkling nighttime city, Maria Eugenia asks the ultimate question: "But why is Abuelita so convinced that this blackguard is such a superior, magnanimous being?"

Uncle Pancho begins to philosophize, in a style not unlike that of Primo Juancho in *Mama Blanca,* on matters of faith, on his vision of marital reality and the complex ironies of nature's balance of sexual power. The all-important key to Eduardo's success—Abuelita's submission to his will—is normal and in keeping with social mores:

"Look: Abuelita, the same as Clara, the same as almost all women who call Caracas their home, are not satisfied with one religion—they have two. The one they practice during all hours, and in every location, and that is the religion they call having a heart and feeling. Of this second religion the God is one of the men in the family. It might be the father, the brother, the son, the husband or the fiancé—it doesn't matter! The essence thereof is a feeling of masculine superiority to which blind tribute of obedience and slavery is rendered. And at that time, once this deity has been created, everything he says is law, everything that exists is placed in his hands, and his anger, combative, arbitrary or grotesque as it might be, proceeds in this way from any offense by the woman to the strict laws of modesty: it explodes suddenly in front of a plate of excessively tough meat, or it is released imposingly when he is in his underdrawers, looking at a badly bleached shirtfront—always, always in the same voice, it will resonate in the environs of the home, majestic and solemn, like the resounding voice of Jehovah over the Sinai. In your case this God is Eduardo, who in all honesty does not have such a bad character—at least he never shouts! . . . And I do not know where this custom of deifying man comes from, from Oriental ancestors, inherited by our Andalusian forefathers, or if it derives from a simple economic problem: could there be any closer resemblance to God in heaven than he who pays all our expenses on earth?"

(p. 122)

Maria Eugenia, thoughtful, thinks back to a feminist conference she once attended in Paris. The chairwoman had been wearing, of all things, cotton stockings—instantly Maria Eugenia's halfhearted fighting spirit gave way to revulsion and a more ardent desire never to be associated with such lack of refinement in clothing. Now, however, regretting the superficiality of that reaction, in light of her new experiences, she continues to stoke her anger (p. 130): "The only thing to which I aspire is the delight in my own personality, that is to say, to be independent like a man, and never to be given orders—My motto will be this: long live suffrage!" But Pancho does not try to reinforce this bellicose attitude. He can always be counted on to say the unexpected. For him, it seems more useful to guide Maria Eugenia by stressing the hidden powers of woman—power that, for a beautiful woman especially, has no boundaries: "Better to be a beautiful woman than a poor man!" he asserts (p. 130). Following, reprinted in its entirety, is Pancho's treatise on the foundation of sexual politics; it is an example of the frankness that earned *Ifigenia* its blasphemous reputation. No doubt this "rebellion of the word," so carefully placed in the mouth of a man, expressed one argument in the author's own rebellion to marriage:

"The equality of the sexes, my dear, the same as any other equality, is absurd, because it is contrary to the laws of nature that detest democracy and abominate justice. Just look. Look around you. All this is made in hierarchies and aristocracies; the stronger beings live at the expense of the weaker, and in all of nature a grand harmony rules based on oppression, crime, and robbery. The complete resignation of the victims is the foundation stone on which this immense peace and harmony is built. The democratic spirit, or be it the zeal for justice and for restoring rights, is a juvenile dream that exists only in theory within the poor human brain. Nature, then, is ordered in hierarchy; the stronger animals devour the weaker, live at their expense and rule over them.

"The human being is at the top of all hierarchies and is the supreme expression of aristocratic character in nature. Today, according to the law of hierarchy, which of the two sexes has been called to rule over the other, and therefore over all of nature? Here is the problem. To resolve it in man's favor, leaving him all his apparent vanity of control, is proof of the greater intelligence a woman can give, and moreover it is the sign of a higher civilization in which we live. . . . Man, in spite of having a pompous and theatrical nature ever since primitive times, plus the basic attributes of power, is basically not constituted to command, but rather to obey, and not being privileged by nature with the special gift of command, he wants at all costs to dominate. That is what generally occurs here.

"These poor women are ignorant of their power. Dazzled by the idealistic light of mysticism and virtue, they always run to offer themselves spontaneously in sacrifice and denigrate themselves by force of their generosity. They live intoxicated in the voluptuousness of submission. Like the martyrs, they habitually exalt their love with flagellation, and in the midst of the chains and torments they bless the Lord. They live a deep inner life of the ascetics and the idealists, finally achieving a greatly refined abnegation that is doubtless the highest superiority.

"But with their superiority hidden in the soul, they are victims of their executioners. And it is in ignoring their obvious strength that they exercise their charms, forgetting themselves, disdaining their power and neglecting their physical beauty, and as soon as the men see them thus denigrated and fallen, they make of them sad beasts of bruden upon whose docile and weary backs they place the total weight of their tyranny and their caprices, after giving it the pompous name of honor.

"And guarding their honor they walk to one side, with whip in hand, ordinary and vulgar like the muleteers, Yes! Crude—the most common—without the slightest refinement of soul or of body! Don't you see that they lack discipline? that they lack that kind of methodical exercise that forms and refines everything, something like what the English call training—that is to say, government, direction, command!"

(pp. 131–33)

Adult Compromises—Lessons in Female Integrity

Maria Eugenia's ambition is really a simple one, found more purely consummate in the love legends of Tristan and Isolt, Romeo and Juliet, Ophelia and Hamlet, in "an old sad story where the lovers die (p. 397)." Her aspiration comes alive to her one day, "in the language of grandeur" (p. 241), while bathing naked in a river pool on the grounds of San Nicolas. There, as if it were induced by hallucinatory drugs, she senses the presence of Gabriel Olmedo pulsating in every leaf, breath of air, and drop of water (p. 251). This is an aspiration toward loss of self—not towards renunciation of the ideal, which she unfortunately achieves, but towards submission to the ideal, which is found in dedication to work held sacred or in the expression of true love, "to realize the glory of love united with the glory of my ambitions" (p. 195). It is deliverance from the shallower aspiration, manifested elsewhere in her diary, toward narcissism—that submission to an image of self, one gazing back from a mirror's glass or an admirer's eyes.

But the chances for realizing the higher aspirations of either true love or independent livelihood, as indicated by her behavior from the very beginning, are never reassuringly weighted in her favor. She has confounded her suitor, Gabriel, with coquetry and an ambivalence sprung from her inexperience with men; her sense of independence is defined in the murky imagery of fortune and fame.

After he had squelched with his monologue any last flickering desire in his niece's mind for marriage, Uncle Pancho endeavored to retrieve her from disconsolation. He explained that marriage need not be the nightmare of slavery he had just depicted, but that, given the right husband, it could offer her the happiness of which she dreamt. And he knew, moreover, just who that man should be: his own good friend, the most handsome, sensitive, and intelligent bachelor Gabriel Olmedo. The meeting between that gentleman and Pancho's young niece would be arranged by another friend of his, the wealthy socialite Mercedes Galindo, who would in her turn conjure this destined happiness under the alchemical magic of her salon. Pancho's judgment was entirely correct so far. With Gabriel Olmedo as catalyst, Mercedes succeeded in introducing new hope into Maria Eugenia's life as she launched their relationship at many an instructive and exciting social occasion.

But the afternoons and dinners at the Galindo mansion compared all too favorably for Maria Eugenia's own good with sitting at home doing embroidery under her grandmother's tutelage. Abuelita made clear her disapproval of Mercedes, denouncing the discussion of books and ideas in her salon as a sign of reproachable degeneracy. The two fictional families, moreover, had had a history of political feuding over exactly the same issues as the Ibarra and Tovar clans upon whom the characters were based.

Gabriel also lacked effective allies in the Alonso household. Only the laundress, Gregoria, appreciated and understood those refinements of his bearing that unsettled Abuelita and Aunt Clara. These two exemplary old ladies were growing increasingly resentful of Maria Eugenia's socializing away from home and looked askance at Uncle Pancho's motivation. With their suspicious eyes, they penetrated her studious pretense of concentrating on her embroidery tasks; indeed, Maria Eugenia's mind would be far off in dreams of Gabriel in anticipation of their next meeting. Sensing her declining control over her granddaughter, Abuelita reprimanded her sharply over a lost stitch, at which the young woman was no longer able to contain her temper. Her "boredom, loathing and disgust" for everything these paragons held dear came pouring out in a torrent. Within the course of her diatribe, Maria Eugenia denounces their lifelessness while praising her own appetite for truth and knowledge:

> "I do not even want the slightest unknown to exist in my mind and have tried to explain—all by myself, for the most part—the origins and formation of life. Yes, if you call using this scientific system of clarifying our doubts or unknowns having lost 'innocence,' then yes! I have lost it! I find nothing inconvenient in proclaiming it and it makes me happy!
> "Even the innocence of married women, or rather the despotic eagerness of making us ignorant in theory of all that other people know and have always known in practice, seems to me one of the worst abuses which the strong forces have committed against the weak. In the first place, to hide the mysteries of life is the same as hiding deep pits in the road; it disorients horribly. . . . Innocence is a paralyzing blindness, which the human imbeciles have crowned with roses!"
>
> (pp. 177–78)

In the long, intimate letter to Christina and the ensuing first chapter of her diary, Maria Eugenia has attempted sincere dialogue between self and self. As yet unchallenged by her relatives, she posits her vision of what is and what ought, in her view, to be, with a wistful longing and sometime self-mocking, sometime self-righteous, insight. After the climactic outburst of truthtelling in Abuelita's living room, the course of *Ifigenia*'s plot is marked by Maria Eugenia's progression from innocence to corruption. Her personality, with its "wretched propensity for philosophizing," is the cause of her "disgrace and downfall" (p. 243). Because Abuelita, Aunt Clara, and Eduardo have considered it their duty as guardians to enforce Maria Eugenia's progression in the opposite direction—from corruption to innocence—she now begins her downward spiral, learning to lie about the feelings so recently exposed in their truth. Only later would she disengage, coming to rest on an interim platform of guilt-ridden, reawakened honesty, from which she would soon plunge into lifelong dishonesty.

Maria Eugenia does not understand the destructive power of honesty and the costliness of her compulsion to articulate ideas until forced to by a severe punishment. After contemplating the full implications of her rebellious granddaughter's outburst, Abuelita decided Maria Eugenia's complete isolation from Caracas and the corruptive influence of Mercedes Galindo was in order. Uncle Eduardo concurred, and the whole family relocated for several months to San Nicolas. There Maria Eugenia now faces an incarceration mercilessly exacerbated by the constant company of Eduardo's irreproachable and unimaginative family. She retreats daily on horseback up the mountains surrounding the plantation to the river, where she loses herself in a virtual garden of Eden. Streams of philosophizing flow from her pen as she describes her secret passion for Gabriel and her mystical bond to nature. Like Parra, who experienced contact "with the universal soul" while bathing in the river at Macuto, Maria Eugenia describes for us her own rite of water-borne nature worship:

> One day, alone and naked, I slid down into the ancient freshness of the pool, believing myself to be the living soul of the countryside. And I remember that day, submerged in the pool, I lost like never before the notion of my own existence, because the encircling water held my awakened skin in some kind of mysterious delight, and because my eyes, roving up on high, forgot themselves.
>
> These daily trips are consoling like confession, because they unload my soul of its burden of sorrow. The river . . . is the confessor who absolves me every day of dark thoughts, gives me council of hope, and leaves me always in the spirit of infinite grace of happiness.

(p. 245)

Like a jack-in-the-box crashing a holy silence, a report reaches the plantation from Caracas announcing Gabriel's marriage to a very rich young woman with petroleum connections, Maria Monasterios. Maria Eugenia, her hopes crushed and betrayed, does not discover until Gabriel returns two years later that Aunt Maria Antonia had simply not forwarded his letters and calls, This aunt, a bitter, impeccably correct woman, contrived also to humiliate Maria Eugenia at the dinner table by exposing her nature walks as "self-indulgent" and her habit of writing letters outdoors as "improper." Maria Eugenia, like Parra, is most vulnerable in her highly developed sense of shame; therefore, in using public derision against her, her aunt struck to the quick. Those pilgrimages to the countryside, now abandoned, were the source of the girl's mental health, and her unselfconscious spontaneity was her only key to self-knowledge. Maria Antonia succeeded, with those two simple blows, in severing her niece's lifeline, one that ran between her private, inner self and the greater world of love and action.

A dark period follows: two years pass without a word being written in Maria Eugenia's diary. The Maria Eugenia who reenters its pages in chapter 3 has been convinced of the folly of her previous self. She moves around the house benumbed, like a sleepwalker, as vacant as a lobotomy victim. Abuelita and Aunt Clara, in the blindness of their moral rectitude, neither understand the complexity and seriousness of her psychological depression and their own part in having created it nor completely trust its permanence. "This girl is too pretty," they say, "and at the same time too liberal in her thinking; alone she might make very bad use of her liberty" (p.318). It is time, they say further, for Maria Eugenia to find a husband, The worst and most unbearable fate in Maria Eugenia's eyes has always been spinsterhood—becoming like her Aunt Clara, an aging child still dependent on her mother, who, lacking the livelier distractions of marriage, has turned the force of her energy to the practice of worship, is for Maria Eugenia a horror of the first order (p. 386): "Some mornings, when I see Aunt Clara with the corner of her veil hanging down her back, leaving for church where she will remain kneeling for over an hour together with many others like her whom people call las beatas . . . well, at times, when I see her leave in the morning, if I am in a sentimental mood, or in a spell of fantasy as Gregoria says, I picture Aunt Clara's soul and the souls of all the beatas coming up to the fount of holy water as if they were a white line of biblical maidens." Therefore Maria Eugenia's resistance to their pressure is nil. The marriage snare, as customarily laid by all proper and marriageable young ladies, consists in grooming oneself carefully and placing oneself behind the grating of the window overlooking the public street, in hopes that one of the men strutting by in his finery or, better, driving by in his fancy automobile will be lured and, God willing, entrapped. Maria Eugenia dutifully performs this ritual. She sits in the windowsill, uncomfortable and self-conscious, looking out toward the street. Other young ladies along the street gaze hopefully from their cages in concert with her. An occasional man passes by to inspect them, undergoing in turn the sharp scrutiny of the ladies' chaperones. Slowly and surely Maria Eugenia begins to perceive, through the prisonlike bars of the grating, a preview of her future. A feeling of humiliation and awareness of the absurdity of her posture wells up inside her. Because she has merely suppressed, rather than killed, her love for Gabriel, her apparent cynicism is really a symptom of her faith in love betrayed and her indifference a mask for her despair. Uncontrollably she begins to murmur, "Who will buy me, I'm for sale! Who will buy me, I'm for sale!" (p. 312) until she is silenced by the shocked women inside her house.

It is as if in answer to this chant that Cesar Leal enters her life. Shopping for a wife in his pompous brown automobile and with his upper–middle-class, conservative airs, he becomes smitten by Maria Eugenia's beauty. Learning that he intends to court her, Abuelita and Aunt Clara are transported with excitement. Even to Maria Eugenia's ebbing spirit, so bitterly resigned to this consecrated prostitution, his attentions are flattering. In her opinion, they rightfully pay homage to the beauty of which she has always been proud. Much later, Gabriel himself would shame her into recognizing the pathos of her mindless submission to Leal's alien sensibility. In his letter urging her to elope with him, he accuses her of having tried to sell her body (p. 447): "You were going to sell it to one man with the law, the church, the society and your family, as if those trammels of endless submission and general approval did not make the sale a thousand times more odious than those that are made secretly, and without legal guarantees or religious sanctions."

Parra found it ironic, too, that women of the highest social classes suffered the most, while the women on the lowest end, the servants, indifferent to "legal guarantees or religious sanctions," appeared to enjoy the greatest freedom of behavior. She bestows on her character Gregoria, as she does on Cochocho, freedom from the compunction to restrain herself with social mores, as long as she does not breach her class boundaries. This attitude is clearly illustrated in the fourth chapter, wherein Maria Eugenia, once having revived her buried love for Gabriel, also revives the habit (of former days) of discussion with the wise old Negress. Gregoria takes the opportunity to express her impatience with Maria Eugenia's tiresome vacillations toward Gabriel:

"I am black and ugly, and whatever you might think as well, but never have I lacked someone to give myself to. Marriage is only for the upper classes!'' she says, taking out a cigarette. "Aunt Clara can say nothing to me about my morals. I'm a good Christian. Married or not married, children are born. I'm glad to be poor and black! I will tell Gabriel that you have lost the courage you inherited from your branch of the Aguirre family!''

(p. 402)

Now Maria Eugenia yearns for the innocence that she was once so proud and happy to have lost. Conscious that she can never effectively regain it, she tries to convince herself that manufacturing a fake innocence to ensure her fiancé's approval calls for great imagination and skill, of which she can be even more proud. In this way she begins to construct on the foundation of her anesthesia a new personality; it is as offensive to both Pancho and Gregoria in its falsity as her intended husband is offensive to them in his stupidity. She avoids them both now. Her flat and glib pronouncements betray her obstinate cover-up. The dialogue is no longer spoken between her and a unified self she aspires to, but between her and a self whose voice she seeks to drown out. Pancho does his best to aim selected verbal darts her way, but they fail to penetrate her augmented determination to persist in her farce. The Maria Eugenia who loved literature and wrote prose seems gone forever when Pancho, intruding into one of the stiff, formal living-room encounters between Maria Eugenia and her fiancé, attempts to expose those former obsessions in front of Leal. Slyly he poses questions about her diary and suggests that she recite some poetry for the company. But Maria Eugenia, knowing full well that her ability to recite Dante or her habit of writing down ideas might scare Leal away, fields Pancho's remarks with profuse denials, and Leal is too dull and self-absorbed to be suspicious.

The logic of Maria Eugenia's final decision to marry a man like Leal, given the idealistic and obstinately independent character introduced in the first two chapters, raised doubtful eyebrows among several of *Ifigenia*'s critics, in spite of the author's many devices—lies and discouragements—that plotted her heroine's defeat from without. Whether Parra adequately developed Maria Eugenia's character flaw or not is for critics and the individual readers to decide. Perhaps, as Parra believed, the cause lay in the public's failure to grasp or appreciate the subtleties of her irony. Or one could say the dangers of combining tragedy with the confessional diary form (can one imagine Othello telling his own story?) and the stridency of its "excessive lyricism" opened the book up to a larger criticism it perhaps did not deserve. It is worth noting that success of the initial chapters, which were written before the reading public intervened, might be due to the fact that in these Teresa herself identified most with her heroine, achieving only later that distance, artificial and less convincing, she assumed when Maria Eugenia's life took its sharp fictional turn from her own in the remaining chapters.

In one of her many letters written to explain and defend her novel, Parra speaks on the subject of Maria Eugenia's motivation:

> . . . The only purpose of my book has been to demonstrate the contrary, that is to say, our mysterious duality, the terrible conflicts that spring with surprise from what we believe ourselves to be and what we are; and finally, as a consequence or synthesis . . . this eternal and torturous question is submitted to the reader: which is the true ''I'' within us—the I that reasons or the I that acts?
>
> My big task, improbable as it seems, has been to intervene continually between Maria Eugenia and the reader, giving a voice to that of which she is unaware. The only thing I consider well written in *Ifigenia* is that which I did not write, that which is carried without words in order that it reach the benevolence of the reader in a low voice and the benevolence of the critic in a high one.
>
> She is illogical, and she is illogical because in spite of this ultramodern mentality that raises her to revolutionary extremes, she is and always will be under the command of her ancestors.
>
> Don't forget that like Maria Eugenia, all sensitive temperaments (women or artists) contain in their soul those two ''I's,'' different and contradictory, that are rarely in agreement: the one that speaks through the mouth of reason and the one that operates for reasons unknown to reason itself. The first is . . . geometric and full of logic, it governs the ego and drives us to success; when it is in control the world calls us intelligent. The other is generally crazy, that poor sublime insanity of the great sacrifices and absurd generosities, the mysterious unnamed visitor that sows disorder, laughs at our wise tutor the ego . . .
>
> The subconscious reasoning that drives Maria Eugenia, her ''nameless guest,'' is without doubt, as revealed to me by an old and wise writer, her inevitable motherhood. And with that, she anticipates and follows it, accompanied by the renunciation and sacrifices of centuries. It is that which has made her fall from the very beginning under the yoke of an inferior yet important man, who dominates her in that absolute way so typical of our countries.[73]

It is only a crisis that succeeds in awakening Maria Eugenia's senses to the truth of their own perceptions—a crisis where love and death meet over the comatose body of Uncle Pancho, that so-athletic symbol of her conscience. This is the erotic event that plunges Maria Eugenia into extreme moral confusion. Pancho, with his threadbare yet honest existence, has personified not only her conscience but the guardianship of her love for Gabriel. None of Pancho's devices has worked to derail Maria Eugenia from her disastrous marriage plans until, by his descent into coma, he serves unknowingly as a martyr for the sake of her happiness. It is his illness that has brought Gabriel back to her—a Gabriel now absolved of his earlier crime and accepted in the household by the tireless nursing of his old friend Pancho, a Gabriel who had declared his love for her.

Maria Eugenia, however, alive to that love and its concomitant sexual message, still cannot bring herself to tell Gabriel what he wants to hear. She is within grasp of the full flower of her most ideal loss of self; as they kiss over Pancho's dying body, she and Gabriel are united in love and death. But the droning voice of ages says that death demands mourning, not pleasure and happiness, in spite of Pancho's dedication in his former health to the couple's mutual happiness. Though she comprehends the message implicit in his unconscious state as a signal to her buried, but living, love for Gabriel, she cannot transcend her feelings of guilt to honor Pancho's sacrificial offering. Two years earlier, when her love had been betrayed by the news of Gabriel's marriage, she had described it in these terms (p. 301): "Ah! love! love! Why put the question to the swaying of the hammock? Yes, I have felt it. Yet, it is this mute subterranean tragedy above which everything passes with indifference, as happens that which goes above the macabre punishment of a live burial."

The door to life and love, entered thus through death, stands open. Gabriel has written a letter stating everything that has to be stated, announcing his plans to leave his own unhappy marriage and travel to Europe and offering—insisting, actually—that she acompany him. Maria Eugenia desires desperately to go. Her excitement is spiced with melodramatic defiance. She decides to meet him at the place and time specified in his letter.

In the middle of the night, she must pack her bags quietly so as not to wake anyone up; she must remain cool and calm. But Maria Eugenia is contemplative rather than active. Her rebellion has existed only within the unlimited boundaries of her own mind, and the variety of roles she is capable of playing have never made it to dress rehearsal. There is a wide gap between her "conduct and her convictions," a gap that unknown forces waste no time in exploiting. Maria Eugenia, fussing unnecessarily over the exact placement of her hat on her head, suddenly becomes inexplicably preoccupied with her image in the mirror. As she strives to effect the exact enigmatic touch desired, other faces begin to flicker around her reflection and she begins to hear the stories of the dead "come to warn the living—that motive of the tortured souls always wandering invisibly around us, the desperate imploring of the recently dead from the horrible punishment of purgatory." She is terrified by familiar objects that now "have a soul and speak to us" (p. 461). A black cat crosses her path, knocks over some boxes, and goes into hiding, bringing Maria Eugenia's terror to almost unbearable pitch. All the devilish associations with black cats run through her mind, even the possibility that:

> Some dominating and terrible spirit became incarnate in the body of that black cat and wanted at all costs to prevent my leaving with Gabriel; maybe it was some very powerful spirit that reads the future. Perhaps it was the spirit of someone who was very interested in me. Someone, someone, who . . . who could it be? Without a doubt it was the one that had me under his power and against my will had made me leave my room, had me come defenseless to the patio and now had me there, as if I were chained, only to keep me from escaping. Only God knows by what dreadful and sinister means to prevent my escape.
>
> (p. 470)

Out on the patio, Maria Eugenia's courage only tenuously survives the curse of the black cat. She tries to reassure herself with positive thoughts: *But I will go! In spite of the cat—with Gabriel, who is alive, strong, young, rich, and loves me madly, will make me happy, and always will want me, yes! Always will want me!"* But new doubt creeps into her head with that last phrase, and suddenly it turns to a question: *Ah! always will want me?* And with that finishing blow to her nerve, she finds herself confronted by the sudden appearance of Aunt Clara, who has been awakened by the black cat. Maria Eugenia begins lying clumsily. Skin-close to revealing her intentions, she finally yields to the pressure. She falls into her aunt's arms with the cry "Oh, don't leave me alone"' (p. 477), delivering therewith her hopes into the lap of her fears.

After the failure of her escape attempt, Maria Eugenia is loath to analyze the riddle of her perplexing conduct. She is stunned and disgusted with herself, and in an infuriating attempt to retrieve her sense of dignity, she writes a short, nasty letter of rejection to Gabriel. We, the readers, find ourselves waving frantically toward the last door where the question mark of female potential is emblazoned and underneath it the taboo against its independent development and expression in society. As if she has heard us, Maria Eugenia calls Leal to cancel her rapidly approaching marriage. It had been moved up to the following week because Abuelita, in her increasing infirmity, expressed her wish to see her granddaughter safely yoked in marriage before she could die easily.

In that period of Venezuelan history, for Maria Eugenia to express herself totally either in love or the mastery of a skill that would bring her a different kind of immortality than childbearing, she would need to draw upon an undivided, guilt-free spirit. But, as she accepts, with Cesar Leal's male vanity, the notion that a career would obviate a family, she reflects the fear of womankind to chuck the trappings of its biologically dictated role from whence its inverted power stems. Maria Eugenia cannot look Leal in the face and refuse to marry him. In a pitiful loss of nerve, she allows him to bulldoze her stammering attempts to be honest, and her pact, bargained for under pressure as it is stamped with her youthful inexperience, is sealed. Divorce, as both Gabriel and Mercedes have testified with their example, brings with it the devastating shame and disgrace of both church and society; therefore it can never be used as an effective escape. Maria Eugenia has been deprived of the lessons only personal experience can bring and pushed not really by the perceived enemy—man—but by a network of older women who tyrannically impose the protection of their greater experience with men and dutifully enforce the hypocrisy of their own sacrifice upon their daughters. Thus, deprived of all the sources from which confidence and self-knowledge spring, having rejected her faith both in the church's corner on the truth and in Gabriel's fidelity to her should she begin producing his children without a marriage license, Maria Eugenia turns her back on the last door of independent struggle (through which Parra herself had had the courage to venture), the door that led right back to the worst unknown of all, the terrifying illogic of her self.

Now even the reflection of her body in the mirror brings neither reassurance nor pleasure; even the silk wedding dress from Paris lies in a dull heap on the bed. The trepidations of marching to the altar with a man she does not love are fanned into a raging fire by centuries of resigned whispers. Hallucinations, described in effusive and turgid prose, ripple the surface of her composure during her last moments of freedom. Her eyes, seeking some grander name for their surrender, retreat like a wild animal's from the memory of running free with its natural mate, to exalt in an imagined biblical mating with God. Around her the earsplitting command of the "seven-headed monster" (p. 493)—society—resounds, striking her down to the "final, definitve repose," the frozen pose of sacrifice.

Notes

1. As told to the author by Teresa de la Parra's cousin, Luis de Llano Sanojo.
2. Personal interview with Sister Marcelle Chevalier and Luisa Margarita Sosa, at Saint Joseph de Tarbes Academy, March 30, 1978.
3. *Distribution de Permios, Religiosas del Sagrado Carazon de Jesus Godella*, Valencia, Spain, years 1094–1907.
4. Letter to Carlos Garcia-Prada, in *Obras Completas* (Caracas: Editorial Arte, 1965), p. 901.
5. As told to the author, Valencia, November 6, 1978.
6. *Teresa de la Parra, Cartas a Rafael Carias* (Alcala de Henares, Spain: Talleres Penitenciarios, 1957), p. 10.
7. Ibid., p. 12.
8. *Ifigenia*, in *Obras Completas*, p. 34.
9. Clara Isabel Gonzalez, "Teresa de la Parra," *Revista del Instituto Pedagogico* (Caracas, April-June 1945), p. 229.
10. *Ifigenia*, p. 185
11. "La Vida Intima de Teresa de la Parra," interview with Maria Bunimovitch, *El Nacional*, December 7, 1947.
12. "A don Miguel de Unamuno (Carta escrita en julio de 1925)," *Repertorio Americano*, San Jose, Costa Rica, February 5, 1927.
13. As told to author by Luis de Llano.
14. Thomas R. Ybarra, *Young Man of Caracas* (New York: Ives Washburn, Inc., 1941), p. 217.
15. Letter received from Luis E. de Llano-Sanojo, August 5, 1979.
16. *Ifigenia*, p. 105.
17. Ybarra, *Young Man of Caracas*, p. 105.
18. Luz Machado de Arnao, "Tiempo y Obra de Teresa de la Parra," *Atenea, Chile*, Jan.-Feb. 1955, pp. 117–18.
19. *Ifigenia*, p. 54.
20. Ibid., p. 70.
21. Ibid., p. 72.
22. Ybarra, *Young Man of Caracas*, p. 116.
23. "*Ifigenia* y un Valiente Defensor de las Aristeguieta," in *Obras Completas*, pp. 512–13.
24. Ybarra, *Young Man of Caracas*, p. 23.
25. *Ifigenia*, p. 147.

26. Ibid., pp. 187–88.
27. Ibid., p. 165.
28. Ibid., p. 200.
29. Verified by the author, *Diocese de Paris, Paroisse St. Augustin, Book,* pag. 214, No. 71, dated 20 May 1924.
30. Interview with Luis de Llano.
31. *Ifigenia,* dedication page.
32. See note 11.
33. Letter to Carlos Garcia-Prada, in *Obras Completas,* p. 901.
34. Armando Rojas, "Romain Rolland y Teresa de la Parra," *El Nacional* (Caracas), August 4, 1963.
35. Nelida Norris, *A Critical Appriasal of Teresa de la Parra,* University of California, Los Angeles, Ph.D., 1970, unpublished, pp. 193–95.
36. "Second Lecture," 1930 in *Obras Completas,* p. 735.
37. See note 11.
38. Ibid.
39. Letter to Miguel de Unamuno. See note 12.
40. *Ifigenia,* p. 72.
41. See note 11.
42. Letter to Rafael Carias, August 21, 1925, Cartas a Rafael Carias, p. 26.
43. Letter to author from Pastor of Paroisse Sainte-Honore D'Eylan, November 8, 1979.
44. *El Nuevo Diaro,* October 23, 1924.
45. Ibid.
46. See note 11.
47. Francisco Guarderas, *Las Paginas de Gonzalo Zaldumbide,* Quito: Editorial Casa de la Cultura Ecuatoriana, 1962.
48. *El Nacional,* January 26, Sec. C, p. 7, 1965.
49. As related to author by Elia de Perez-Luna, Teresa de la Parra's niece.
50. Letter to Carias, June 22, 1933, in *Cartas a Rafael Carias,* pp. 153–55.
51. Ybarra, *Young Man of Caracas,* p. 33.
52. Ismael Pereira-Alvarez, *Revista de Instruccion Publica,* vol. 1 (1905), p. 145.
53. "La Mujer Venezolana," *El Universal,* Caracas, July 21, 1920, p. 1.
54. Letter to Carias, January 11, 1935, in *Obras Completas,* p. 882.
55. "Diario de una Caraquena," *Acutalidades,* Caracas, 7 and 14 December 1919.
56. See note 9.
57. *Ifigenia,* p. 250.
58. Letter to Zea-Uribe, December 1930, in *Obras Completas,* p. 813.
59. "Homenaje al Principe Don Fernando," *El Nuevo Diario,* Caracas, 9 May 1921, n.p.
60. Personal interview with Elena Mederos-Gonzalez, June 11, 1978.
61. Letter to Vicente Lecuna, in *Obras Completas,* p. 810.
62. Interview with Maria Bunimovitch. See note 11.
63. Interview with Rafael Carias, Caracas, August 25, 1978.
64. Letter to Miguel de Unamuno, 1925. See note 12.
65. Edmund Chispa, "Mujeres de Avila," *El Nuevo Diario* (Caracas), February 23, 1923.
66. Letter to Unknown, December 29, 1932, in *Obras Completas,* p. 930.
67. Letter to Carias, March 5, 1927, in *Obras Completas,* p. 851.

68. Letter to Guzman-Esponda, June 1926, in *Obras Completas*, p. 888.
69. "Unas Palabras Mas Sobre Ifigenia," March 31, 1927, in *Obras Completas*, p. 518.
70. Letter to Guzman Esponda, in *Obras Completas*, pp. 884–890.
71. "Unas Palabaras Mas. . . ," in *Obras Completas*, pp. 514–521.
72. Luis Eduardo Nieto-Caballero, *Colinas Inspirada* (Bogota: Editorial Minerva, 1929), pp. 62–63.

CHAPTER THREE

Parra Matures as Writer and Person

The New Freedom

In 1922 Teresa de la Parra envisioned her fate much differently than she had envisioned the fate of Maria Eugenia Alonso. Boredom, renunciation, and sacrifice were to have no part in Teresa's own life. In Caracas, as she entered the first stage of her personal fulfillment, French artists at the forefront of Western culture were entering the last stage in the expression of the individual human journey. World economics was defined now in mass movements; industrial labor and world war urging upon mankind—in unsubtle terms—the visualization of a terrifying new order. "Machines created for the service of humanity" became a phrase reversible to "humanity created for the service of machines." In popular culture, humankind saw itself struggling to oblige the new economics that had begun reshaping and stamping out its members like cookie-cuttings distinguishable neither by class nor by personality. For the majority of people who were poor, this was a beneficial turn of events. Along with the besiegement of individualism came an assault on the barriers of prejudice and gentility that had fostered the development and well-being of some individuals at the expense of others. New voices in politics, science, and art participated in this wholesale dissection of the social contract, especially in the context of the first great war. In European painting, for instance, surrealists and expressionists had taken an exploratory step further into the shocking fantasies and realities of the human mind, while a more experimental group entered the realm of cerebral abstractions.

The chief direction of the most influential writers in Europe during the 1920s was toward introspection. We know Paris of that decade through the books of many English and American authors who flourished in its international, avant-garde atmosphere. The city was a crossroads for writers and thinkers throughout the Western world. In Paris and elsewhere, writers such as T. S. Eliot, D. H. Lawrence, James Joyce, Thomas Mann, and Marcel Proust, taking their individual searches to the limits of the expressible, were making their mark on the intellectual life of the time. Spanish-speaking philosophers and writers pursued similar lines of thought, though their products languished in the shadow of the great European works. An overriding theme of the "tragic sense of life" pervaded the work of these writers of the twenties, whom the more politically committed writers of the thirties, such as George Orwell, criticized for their self-absorption: ''. . . What purpose they have is very much up in the air. There is no attention to the urgent problems of the moment, above all no politics in the narrower sense. Our eyes are directed to Rome, to the Subconscious, to the solar plexus—to everywhere except the places where things are actually happening.''[1]

Parra, possessed of an inborn melancholy and—in the self-descriptive words of Maria Eugenia—a "wretched propensity for philosophizing," was in 1922 still optimistic in her thirst for the earthly ideal: ideal love—perhaps—and absolute freedom of movement and expression —assuredly. Step by step, *Diary of a Young Lady Who Wrote Because She Was Bored* worked its way into the conscience and consciousness of South America's educated male elite. Teresa, now writing behind the thin veil of her pen name "de la Parra" and marveling at the new life opening up to her, followed closely behind. Her success came, just as she had imagined, like the "smell of the sea, carrying its message of hope from foreign lands.''[2]

It was not such an unlikely success as one might initially suppose. When the first chapters *Young Lady* . . . were made public in *La Lectura Semanal* in June 1922, the ordinary folk of Caracas were the first to show their approval, as the heavy sales testified.[3] They devoured it for its readability, its bombardment of upper-class gentility, and its speaking of the unspoken. Accompanying Parra's story in the magazine, an optimistic comment relevant only indirectly thereto pointed to the overall awareness of women's complaint at that time even in Venezuela: "In a few generations we shall produce women with as sound a constitution as men's. Civilization, mitigating the conditions of city life, will no longer allow women to drop off like flies under the age of forty."[4]

Encouraged by the preliminary response to her writing, Parra entered a literary contest sponsored by the city of Ciudad Bolívar, with a second excerpt from her manuscript. For this event, she had chosen a section of her novel that she could most easily edit into an independent short story. It consisted of one of Maria Eugenia's flashbacks to her precocious convent days in Spain, when she and her special schoolmate Cristina Iturbe had sought the true identity of Cristina's mother. The mother had supposedly died in childbirth, yet the hushed tones in which Cristina's guardians still spoke about her aroused her daughter's suspicions. It was the young girls' hope to discover that Cristina's mother had actually been a great actress, so that Cristina's loneliness in the world would be consoled and her own hopes for a future in the theater encouraged. Guided, however, by the mysterious key phrase "natural child" overheard once in conversation, the two innocents gradually uncovered in its meaning the ugly truth of Cristina's disgraceful parentage.

Parra entitled this excerpt "La Mama X." There seemed to be no dispute among the judges as to its artistic excellence. Unfortunately, however, the contest rules specified that entries should be representative of national culture, "La Mama X" took place entirely in Europe. The judges were divided on whether to award the story first prize; therefore they reached a compromise by awarding Parra a specially created prize of recognition.[5] Several months later, in April of 1923, "La Mama X" reached the Caraquenian public through the pages of *El Nuevo Diario*. Major publicity—again in that newspaper—had prepared them for this event, since earlier in the year Teresa had been interviewed by a noted Caraquenian journalist, Edmund Chispa, in an article titled "The Women of Avila." Her mood seemed overflowing with cheerfulness at that time; flushed with her recent critical and commercial success, she had revealed to Mr. Chispa that plans were already underway to publish her novel in Paris.[6]

Parra's optimism was well founded. Her Caraquenan readers had paved a smooth runway from which her novel glided into the welcoming arms of French readers as well. The place and time could not have been more propitious. By the time she boarded the vessel *Macoris,* in August of 1923, bound for France via Havana,[7] everything had been arranged for her. Any one of her friends and any member of her family was in a position to influence the publication of her novel in Paris; international and academic and diplomatic circles were accessible to her as both granddaughter of Luis Sanojo and daughter of Rafael Parra. Teresa's friend Emilia Ibarra, so wealthy that she was said to bathe in honey, also enjoyed influence on people of many professions on both sides of the Atlantic through the medium of her salons. Even without this help, the gentlemen at Caracas's two newspapers, along with Jose Pocaterra of *La Lectura Semanal,* maintained ties to the Franco-Ibero Publishing Company in Paris. Thus Teresa would arrive in Paris carrying the address of the famous French writer and critic Francis de Miomandre. A laureate member of the Academy Goncourt, he would later be the one to translate the whole of *Mama Blanca* into the French language. Already, portions of Parra's unedited manuscript had been submitted through him to a contest for best Latin American novel sponsored by the magazine *Revue de L'Amerique Latine* (hereafter called *RDLL*); that magazine's editor, Peruvian writer Ventura Garcia Calderon, was so impressed by what he read that he told Parra her chances for winning the contest were virtually assured.[8]

Parra was now returning in triumph to the city that Maria Eugenia had left in retreat; the elation Teresa felt in her arrival stands in contrast to the "presentiment of sorrow" that overtook Maria Eugenia as, "eyes lost on the horizon," she beheld from the ship's tower her whole life, past and future. For Teresa in August of 1923, this was the first journey since her return from Spain thirteen years previously, and if melancholy contemplations like Maria Eugenia's in the following passage did in fact describe the past, they hardly described the present: ". . . When a steamship stops moving, after having traveled a long way, it seems that along with it all our dreams have stopped and all our ideals are silent. The gentle slipping away of something that directs us is beneficial to our spiritual fecundity. Why? Could it be that each time our soul finds itself running without any assistance from its feet, it dreams, perhaps, that it is flying far away from land and detaching itself completely from the material world?"[9]

At almost thirty-four years of age, Teresa posed as her most immediate object of desire the material world with all its sensual delights. Animated within a Parisian fantasy future, she charmed the welcoming party gathered in her honor during the *Macoris*'s Havana stopover, and this was how a twenty-four–year–old Lydia Cabrera encountered Teresa for the first time and was infected with Parra's spirit, enthused, and encouraged to venture forth, too. Teresa discovered that the Cuban had her own manuscript on African folklore waiting an opportunity for publication; promptly she offered the benefits of her own connections. They exchanged calling cards. It wasn't until a year later that Lydia followed Teresa to Paris, at which time their friendship entered the first stage of its lasting course.[10]

Paris gathered exiles—self-imposed or otherwise—to her center; anyone and everyone wishing to contribute his or her small part and, in turn, wishing to partake of greatness, flocked to the city. Often coming from conditions of oppression in other countries, these exiles were finally free, once in Paris, to live according to their ideals of full personal liberty. As soon as Teresa arrived, she was plunged into a world both reassuringly familiar and excitingly strange. Emilia Ibarra, widowed since 1920, stood tall against the cityscape with her continued patronage, and younger sister Isabelita was also in residence with her husband. The men of the *Magazine Review de L'Amerique Latin*—Garcia Calderon, Miomandre, and Zaldumbide—flocked around Teresa. As Mistral, who did not arrive until 1926, would later say, "So beautiful was the Venezuelan that her beauty made one forget her literary status. . . . A woman dressed by Paquin or Ducet . . . she creollicized the gatherings (of Frenchified South Americans in Paris) within twenty minutes, letting fall her Creole expressions into the conversations, which were usually full of red-and-white political commentary. The conversation would change its course, warm up, become witty. . . ."[11]

Teresa indulged her love of fashion only as much as her modest budget would allow. Ever conscious of refinement in speech as well as in dress, she enrolled in elocution classes taught by an "attractive former actress" in order to improve her French diction. At the Sorbonne, she attended lectures on contemporary French literature, through which she became familiar with the names "Colette, Gyp, Tinayre, and [those of] other male and female celebrities."[12]

But most important, Teresa spent her first winter in Paris awaiting the results of the contest for best new novel to come out of Latin America. Ten thousand francs were to accompany first prize; she had heard from Garcia-Calderon and through the grapevine that the award would be hers, though the jury did not make it official until later in the year. (The formal announcement was not made until as late as February of 1925.)[13] This delay greatly frustrated the progress of publishing her novel; to Carias she lamented her misfortune that the official announcement, "for whatever reasons of intrigue or economics," was not being made: "I find myself, as time passes by, in the dilemma of continuing to hope indefinitely, consumed by impatience . . . or whether to renounce the prize and publish the book at my own cost."[14] During this period she also appealed to the Gomez administration for funds to cover her publishing costs. At some point, she did begin to receive a pension, but it was discontinued later on.[15]

The thrill of arrival lasted exactly eight months. Teresa's "second mother," Emilia Ibarra, the one most responsibile for Parra's current success, died of cancer in May 1924.[16] So integral had Emilia been to Teresa's new life that now, "abandoned and alone, alienated from life, disenchanted as if all my spirit had died with Emilia."[17] Teresa left Paris immediately to find solace at her sister Isabelita's house in the Swiss countryside. The letter Parra wrote from there to Carias in July of 1924 was full of a brand-new sense of doom. She felt her "evil star" was on the rise; she suggested having first considered, then rejected, uprooting herself completely and moving back to Caracas; she expressed new impatience with people other than trusted friends. Finally, she indicated a new scorn for the exile mentality that "denounces its own, without ever arriving at a comprehension of the foreign—they play the role of intruders in a foreign house." Her letter ended with a sad analysis of the restlessness that, from this time on, she would regard as a kind of curse: "At times I think in Caracas I was happy and that I have been ruined by this nomadic inquietude that we Venezuelans all carry in our souls. . . . This restlessness, which is perhaps responsible for the religions and the arts, this thirst for the ideal, is not cured in travel, believe me. We have merely transferred it to our bodies, sacrificing the familiar tranquillity of our homes and the sky. . . ."[18]

As the year 1924 progressed, Spanish-speaking lovers of contemporary literature gradually became aware of the new novel, soon to be published, by Teresa de la Parra. In June, the first fragments, translated into French by Miomandre, were published in the *RDLL,* under the title *Diary of a Bored Young Lady,* with a footnote giving public thanks to "our friend Gonzalo Zaldumbide, through whom we have come to know these pages."[19] By September 1924, the complete Spanish version of *Ifigenia* reached print at the Casa Editorial Franco-Ibero-Americana and the *Paris Time* of Septembere 30 announced its arrival to the book world in an article titled "Issues by Ana Teresa Parra: A Writer and Woman Pioneer."

But everything connected to *Ifigenia* seemed to have gone sour for

Teresa now that Emilia could not share in it. Parra's mother and sisters, who had never been thrilled by the novel's indiscretions, nevertheless resurfaced as her main source of emotional and financial support. According to the tradition her family had always observed in the past, separate rooms became permanently available to both Teresa and her mother for the rest of their lives in the many houses belonging to Isabelita and Maria that were scattered throughout Paris, Switzerland, and southern France.

Parra did not need any training to develop her "tragic sense of life." The next four years were to be defined by the effects of success on a small-town innocent; between 1924 and 1927, she appeared to suffer all the symptoms of an awakening induced by the barrage of praise and criticism following in *Ifigenia*'s wake. How often she must have regretted using her real name![20] Her new audience of admirers and detractors tried to pin her down on every implication of her novel's text—what was autobiographical and what wasn't, why she had decided on such an ending, and above all, why she had even written such a disgraceful expose of her own family! Already her fans hoped for a sequel, in which Maria Eugenia's renunciation might be revealed as a merely temporary capitulation.[21] Teresa, reeling from all the attention, pondered Maria Eugenia's fate in private. In the good company of friends and colleagues with whom freethinking discussions were common, Parra embarked on a new course of self-improvement that promised a closer integration between her personal morality and her need for public approval. The ethics of her art became the prime focus of this self-refinement. Had Maria Eugenia been, in truth, too frivolous to take seriously, and if so, what exactly was her own relationship to her protagonist? As Teresa wrestled her tendency to indulge a thirst for the superficial and illusory, the clothes became less glittery and the phrases less gilded. She began to realize that the great outside world in which she had sought her release from the seclusion and silence prescribed for her sex was shallow with greed and gloss and empty of all soul. She found herself surrounded by jaded and cynical sophisticates on the one side and childlike, radical experimentalists on the other. No rulebook existed for women caught in this modern bind. Virginia Woolf, whose literary star was ascending at the same historical moment, expressed in 1936 her analysis that the ". . . daughters of educated men are between the devil and deep sea. Behind us lies the patriarchal system, the private house, with its nullity, its immorality, its hypocrisy, its servility. Before us lies the public world, the professional system, with its possessiveness, its jealousy, its pugnacity, its greed. The one shuts us up like slaves in a harem; the other forces us to circle, like caterpillars, head to tail, round and round the mulberry tree, the sacred tree of property. It is a choice of evils.''[22] Woolf's advice to the next generation of women was to ''retain the outlook of the loser even after you've won.''

It was becoming rapidly apparent that Teresa's enthusiastic feminity was a double-edged sword. Many contemporary critics, stung by the loud and abrasive sounds of the Anglo-Saxon women's movement, with which they sympathized in heart, praised Teresa's style with relief and thrilled at her many-sided revelations of a young womanhood traditionally hidden from them. Others, however, saw in her manner a barrier to masculine seriousness, and from her novel they turned their heads as they did from the world of women, which, trivial and irrelevant, existed alongside the larger world without affecting it. Indeed, in the emotional flurry that her novel had begun to instigate, much of the criticism devolved around its moral and political, rather than its artistic, merit. As early as 1923, a prominent Venezuelan critic, Don Lisandro Alvarado, had pointed out that *Ifigenia* revived the age-old and bitter philosophical struggle between philogynists and misogynists.[23] Teresa, believing that the bulk of intellectual commentary leveled at her novel was by men who had no faith in her as an artist, stood proudly by her gender and made no attempt to modify her writing style.

In 1926, Teresa could no longer stand the misogyny she divined behind those ''brilliantly prepared arguments'' and exploded in an article, published in Caracas, called ''*Ifigenia:* The Criticism, Critics, and Would-Be Critics.'' Stressing somewhat bitterly her humble approach to writing as an ''amiable and conciliatory recourse, at times very sincere,'' which she permitted herself to ''recommend to all authors,'' she lit into a group of critics she labeled ''false intellectuals'':

> One time, for example, one of them said to me with a patronizing air, that my novel *Ifigenia* was full of ''femininities.'' I believed sincerely that he meant great praise and started to express my thanks with my most pleasant smile. But in time I realized that ''femininities'' did not constitute a good quality, but rather a grave defect. Then, with the same smile I was prepared to give him in thanks for the praise, I thanked him instead for the warning and promised in the future I would never commit another ''femininity.'' The truth is that I could never change myself, because I have not really managed to understand what they wanted to tell me.[24]

To the group of Latin Americans at the *RDLL,* the theme of Euripides' tragedy *Ifigenia* seemed to be at the forefront of discussion. Mexican author Alfonso Reyes had recently published his own modern adaptation titled *Ifigenie Cruelle,* from which he gave a reading in 1925 at the home of Gonzalo Zaldumbide.[25] Both Zaldumbide and Miomandre took charge of publicizing Parra's *Ifigenia.* It was Miomandre who convinced her to change the long original title to one more befitting the tastes of its new international readers.[26] Teresa, feeling inept in commercial matters, was amenable to his suggestions and made the relevant changes—all minor—in chapter headings and, toward the ending, in portions of the text. The final package arrived on the South American continent early in 1925. Response from critics returned in slow trickles to its author in France, so that she was unable to tally its total effect until the end of that year. In the meantime, complete French translations were already in progress. Although Miomandre had rendered a fragment into French the previous year, the total job fell to many diverse hands. Originally, Teresa had entrusted it to Marius André, one of *RDLL*'s contributing writers. He had hardly bent himself to the task before she changed her mind, retrieved it from him, and, with typical impetuosity, allowed instead an "exquisitely refined bohemian couple" who had written her of their suffering and need of work, to complete it: ". . . Marius André, with a name and connections and everything necessary to launch upon the French *Ifigenia,* to have been published at the beginning of 1926, said indignantly: 'Only a woman would do such a thing; where did she find these translators?' The fact is that *Ifigenia* is being translated with true conscientiousness and affection, something a well-known writer would never have done due to his desire to publish immediately.'"[27]

Publication details about this final French translation are confused. Teresa announced its completion to Carias in March 1927,[28] but dates and names referring to its release are inconclusive. Marius André succeeded in translating the whole of "La Mama X" into French, which *RDLL* in turn printed under the title of "Cristine, Enfant Naturelle."[29] Other fragments, with yet other translators' names, appeared in print elsewhere around Paris during the year. The reviews praised their author to the skies. To the French-speaking readers, *Ifigenia* provided in its tropical setting a flavor of the exotic and in its raw and genuine social conflict a vivid picture of the fundamental issues shaping women's destiny as a whole. The following critique was written by Marius André:

Perhaps the public thinks, as I do, that the Latin American writers manifest their superiority in the short story, poem, and critical essay more than in the novel. Certain indications, however, make us think it will not always be this way. This shocking *Ifigenia,* by Teresa de la Parra, which I am not alone in regarding as a chef d'oeuvre—is it not a novel? This book that paints the life of a young girl in Venezuela with a hallucinatory brush reminds us of Marcel Proust. Through the subtle precision of analysis, through the very rhythm of the sentence, through the ensorcelating charm and mystery of style, this singularly personal and original novel belongs to the art of Swann.[30]

Max Daireux, also a member of Parra's social group, went so far as to say: "Teresa de la Parra belongs to the class of the best writers of South America," praising her "magnificent prodigality, her mixture of malice and sensibility," and the "indefinable charm of the simple style; the breath of poetry enlivens like the breath of those perfumed breezes filling the sails of light boats on tropical seas."[31]

Verbal Wars

Spanish philosopher Miguel de Unamuno gave Teresa these words by which to live in 1925: "Do not concern yourself with what they say or don't say about your novel: withdraw into yourself—throw away the mirror, Teresa. . . ."[32]

She emerged from the events of 1924—ups and downs jolting her along her uncharted course—as if awakening from the effervescent Caraquenan daydream to find herself in a dark, noisy place with no name. Emilia Ibarra's death, besides leaving Teresa stranded with a scandalous book to defend, bequeathed her a mixed inheritance: on the one hand, the general provisions of Emilia's will secured Teresa's financial independence for an indefinite number of years, and on the other, it embroiled her in two years of bitter haggling with the wealthy and powerful—and very resentful—Ibarra Barrios and Guzman relatives. At stake were a yearly stipend and a small rental house in Caracas; the relatives, drawing added bile from the century-long political feud between the families, lodged an accusation against the less fortunate "Godo" Teresa that her twelve-year-long devotion to her Semiramis had been motivated by greed. Teresa responded by telling them the following: "I would have accompanied Emilia through illness or poverty; never, out of very natural reasons of delicacy, did I try to influence her on my behalf. On the contrary, when Emilia said that should I have a child one day, everything, everything would become mine unconditionally, and I contested that I had no intention of marrying, and I even said this to her several times in the presence of various members of her family."[33]

"Cruel publicity,"[34] too, was a major factor in this sudden disenchantment with the whole business of fame. "How different the praise of the public and the critics to the look of interest, the laugh of joy and satisfaction with which Emilia, in the evening, greeted that I wrote during the day," she wrote Carias in 1926.[35] For at this stage it was the praise that had grown stale; except for two successive articles in the Caracas newspapers during the summer of 1925, reporting proudly her success with French critics of the *Review de L'Amerique Latine*, South American critics had not yet responded to the book. Teresa still wrote Carias anxiously for detailed reports as soon as that response should come, emphasizing that it was the only one that truly mattered to her. Her disgust with city life altogether seemed linked to two additional factors: she found herself unable to write, and her flirtation with Gonzalo Zaldumbide was coming to an end. She fled Paris to spend the summer of 1925 at her sister's home in Switzerland, where she could enjoy "spiritual repose":

> In Paris, not only do I not write, but neither do I read a single sentence. The agitated diversions that drive me away from myself are causing me immense discomfort; how welcome now is gentle boredom, giving off its dreams and longings for the ideal! I am writing you from the shores of the lake, in a poetic restaurant, in full view of small steamboats and launches, within hearing of a nearby orchestra, and all this situated against a picture-postcard landscape, the most cinematic in the world. I, dressed in white, feel myself to be quite the "romantic heroine."[36]

At one time Teresa had cried out through *Ifigenia's* pages for the opportunity to pursue the independent development of her personality, free of male domination. Now that such freedom was achieved and the workings of her personality exposed to the world in those pages, she was not pleased with her reflection in the public eye. And, as we can well imagine, neither was her mother, upon whose maternal affection Teresa now depended more than ever. Teresa's true self, like any other truth, was a stable equation made up of ever-shifting elements, and the voyage to its discovery must, she now felt, begin from ports of solitude, where she could listen to the welling up of deep-rooted currents inside her own mind just as she had done, when younger, in Caracas.

Miguel de Unamuno, towering patriarchally over the Latin community of Paris, was flatteringly sensitive to Teresa's predicament. Much to her surprise, he read the book she had presented to him at a social gathering; furthermore, he voiced publicly his enthusiastic response to it, which he tempered with the kind of criticism that Teresa—gratefully—accepted.[37] Unamuno had made the problems of the fallen Catholic and disillusioned intellectual the subject of his life's work, the opus of which titled *The Tragic Sense of Life*, and therefore his advice to Teresa reflected an authentic concern with the issues raised in her novel. He had come to Paris only months after Teresa's arrival, banished at the age of sixty from his Greek chair at the University of Salamanca, where he had irreparably offended the Spanish government with his socialist teachings. Teresa was obviously new to the literary world, its jealousies among authors and publishers, its vanities, and of course, its various unsavory parasites. Unamuno's seasoned counsel to "throw away the mirror" and let the comments fly over her head had already occurred to her "many times," yet she had not found the self-discipline to be able to commit it to action, much to her "sadness, remorse and humiliation": "No, I did not invent the mirror, Don Miguel. If, like Narcissus, I spend my days in its insipid attraction, it is out of sheer nonsense, out of an obstinate spirit of association; the inertia of the blank page . . ." Proof of her dwindling enthusiasm for the mirror, she went on to assert, was that ". . . many, many times, while watching the mannequins of the large fashion houses file past in show, my poor eyes, overwhelmed, turn around in the anguish of indecision and the anguish of the inaffordable prices; my spirit suddenly goes flying down the road to the other show, to the exposition of second-hand booksellers, the old friend full of . . . rich surprise, of whom I am constantly reminded and whom I have yet to go visit!"[38]

To this turbulent stream of self-castigations and self-indulgences was soon added the criticism from South America, and as she seemed to have anticipated, by 1926 it had become torrential indeed. In the establishment circles of Venezuela and Colombia, everything, from the realistic, moody description of Caracas in the beginning of the book to the descriptions of misery underlying family life throughout it, was seen as an insult. As late as 1928, harsh religious judgments by a Colombian Jesuit came down on Parra's use of the words "obligation, honor, family, religion, morality, society and social need."[39] Not only did he feel that Maria Eugenia was immoral, but that her author was equally so. From his point of view, the novel clearly posed a danger to readers without strong moral principles.

Ifigenia soon became forbidden reading for young women in Bogota, and in Caracas, the upper classes discouraged it strongly. As it usually happens with things that are so fiercely withheld for the ostensible purpose of protecting the morals of youth, *Ifigenia* also became an object of compelling curiosity. It attained a clandestine following that spread through the Spanish-speaking countries. To give an idea of how strongly the book was obstructed in Caracas, writer Roberto Blanco reported the following incident on his first trip there in 1928: "The first book I requested at the bookshops was *Ifigenia,* thinking it would also be the first book that would proffer itself to me. The masterful work of Venezuelan realism was not there. It was almost unknown. . . . The most I got was a mysterious response. Privately they spoke to me, and I understood then that this book could not be in good standing here and that bad times could come to whomever did business with it. . . ."[40]

In spite of praise existing elsewhere in Blanco's belated essay—for instance, his stating that Parra was a woman of vision and inspiring example, a redeemer even of women in Latin America—the initial attacks on *Ifigenia*'s morality wounded Teresa strategically. Not only did they perpetrate an injustice on the many women she felt Maria Eugenia represented, but because of the ambivalence of her identification with her "other self," they also challenged her sense of pride; in no way did she consider herself as weak as her protagonist. Artists, in making art, must always risk the mortal wounds of ridicule—Parra's courage in expressing herself had not encompassed that eventuality. Somewhere inside her pity for Maria Eugenia's defeat lay a matching contempt. This ambiguity, which her novel reflected, did, ultimately, allow for different interpretations, in the same way as do the ambiguities presented by real life. The more she tried to explain it, the more confused she became. For to her the book was written by Maria Eugenia, not by herself; it lived a separate life of its own, and all the exceptions after the fact of its creation seemed futile to her. We must remember, after all, that during the writing of her novel, Teresa had proudly considered it a "disinterested protest." As her voice rose in defiance or vacillated in wordy embellishments, its identity became lost in resemblance to the voice—capricious and charming—that we learned not to trust in the pages of *Ifigenia*.

Parra did concede that *Ifigenia* suffered, perhaps, from "excessive lyricism," but only later, in 1932. For now she took refuge from attacks on its rambling style in witticism and facetious excuses that she had purposefully avoided creating "strong literature" by elaborating on the ordinary details of the small, humble side of life. In one letter, she wished to suggest that the misunderstanding over her novel's ending even by many of its supporters was due to the fact that most of her critics were men. Unlike her female readers, who, she claimed, were moved by the ending, men (i.e., her correspondent Guzman-Esponda), were disturbed by it. Perhaps the idea pricked at them that their own wives and mothers, now resigned and peaceful, might have undergone a similarly painful experience preceding their capitulations to careers in the home.[41]

But most of all, Parra did not want to be remembered as the author of a harmful book. The insult perceived in *Ifigenia* by South American critics seemed to her much out of proportion to the "benevolent criticism" she had intended. Because her innocent and desperate cry for independence was bringing dishonor to her mother's name in Caracas, Teresa became increasingly insistent that not the slightest criticism had been implied in her novel—it had simply represented even-handedly a realistic situation. When, in December of 1926, Chilean critic Armando Labarca published an article in *El Universal* praising *Ifigenia* for its author's gift of observation, he thought to support its convincing view of the "ridiculous aspects of people and things, of gentle conventionalisms and the impositions that abstain from logic."[42] But Parra refuted even this much insinuation that she had made anything or anyone in her novel loook ridiculous, and Mr. Labarca, exasperated, published another article praising her instead for her new talent for writing charming and contradictory letters.

It is probable that Teresa's overly sensitive retaliation to Labarca's comments—so well intentioned—reflected an anger stoked elsewhere. A vicious pamphlet had recently been mailed by an anonymous person, writing under the pseudonym Carlos Villena, to the Venezuelan embassy in Paris, containing a long list of writers, critics, and publishers to whom the embassy should forward copies. The writer's purpose was to stop *Ifigenia*'s second printing and to cast aspersions on Teresa de la Parra's character. His motivating spirits were racism, misogyny, and snobbism, and his chief point of attack was a remark made in *Ifigenia* by—naturally—Uncle Pancho. Women from great families, Pancho had declared, even the Aristeguieta, were so bored and unhappy in their forced isolation that when war broke out and their men departed, they took in lovers of other races. This inflammatory statement did not go over well at the Galindo table; Mercedes Galindo, especially, defended the virtue of her Mantuana forebears and the purity of their descendants' white blood. For the anonymous author of the pamphlet, however, the context of Pancho's remarks was immaterial—the mere printing of such thoughts on the page constituted sacrilege.

Parra made inquiries to identify the anonymous critic. As she had suspected, he proved to be a descendant of the Aristeguieta family, a widely published journalist and the secretary of the Venezuelan delegation to Peru and Bolivia, Dr. Ignacio Vetancourt-Aristeguieta. "Where has Parra learned her history of Venezuela?" he asked. "She has no understanding of the different levels of society." Proof of the author's inexperience, he charged, was Maria Eugenia's preference for the company of the Negro laundress, Gregoria. "One might also cite the fact that, despite what she says, Señorita Parra has lived in contact with the present-day community of Caracas in which white women, tortured by hunger, had no alternative but to suffer the amorous pleasures of negroes, half-breeds and mulattoes. They are flowers trampled under the hairy feet of pigs."[43] The Venezuelan embassy fortunately did not comply with Dr. Vetancourt Aristeguieta's request to pass on his warning; Parra, in the meantime, planned her counterattack with care. In November of 1926, she published an article titled "*Ifigenia*: Criticism, the Critics, and the Would-Be Critics," in which she divided her critics into three groups: the public, "cordial, open and silent like an absent brother"; the truly intelligent ones, "flexible and understanding"; and finally, the "false intellectuals," who constitute in this article the target of her wrath. These "would-be critics," mentioned previously for their misogynist tendencies, prey with their brilliantly documented, self-righteous arguments upon the weakness of the artist, betraying in their love for the sound of their own voices not the slightest desire to comprehend the results of the artist's labor. Indeed the effect of their words is to stifle the artistic impulse altogether: "To live peacefully after writing and publishing a book, the writer should never discuss its theme with an intellectual. One should merely listen attentively to their judgments, cares and warnings, though they make no sense."[44] She blamed the "false intellectuals" failure to absorb the subtleties of her book—subtleties that others less educated but more intelligent had easily understood—on their malicious intentions.

The above article was the first, published along with two others, in a series containing Parra's angriest defenses of *Ifigenia*. The second one, "*Ifigenia* and a Defense of the Aristeguieta," she sent to *El Universal* in December, 1926. In it she answered specifically the pamphlet written by someone so "manly" that he had not had the courage to sign his own name to it. Mocking further his possessive attitude toward the Aristeguieta name—"he takes it out every day and polishes it—it is his crown!"—she referred to him as a "modern knight of the Round Table." Her own proud ancestry, consisting of families who contributed to every facet of her country's history, from the founding of the colonies to the War of Independence, stood as her best defense of the charge of disrespect: "I cannot respect the nobility of my country, as he says, because one very simply reason prevents me: for this kind of respect it is necessary to have distance, and in this case no distance exists. It is exactly as if he were counseling me to respect my hands or my hair."[45]

Dr. Vetancourt-Aristeguieta responded immediately, in January 1927, to her second article; under his real name this time, he attacked Parra for having so irresponsibly created a character who, albeit fictional, was decidedly immoral. In her March 1927 retort, called "Some More Words about *Ifigenia,*" she attempted yet again to defend the creation of her embattled heroine. She identified the real issues at stake as the freedom of an artist to create characters with independent morals: Aristeguieta's argument raised the hackles of all artists reliving the age-old struggle against the hypocrisies of censorship. Other prominent critics in Colombia, a country more tyrannically conventional than Venezuela, praised *Ifigenia* without any complaints about its morals, she emphasized. Although she claimed not to have had the slightest intention of preaching morality, its tenets—she contended—were well represented in her portrayals of Abuelita and Aunt Clara. Maria Eugenia was badly judged, moreover, because although she "reveres certain moral principles neither in theory nor in minor points of practice, she does follow them irrespective of that judgment when life presents her with the necessary occasion."[46] Maria Eugenia is, Parra said, "a noble inverse of people who proclaim their virtue loudly and with ostentation, all the while keeping the evil of their true intentions hidden." The humble people, those who are unpretentious and close to daily life, are the only critics she wishes to have. She invoked Unamuno's definition of *intelligence* in order to put Dr. Vetancourt-Aristeguieta in his place once and for all: "Who are the intelligents? Those who have more ideas than words. And the foolish? Those who have more words than ideas."[47] At this point, in the final paragraph in Maria Eugenia's defense, Parra became carried away by the fury of her rhetoric and we see a perfect example of the contradictions for which Labarca was to compliment her that same year: ". . . The severe judgments directed towards the mentality of Maria Eugenia . . . calling her cynical, immoral or an infidel, are the hypocritical judgments of pharisees. Maria Eugenia represents a type of modern woman whose renunciation is unique and truly sublime, since to respect a moral that she considers unjust and to sacrifice life for an ideal that she does not have amounts to being twice virtuous and seven times heroic."[48] Here, Parra's bias against the phony morality that pressured Maria Eugenia to her renunciation appears to have remained intact since the time of her Chispa intereview in 1923, when she blamed the tragedy on "prejudice and imaginary deities."[49] The pious renunciation itself, howeer, that at one time represented merely a cover for bitterness and despair was now, she insisted, to be seen as a glorious achievement. Was not *Ifigenia* intended as lament? Since the most positively drawn, dignified characters in both Parra's novels are the ones who are true to their personal codes of honor against great social odds (Pancho, Gregoria, Cochocho), we can only assume that her distaste for the speciousness of Dr. Vetancourt-Aristeguieta's person prevented her from conceding to him that Maria Eugenia's lack of backbone was correctly diagnosed, yet the moral of the story lay in the opposite direction: the forced dependency of her sex prevented the young woman from resisting a morality she considered false.

Parra was too personally involved to yet answer her own question as to which goal was most worthy of sacrifice—personal integrity or the will of one's ancestors. When those forces clashed, which embodied the true will of God? To her, the "desire for complete personal independence" was the rational opposite to the "ancient and pervading struggle for social survival."[50] Her private letters following *Ifigenia*'s publication betray the hint of an inner labor focusing on these implications of her novel. It wasn't until after *Mama Blanca* came into being that we can detect any evidence that Parra achieved a tolerable compromise. Speaking to Carias in 1928, she revealed a kind of weary familiarity with the feeling of martyrdom that life imposes on those faithful to the abstract configurations of their hopes and dreams. "I see in the final phrase of your last letter than you find yourself in one of those melancholy hours that blows across our souls from time to time like a desolate wind. Think, my good friend, of it as the tribute you must pay when you have a sensitive soul, a subtle intelligence, and eyes positioned highly towards pure ideals."[51]

Parra had already resisted the compromises of marriage that had trapped a less agile Maria Eugenia. Once Teresa had established her independcence as a "rebel of the word," however, the immediate and obvious problem she faced was whether and how much to restrain herself in her speech and her writing; the accusations and misunderstandings had hurt her mother at least as much as they had hurt her. Isabel's concept of a woman's proper role in life was the opposite of Teresa's, but the tension caused by this philosophical difference took second place to Teresa's desire for a mutually tolerant understanding. The fact that Isabel, the same as Abuelita, dedicated her efforts to a saintly ideal that never questioned submissiveness to men did not forever invalidate the words *sacrifice* and *renunciation* in Teresa's mind. She already suspected her future to be a solitary one, and she recognized its frontiers by the barricades of life itself, the years, the gathered karma. These, if she would skirt them with grace, might yet be scaled with the aid of contemplation, and the words Isabel lived by, freed from the conventional behavior that galled, might even find a working place in Teresa's task of self-improvement.

To learn how Parra defined those words, *resignation* and *sacrifice,* Miguel Unamuno questioned her regarding their use in *Ifigenia,* where Pancho states, ". . . The great harmony of the universe is based on the complete resignation of its victims," by suggesting that resignation, at times, hides a divinely motivated scorn directed towards a tyrant, Unamuno elicited a response from Teresa that helps us understand her sympathy and support for Maria Eugenia's last speech: "Most certainly! I think also that in all resignation, as in all sacrifice, there is a divine scorn, towards something or someone, a divine, inactive scorn that asks neither vengeance nor justice, and which sleeps tranquil with the sweet dream of serenity."[52] Maria Eugenia's passionate dedication of her soul, in the ending, to the spirit of Christian sacrifice can therefore be seen not only as a weak and reactionary mental escape from reality, but also, once Leal was rendered inevitable and inescapable, as the only available avenue by which she could express her scorn for his will, Teresa never denied that oppression must be avoided in the beginning. In the above comment, she demonstrated her awareness that in sacrifice to greater being can be found a dignified form of submission, capable of offering a haven of solace for the oppressed on earth. When Carlos Villena, persisting in his campaign to stop *Ifigenia's* second printing, concluded his analysis of the ending with a racist slant against Francis Miomandre, he meant it to denigrate Parra's religious sense. Perhaps Villena was an accuser who, in spite of his insulting tone, named a truth that Parra could have conceded; only the lowliness of his own personality is betrayed by this pejorative comment: "The book, already close to completion, very likely took on a collaborator in its manufacture, probably Jewish, who conceived of the ending, pretending therewith that the spirit of sacrifice can exist beyond the Christian religion, and even beyond all religion."[53]

Mama Blanca

The year 1927 was an eventful one. The negative criticism of *Ifigenia,* which had reached its greatest force and effect in Aristeguieta's stormy outrage, receded to a final position of lesser importance in the overall picture; amidst the now-distant flashing and thundering, a new serenity came shining through with the calm promise of a new novel. The shape of Parra's new feeling was Venezuela, and its tenor was instructed by the lives of the Spanish mystics. The women saints, driven to the shelter of the convents by an uncomprehending and intolerant society, became her special comfort and her counsel—her "persecuted friends," as she called them. Yet this emphasis on the mystical did not blunt her intellectual curiosity in the slightest: "I have not lost interest in the knowledge which today has dealt me the turn of bearing the cross on my back—as it did to my holy women," she wrote to Carias in March 1927.[54] Nor had her new resignation to spinsterhood (demonstrated that same year by her request of Guzman-Esponda to show more respect for the word) made her life in any way similar to that of Aunt Clara and the Beatas. *Ifigenia* was enjoying "immense success," Parra reported to Carias; not only had exiled Spanish royalty—the Infanta Eulalia Paz—laughed enthusiastically at passages that had scandalized the Venezuelan moralists, but at a recent book festival, three dozen copies of *Ifigenia* had to be hauled up from the warehouse because the first twelve copies sold out so rapidly; meanwhile, other French- and Spanish-language novels remained untouched on their shelves.[55] *Ifigenia*'s success continued to grow throughout the year, with the planning of an illustrated luxury edition as well as editions in German and Russian, while a second Spanish version was scheduled for the next year. Parra's success was such that one of the fashion houses mentioned in *Ifigenia* offered to furnish her with an outfit of clothes identical to the one Maria Eugenia claimed to have bought there with her small inheritance.

But while she outwardly enjoyed the fruits of her success, privately She felt "frightened and anxious." She had not written anything in five years: like Maria Eugenia, whose romantic outdoor letter writing stopped as soon as it became a subject of discussion and disapproval at the dinner table, Teresa felt that her fame was directly responsible for her writing block. "I attribute my disinclination for writing to my distaste for fame," she had written Carias in 1926.[56] She felt guilty because of this abstinence; rumors that she was not a serious writer were circulating in Venezuela, along with the insinuation that socializing and vacationing had taken precedence over her contemplative life. If the possibility of marriage had once contributed to this conflict between social temptation and professional duty, now, perhaps because of Zaldumbide's marriage in the spring of 1926, it had vanished as a disruptive factor. That Parra felt marriage and writing were mutually exclusive is implied in her 1925 remark "Neither institutions nor marriage, but to run astray—until overwhelmed by fatigue, I return to writing again." Thus, in Teresa's resolve to write again, she had transformed her defiance of marriage into a positive recognition that the institution was not for her, and in her desire to reconnect to deeper wells of experience, she sought discipline with which to combat the distractions of fame. "I feel this fame," she wrote to Don Lisandro Alvarado under the guise of Maria Eugenia, "disfiguring her ["her" being her creator, de la Parra] like smallpox, is undeserving of envy and incapable of exciting either my or anyone else's rivalry. I allow her then to be content and happy and to live thus in the shadows." Continuing in the coquettish style of Maria Eugenia, Parra describes the "horrible boredom of excessive entertainment" she must endure in Paris. How ironic that "the same reclusive life that once made me a revolutionary, now merely makes me traditional." Her revolutionary urges these days were directed toward the restoration of flowers and humid earth to patios ruined by "abominable mosaic tiles." But crying out would be useless: ". . . My voice would be lost in the noise of the jazz band; I would end up dancing the Charleston without the slightest desire to do so. . . . The best restorations are those presided over by nostalgia and illuminated by sweet melancholy."[57] Such tongue-in-cheek denouncements of Parisian life meant by no means that the two Teresa de la Parras—Venezuelan and Parisian—had resolved their conflict of cultures. But in 1927 the balance leaned heavily in favor of the Old World. Feeling totally independent, Teresa began to revise that Old World in terms more suitable to her current one and in terms more favorable to herself than those under which Maria Eugenia, so tender of soul, faced certain devourment.

Parra was fortunate to be surrounded by a group of writers who were strong and articulate about their art and their ideas. Similar or related obsessions, communicated through their personally distinctive points of view, gave their discussions momentum. Gabriela Mistral, joining this group in 1926, a contemporary of Parra, but there the similarity ends. Her beginnings were humble, her brilliance as a schoolteacher and poet demonstrated at an early age. When she arrived in Paris, she remained for several years an observer to Parra's activities rather than the highly respected friend she became only later on in the decade. One of Mistral's writing forms was a poetic letter she called *"recado,"* or "message," in which she singled out contemporary events and personalities for comment and praise. She dedicated two such *recados* to Teresa: one in 1929 to praise the just-published *Mama Blanca* and another in 1936 to both mourn Parra's death and observe, as in an obituary, the significance of her life. At the time when the two writers met, just as Parra's idea for *Mama Blanca* was germinating in her mind, Mistral saw in Teresa a dual personality, divided clearly by a line separating city on the one side and country on the other. These two qualities opposed one another like good and evil. The metaphorical comparison underlying Parra's transition from the influence of the unspoiled plantation to that of the impersonal city occurred simultaneously with her transition from childhood to adolescence. Mistral saw in Parra a child of the Venezuelan llanos, stripping her fellow South Americans of their "false Gallic principles" in a matter of minutes with her quick and unassuming wit. At the same time she saw the lady of high society floating elegantly through the streets of Paris, adorned with expensive clothing and jewelry. Although Mistral despised the city, and especially the foreign city, for its deracination, she considered the blending of city and country values a uniquely American characteristic; it was important to her at the time, she said in 1929, that Parra maintain such a blend and not abandon totally her Venezuelan roots in her writing. Mistral's own mind was made up, and so was the mind of Teresa's good friend Lydia Cabrera; both were deeply involved in studying the primitive cultures of Indians and Africans, respectively, as these affected the American hemisphere. For the intensely homesick Mistral, South American landscapes formed the very shape of her visionary poems. Having encouraged Parra to emphasize her Creole heritage, Mistral in 1928 also encouraged her to attend anthropological courses on American Indians. Teresa began to express a new scholarly fascination with her national identity in her letters. To Guzman-Esponda she wrote: "Perhaps since I was educated abroad in Spain, I am patriotic about all of Latin America. I think the same as those 16th century thinkers, dreaming of Latin America, evoking all the cities that have the same idiosyncracies and language."[58]

There there was Miguel de Unamuno, who, having first challenged

Parra to build up her inner strength, helped her to loosen some of *Ifigenia*'s knots via dialogue on the subject of spiritual hunger. As a person painfully at home in the distress-filled paths that wind around but seldom lead to religious faith, he commented insightfully on the sadness with which Maria Eugenia stated, "The only object of faith is hope." He would not be surprised, he said, to see her ending up "pious, rather than mystical, and much less ascetic": "Maria Eugenia's true tragedy is expressed here in her thirst for immortality—if not in the Judeo-Catholic sense, then in the other of which I have already spoken—the hellenic and platonic. It is for that reason that she writes, not out of boredom."[59]

When Parra shifted her ambitions from literary success towards a higher communication with the saints, the change as viewed on a larger scale affected solely her means to an end, not the end itself. Cabrera attests to the fact that her friend was a deist from beginning to end and her relationship to the church remained distrustful. Thirst for immortality inhabits many an apparent thirst for earthly success, which in turn is seen as a living, permanent influence on the world. But for Parra, the bubbles of literary success had gone flat and could no longer excite and satisfy; neither did she seek relief by riding any political bandwagon. Knowing that it takes more than the quixotic impulse to move the sludge of institutionalized prejudice, Parra decided to leave that job to people with more Spartan temperaments. Instead, like Mama Blanca, she opted for the "clarity of soul that is loved but not admired." It is difficult for "wretched philosophers" such as herself, and such as Cousin Juancho, to take a public stance toward a perceived truth, since as the issues became neutralized by endless debate, the stance toward truth becomes but the feigning of a stance toward an illusion. Parra held ideas and truths in her heart whose radical nature she revealed in both her novels, but the lessons of *Ifigenia* taught her that these convictions would turn their force against her unless she used only the finest-honed tools of her craft to communicate them. Because harmony and subtlety and charity were too much a part of her personality, her deal with the ancestral ghosts was struck as if between diplomats. Like Aunt Inés and Emilia Ibarra, Teresa wished to like everyone and to have everyone—dead and alive—like her back. With such a double-burdened conscience, her responsibilities felt heavy indeed.

In "Two Judgments in Defense of *Ifigenia*," Teresa stated sarcastically to Dr. Vetancourt-Aristeguieta that the "public's kindness and the genuine critics' praise"—unlike his own exaggerated fantasies, which brought her great satisfaction—had left her spirit burdened with "certain responsiblity for the future" and her conscience burdened with the "im-

112

mense discomfort of thinking I do not deserve it." She felt compelled to pinpoint the location of her responsibilities, although they promised to lie along a narrow path. The example of one of her holy women, Sor Juana de la Cruz of Mexico, did not offer much in the way of guidance or comfort. In the Mexican convent where Sor Juana had built up one of the largest libraries in the country, where she had conducted scientific experiments and received admiring visitors from all over the world, she had also, the church charged, neglected to affect the proper humility and submissiveness toward church doctrine. Sor Juana responded to their censure by retreating into a stunned silence that lasted until her death.

Parra, a twentieth-century woman more intelligent than ambitious, withdrew into herself with a sound not unlike the surreptitious closing of a clamshell. For the "horrible indiscretion of publishing in Paris under her own name" she felt she had suffered enough. Her new emphasis became mysticism (a word that Martinez states Parra used in a free sense, synonymous with religiosity), the deliberate censoring of her public voice, and the fascination with uncorrupted states of being. These disciplines promised to merge in the reverse prism of Parra's Venezuelan childhood. Going back to childhood—a Rousseauean disrobing that sheds acquired tastes and prejudices—was the prescription for other European artists as well, faced with the dead end of their own cynicism. Their search for lost innocence, for a symbolism freed from convention, expressed in the art of the Dadaists, had not failed to arouse Parra's notice, even if it did fail to arouse her emulation. She was determined to find her own way back to a state of enchantment through her new novel, while avoiding a Maria Eugenia–style escape into numb convention. The prepubescent world of trusting innocence she entered through *Mama Blanca* is only vaguely parallel to the regressive farce by which Maria Eugenia tried to unlearn her knowledge. Teresa's real-life move toward renunciation would come much later, in response to the ineluctable force of disease. For now, she forcibly applied new awarenesses and experiences learned from the distance of time and travel to her reassessment of a past once shunned, thereby achieving the advantage of a more fortuitous reentry to Venezuela.

The four years she had spent away from Venezuela meant much to her; she felt it was just this physical distance that had given her the enriched understanding of her homeland. She was not sure, however, if such travel benefitted her countrymen in general. The year 1927 marks new infusion of this feeling in her letters: European culture is spiritually and morally bankrupt, especially when forced on others—or "exported."

The typical "blasé, disenchanted" hero predominating in South American literature was the victim of an "artificial, venemous," exported culture, she wrote to Carias. All South Americans must solve this dilemma: "Is the travelling by which a foreign culture is absorbed and through which disenchantment sprouts, useful or damaging? The best way to solve this is to go not outside, but inside, with books and dreams by which to love Dulcinea faithfully, longing for something that we believe we will attain upon boarding the trans-Atlantic steamships."[60]

In May 1927, Parra traveled to Spain, where she spent an "enchanted month" reading history books and visiting the ancient cities and monasteries: "It was like a journey through the centuries, in search of the profound and not the superficial." All the while she was nurturing the idea for her new novel "in her soul."[61] Like the very world of innocence itself, her embryonic idea was too fragile to allow any rancor left over from *Ifigenia* to sterilize and destroy it. It was like the final destination of a trans-Atlantic voyage, far in the distance, which would prove to herself and to Venezuela that—yes—the answer to the South American dilemma in her case was "useful." She felt no resentment or bitterness toward Caracas, she had written to Carias the previous March, even though its residents were guilty of "exaggerated patriotism, envy, narrowmindedness, and misunderstanding of irony." On the contrary, since the only criticism that really hurt her had come from Aristeguieta, she held the city of Caracas in her warmest affection. Venezuela was, moreover, the "quarry from which everything in art is extracted. . . . Today I do not feel capable of writing anything but Creole subjects." The demons of diversion conspired to sway her from the determination required to undertake the grueling rigors of writing; Paris in the springtime, her family, and friends stood between her and isolation. Finally, toward September of 1927, Teresa went to the shore of Lake Geneva, rented a small house, and began to write.

"I believe this book, less difficult than *Ifigenia*, will also be better," she wrote to Carias on October 1. In fact, she indulged in none of the vices afflicting her first novel. The polished skill she demonstrated in *Mama Blanca*, compared to *Ifigenia*'s rought-cut brilliance, impressed Mistral as the greatest leap in quality she had ever seen in any other prose writer of the Spanish language. *Mama Blanca* derived its anti-rhetorical language from the Spanish classical authors Parra had read in those four years after *Ifigenia*; the result, as Mistral poetized it, was like the fine white clay used for porcelain, which exudes from the mineral earth.[62]

Parra's thoughts poured onto the page in three short months; they bespoke neither adolescent torment, adult temptation, nor moral ambiguity. Her values and preoccupations, essentially unchanged since *Ifigenia,* emerged this time in words so carefully chosen that no Venezuelan could find the slightest intention of insult therein. If *Ifigenia*'s well-groomed characters were unsure of, oppressed, and broken by their ideals, *Mama Blanca*'s disorderly characters were self-assured, persistent, and dauntless in the pursuit of them. Parra's themes echoed from first novel to second—the female point of view, the older woman guiding the younger, the irony of life, the hypocrisy of social mores, the clash of individual codes of honor, the pantheism. In *Mama Blanca,* however, Parra's anti-intellectualism had intensified and her belief that value was to be found in obscure places predominated. Whereas *Ifigenia* was born of a restless longing to leave, to spread outward, *Mama Blanca* was born of a wistful longing to return, to voyage inside the memory itself.

Parra disappointed her French fans with *Mama Blanca.* Miomandre's translation was published in two parts in 1928 in *RDLL,* before the second Spanish edition came out in 1929. Reactions of critics on each side of the Atlantic reversed the trend established by *Ifigenia;* what the French found tame, the South Americans found lovable. In short, *Las Memorias de Mama Blanca* fulfilled exactly the role Parra had assigned to it. The opinions of people she valued voiced the kind of praise she valued. Mistral, in a state of figurative "starvation," felt nourished by it; Venezuelans felt the pleasurable sting of nostalgia, so precisely had Parra remembered their collective Creole past. Romain Rolland, one of her idols, wrote her a complimentary letter in 1929, to which she responded with this flattering acknowledgment: "I maintain . . . a sentiment for you that has unfolded and grown with time. Like the Gospels and the Imitation of Christ, you have helped me to face myself in an interior life; you have shown me, as one would show a child whom one takes care not to intimidate, the marvelous path of simplicity expressed in profound words. I have learned to love the humble and the unhappy and am not afraid to admit it. My *Mama Blanca* is nothing but a long letter, impregnated with my past, that I sent from Vevey to you in Volleneuve. . . ."[63] Zaldumbide also reported having received a note of gratitude from Teresa for having helped to shape that state of mind necessary for producing work like *Mama Blanca.*[64]

The new novel stimulated the imaginations of South Americans who hoped to incorporate its philosophy in redrawing their national self-images. Mistral, who spent many years assisting the philosopher/poet/educator Jose Vasconcelos in the reform of the Mexican educational system, saw in *Mama Blanca* a paradigm for children's books of the future. It was exactly that lightness of touch and refinement of sensibility that should replace the dreadfully somber and didactic tone of the classical literature Teresa herself was subjected to as a child. Parra, in grafting that same classical heritage onto the folk element, had succeeded in crystallizing the South American experience into a form that children, especially, could understand, accept, and be proud to emulate.[65]

Thus Parra's little masterpiece, as it came to be called in Venezuela, arrived on the South American shore to silence the squawking of offenses and numbling of defenses accumulated over the years. As harmony settled over all battlefronts, the terrible burden of responsibility and the cross of the persecuted metamorphosed to the more welcome weight of Parra's new maturity.

Notes

1. *Inside The Whale* (London: Penguin, 1957), p. 27.
2. Letter to Carias, January 11, 1935, *Obras Completas,* (Caracas: Editorial Arte, 1965), p. 882.
3. Teresa de la Parra, "Unas Palabras Mas Sobre *Ifigenia,*" March 1927, in *Obras Completas* (Caracas: Editorial Arte, 1965), p. 520.
4. Dorf Wyllarde, in Jose Pocaterra, "Diaro de una senorita que se fastidia," *La Lectura Semanal,* Caracas, June 4, 1922, p. 1.
5. Irma de Sola-Ricardo, *Teresa de la Parra: Semblenza de una escritora* (Caracas: Impresion Editorial Arte, 1982), p. 13.
6. "Mujeres de Avila," *El Nuevo Diario,* Caracas, February 23, 1923.
7. Miguel Aristeigueta, "Teresa de la Parra," *El Universal,* Caracas, August 24, 1923, n.p.
8. Letter to Carias, in *Obras Completas,* p. 859.
9. *Ifigenia,* in *Obras Completas,* p. 35.
10. Personal interview with Lydia Cabrera, August 25, 1978.
11. Gabriela Mistral, "Dos Recados Sobre Teresa de la Parra," *Repertorio Americano,* San Jose, Costa Rica, September 26, 1936.
12. Teresa de la Parra, letter to Carias, March 2, 1924, in *Teresa de la Parra, Cartas a Rafael Carias* (Alcala de Henares, Spain: Talleres Penitenciarios, 1957), p. 21.
13. "La Vie en L'Amerique Latine," *Revue de L'Amerique Latine,* Paris, February 1925, pp. 175–76.
14. Letter to Carias, July 1924, in *Obras Completas* p. 858.
15. Interview with Seida de la Toree, December 6, 1979.
16. See chapter 2, note 29.
17. Letter to Carias, in *Obras Completas,* July 1924, p. 857.
18. Ibid., p. 859.
19. "Journal d'une Demoiselle qui s'ennuie," fragment, translated by Francis de Miomandre, *Revue de L'Amerique Latine,* June 1, 1924, Vol. 7, No. 30, p. 526.

20. Letter to Don Lisandro Alvarado, 1926, in *Obras Completas,* pp. 893–94.
21. Max Daireux, "Le roman de Teresa de la Parra: *Ifigenia,*" *RDLL,* August 1, 1925, Vol. 10, No. 44, p. 158. k (translated into Spanish for *El Universal,* September 24, 1925).
22. *Three Guineas,* as quoted in *Women of Letters: A Life of Virginia Woolf,* by Phyllis Rose (New York: Oxford University Press, 1978).
23. "Opiniones, *Ifigenia* y Don Lisandro Alvarado," in *Epistolario Intimo,* Teresa de la Parra (Caracas: Linea Aeropostal Venezolana, Ediciones Gratuitas, 19539, p. 197.
24. "*Ifigenia,* Los Criticos, y Los Criticones," in *Obras Completas,* p. 468.
25. "*Ifigenia* Cruelle," *RDLL,* Paris, December 12, 1925, p. 107.
26. "Ana Teresa Parra: A Writer and a Woman Pioneer," *Paris Times,* September 30, 1924.
27. Letter to Carias, December 3, 1927, in *Teresa de la Parra, Cartas a Rafael Carias,* p. 81.
28. Letter to Carias, March 5, 1927, in *Obras Completas,* p. 855.
29. "Christine, Enfant Naturelle," translated by Marius Andre, *RDLL,* October 1, 1925, Vol. 10, No. 46, pp. 322–426.
30. Marius Andre, *RDLL,* p. 192.
31. Daireux, "Le roman de Teresa de la Parra: *Ifigenia,*" p. 157.
32. "A don Miguel de Unamuno" (dated July 25, 1925), *Repertorio Americano,* San Jose, Costa, February 5, 1927.
33. Letter to Carias, August 2, 1927, in *Teresa de la Parra, Cartas a Rafael Carias,* p. 63.
34. Letter to Don Lisandro Alvarado, in *Obras Completas,* 1926, pp. 893–94.
35. Letter to Carias, June 21, 1926, in *Obras Completas,* p. 849.
36. Letter to Carias, Aug. 21, 1925, in *Teresa de la Parra, Cartas a Rafael Carias,* p. 26.
37. "Unas Palabras Mas Sobre *Ifigenia* y; Las Aristeguieta," in *Obras Completas,* p. 521.
38. "A don Miguel de Unamuno. . . ."
39. J. M. Ruano, S. J., "La Novela *Ifigenia,*" *La Religion,* Caracas, March 15, 1928.
40. "Teresa de la Parra Ensena a Muchos Miles de Hombres Come Se Debe Ser Amplio y Heroico," *Billiken,* Caracas, August 1928.
41. Letter to Guzman-Esponda, June 1926, in *Obras Completas,* p. 890.
42. "La novelista Teresa de la Parra: Escritoras Venezolanas," *El Universal,* Caracas, December 8, 1926.
43. "*Ifigenia,* y un Valiente Defensor. . . ," in *Obras Completas,* p. 504.
44. "*Ifigenia,* La Critica, Los Critocos, y los Criticones," in *Obras Completas,* p. 499.
45. "*Ifigenia* y un Valiente Defensor. . . ," in *Obras Completas,* p. 506.
46. "Unas Palabras Mas. . . ," in *Obras Completas,* p. 518.
47. Ibid., p. 521.
48. Ibid.
49. Edmund Chispa. See note 6.
50. "Unas Palabras Mas. . . ," in *Obras Completas,* p. 518.
51. Letter to Carias, in *Obras Completas,* p. 860.
52. "A don Miguel Unamuno. . . ."
53. Carlos Villena, *Estudio Critico de la novela Ifigenia* (Bogota: Imp. de la Sociedad Editorial, S.A.), n.d.

54. Letter to Carias, March 5, 1927, in *Obras Completas,* p. 851.
55. Ibid., p. 852.
56. Letter to Carias, November 24, 1926, in *Teresa de la Parra, Cartas a Rafael Carias,* p. 78.
57. Letter to Don Lisandro Alvarado, 1926, in *Obras Completas,* p. 897–98.
58. Letter to Guzman-Esponda, p. 884.
59. "A don Miguel Unamuno. . . ." in *Obras Completas.*
60. Letter to Carias, May 7, 1927, p. 856.
61. Letter to Carias, Mar. 5, 1927, p. 853.
62. Gabriela Mistral, *El Mercurio,* "Teresa de la Parra," Santiago de Chile, June 23, 1929, p. 4.
63. Armando Rojas, "Romain Rolland y Teresa de la Parra," *El Nacional,* Caracas, August 4, 1963.
64. Francisco Guarderas, *Las Paginas de Gonzalo Zaldumbide* Quito: Editorial Casa de la Cultura Ecuatoriana: 1962.
65. Mistral, "Teresa de la Parra," p. 4.

CHAPTER FOUR

Parra at Forty: The Thinking Woman's Romantic

Departure from the Novel, the Latin Press, and Exploring the Past

In the space of those three months and the waning days of autumn 1927, Parra divested herself of her responsibility to literature. *Mama Blanca,* a slender ivory bone thrown to wolves, signaled the end of its author's four-year battle with the written word. A creative lull blanketed her next two years with peace. But her desire to improve upon her medium of expression had, if anything, increased rather than abated. Presenting to the outside world the substance of a mere shadow, she breezed through Cuba and Italy—two significant voyages—and otherwise she cast about alone in her personal library. Meanwhile, her spirit, ever-curious and so recently poised at her Venezuelan childhood as if on a threshold, could not resist exploring further the ages before her actual birth into which it had thereby gained a footing. Parra had discovered the liberating potential of history. Leaving behind an alternate self more polished than ever to contend with the "vulgar" affairs of every day, she went wandering like a Rilkean "seeker of the inner future in this past in which so much that is eternal is enclosed."[1] Her allegiance to the obscure, to things unofficial, outlawed, and unspoken, was now hard and fast. Thus when she launched herself on her backward journey, it was not to experience the history that was "a banquet for men only," but rather to discover a greater history, embodying greater truths, calling for release from the written lines between which they had been imprisoned for too long.

In Vevey, Switzerland, where she walled herself in from friends in order to let her childhood memories run free, she had hoped to achieve complete transparency of the word. Other writers, her contemporaries and self-styled men of the modern age, were following this same literary

119

trend. At their best, they were moral architects; their binding characteristic was the desire to wrench a transcendent consciousness out of the multidisciplinary expression of the conflicts—religious, political, and artistic—that plagued their epoch. Romain Rolland, trained in history and musicology, was an avid socialist and an Indiophile. He devoted himself to utopian causes and the futuristic characters of his imagination. Miguel Unamuno, another socialist, who represented to Parra the true intellectual, echoed the Taoist principle in his phrase "let feeling think and thought feel." Gabriel Miro (the father of Teresa's good friend Clemencia), less vocal about politics than about his craft, insisted on "telling by insinuating." (Compare Parra's 1926 statement: "*Ifigenia* insinuates much more than it says, and these paths of insinuation are not seen but felt and sensed—in the abstract—like the diverse states of mind crossing the verses of a poet.")[2] None of these men—writers/philosophers/social idealists—to whom Parra felt so akin found their aspirations fulfilled through an exclusive commitment to literature.

Parra, perfectionist that she was, felt obstructed in her desire to make her prose "harmonious with life." Considering her literary vocation "so intermittent and fragile,"[3] she fancied the gift of some magic wand by which a poet, a James Joyce, or the new techniques of the cinema could transmute the opacity of the word. That *Mama Blanca*'s language would win it the status of a standard text in two North American universities for demonstrating the ideal use of Castilian[4] would doubtless have pleased, but hardly have satisfied, her. In her own judgment, her efforts merely transformed the animate word to the inanimate, and her novel would exist as a redundancy to the already superfluous—the "carnival of pringing"[5] that she so disdained.

This desire to transcend the word was the symptom of a grand-scale motivation. Call it the desire for immortality or for total integration of purpose; call it simply the ever-onward motion of the explorer. It encompassed a superhuman effort to transcend human limitation itself and contributed essentially toward fulfilling the tragic sense of life. The poet Rainer Maria Rilke, another of Parra's literary beacons, envisioned in his brilliant *Duino Elegies* a creature in whom this transcendence was actualized—"an Angel in whom that transformation of the visible into the invisible already appears complete, one who vouches for the recognition of a higher degree of reality in the invisible."[6] J.B. Leishman described it as an "ideal of a complete and undivided consciousness, where will and capability, thought and action, vision and realization are one."[7] Reality did not have much of a chance when compared to that winged ideal. When serene old Mama Blanca visited Parra by the mountainside

120

lake, she unfurled her Venezuelan tapestry, subtle-toned but infinitely textured, to a fireside hallucinator, fitful and fragile. Possessed in her vassalage to the written page and all the while pointing one foot toward the open door, Teresa suffered bouts of *Weltschmerz* in her at once dreaded and desired separation from Paris and friends: "Alone, surrounded by a very pretty but sad countryside, I write all morning; I lunch, then walk for an hour, return to writing, return to walking, and at night, next to the lit fireplace, alone, listening to the fire crackle, I sometimes listen to the radio that gives news of the latest aviators to drown while crossing the Atlantic. . . ."[8]

The present retreated with the flick of a pen. Now the "inner future" could begin unfolding. Only three months out of her Swiss seclusion, Teresa announced to Carias that she was traveling back to the American hemisphere. At first, in January, she had reported her indecision whether to go or not.[9] But this was an opportunity for carefree activity; invited by the Cuban government, she would attend the seventh Latin Congress in Havana as a foreign correspondent for Caracas's newspaper *El Universal*. At the end of February 1928, Parra and fifty-eight other French- and Spanish-speaking writers boarded the ship bound for the Caribbean island. They had been organized by the French writer Maurice d'Waleffe, and among them were Miguel Angel Asturias, Fernand Gregh, Charles Lesca, Francois Porche, Jerome Tharand, and Irene Vasconcellos.

When the group arrived in Havana two weeks later, the people of Cuba submerged them in an unexpectedly vivacious shower of hospitality. Teresa found herself caught unawares by the unaccustomed rapport she felt with the rhythm of her surroundings. Two years, later she would describe Cuba as having:

> . . . a strong criollo character to its traditions and folklore that miraculously defends it from spiritual invasion. Exaggerated Americanism has not yet penetrated the spirit of its social classes. The people of Havana have an old and genuine criollo character in spite of the English language, tourism, dollars. . . .
>
> A large number of Cuban women are working and studying without having lost their femininity or their respect for certain principles and traditions."[10]

The year 1928 was a big one for the social advancement of Latin American women, who had become restless in their awareness of greater progress in the North American and European countries. Primarily, hopes centered around the activities of the Organization of American States (OAS). That year, during its annual congress scheduled to take place in Cuba, that organization would give birth to its progressive offshoot, the Interamerican Commission of Women. Also, smaller groups with more specific goals pertaining to their individual countries were contributing to the flurry of organizing activity. The ambient tone was not one of loud and angry demand—the women of the northern countries had covered that thankless ground already—but rather it was an atmosphere where both Parra's nostalgic and iconoclastic tendencies were appreciated and understood. She found herself swamped not by "cruel publicity," but by adoring publicity. The mystique of Teresa de la Parra, writer of *Ifigenia,* the first "woman's" novel in the Spanish language, dominated the congress. Her picture was snapped with the president of Cuba, Gerardo Machado, who was assisting in the ten-day panoply of events. She was, according to a Nicaraguan observer's dramatization, "a sensation, the object of a thousand kindnesses, recipient of a thousand gifts [among them a pair of parrots] . . . and, like in a Greek story, Jupiter fell in love with the Muse. The Jupiter of this story was Gerardo Machado. I must warn you, that everyone was enamored of Teresa. . . ."[11] Once again, rumor and speculation hounded her private life, but this time, perhaps out of the clear conscience of her innocence, Parra did not seem to mind. Lydia Cabrera insisted on the merely friendly nature of the relationship between Parra and Machado, as she, providing her friend with shelter in her villa during the visit, was in a position to observe it.

The focus of Parra's attention was elsewhere. Standing at the Cuban gates to Latin America, she was filled with the first of many impressions that she would incubate for the next two years, before unleashing them in her meticulously "written" oral message to the Colombian people. If the post-*Ifigenia* years taught her disillusionment and cynicism, the post–*Mama Blanca* years were to revive in her the romantic heart of Blanca Nieves, forever locked in battle with the positivistic heart of Violeta. Venezuela, and South Amereica itself, had come to symbolize the idealistic striving of that romantic heart, and Teresa was now ready to take her place unashamedly alongside the Don Quixotes, Primo Juanchos, and Panchos to claim its heritage her own.* Although Teresa lived her chosen life outside the mainstream of female endeavor with a certain bittersweet resignation, the hope to render greater clarity and significance to her precarious outsiderhood dangled its new guiding question over the

*She began to make requests of Carias for books on South American literature and history.

path ahead: were there not others, even a whole cycle of Teresas, who had lived barely tolerated and overly envied in the margins of society?

To find accommodation for her uncompromising soul, to realize an opportunity for blameless action—these became actual possibilities as Parra stood viewing the Cuban culture. Here the modern world embellished the old rather than threatened to destroy it. Now, in her maturity, she could respond with greater conviction to the ethical nature of her idealism and the feminist nature of her ethics. She accepted an invitation to speak to the twenty women involved in the formation of the Lyceum, a feminist group. Seeking advice about how to organize a cultural institute for women that would work to provide a more "transcendent role and greater responsibilities" for them, this group placed the burden of its questions to the author of *Ifigenia*. Maria Eugenia's cry had been unique in inspiring these women to vocalize their own dissatisfactions; Parra's tireless sifting of values as well as her professional status as a writer gave them hope. The founding spirit of the Lyceum was Cuban feminist Elena Maderos-Gonzalez: "We did our job not for publicity's sake, but for communication with the decisive factions of society. We had no rules, our protests and ideals were unrestricted. We did everything almost without knowing the repercussions. Parra's intellectual efforts were a great stimulus to us—we remember her and owe her due respect."[12] When Parra spoke to them, sometime after March 22 and the closing of the Latin Congress, she stressed that economic independence for women was integral to social change and that proper training, or new modes of education, were the stepping stones to that vantage point.[13] This small concession to the women's movement represented Parra's first public admission, since the unwittingly political implications of *Ifigenia,* that she recognized the need for outward change in order to eliminate the extreme legal and traditional disadvantages under which she, even and especially as a member of the privileged class, would have suffered had she remained in Venezuela. As Maderos-Gonzales stated, the feminist groups were embryonic and the idealism strong, but also derision by men was guaranteed and the notion of the working woman, only recently accepted in Cuba at the time, was still considered an impiety in nearby Venezuela.

Back in 1926, Parra had been invited by the Venezuelan government to attend a "Congress of Women." Her letter reporting the invitation to Carias does not reflect any unwillingness to attend; rather, she claimed the invitation arrived "too late" for her to be on board a vessel.[14] Given her state of conflict over *Ifigenia*'s various successes and failures in that year, it is not likely that she would have attended even had she been given ample time. The fact, however, that she even considered taking that opportunity reminds us of her insistence on extracting her literary subjects from the Creole quarry; here, too, any expression of her feminism would have to occur not within a French or an international, but within an exclusively Latin American context. Her 1928 response to her countrywomen's call for help was made possible by two concurring factors: her new sense of literary accomplishment achieved with "the most Creole of Creole novels" and her new contact with women, like herself, who wished neither to lose the security of their sexual identity nor acquire the taint of political hypocrisy because of their social activism.

Parra received much admiration and sympathy from her new audience. She was a woman who affected other women strongly. Approaching forty years of age, she had not lost the green-eyed charm and spirited curiosity that characterized her youth. In an interview given on April 1, she claimed that she much preferred honors that flattered her physical rather than her intellectual and moral attributes, because the responsibility empowered to her by the latter filled her with such anxiety. They meant "Let's get to work!"[15] Parra obviously took great pleasure in complying with what Anatole France called "a woman's first duty": to be beautiful. In that mutually satisfying, if time-consuming, procedure, she was able to dispense with her immediate responsibility to male expectation. But the women of the Lyceum limited their request for aid to specifics and therefore taxed her sense of responsibility to them only minimally, so that she must have taken at least some pride in the respect they showed for her intellectual gifts, otherwise considered so troublesome in her family. Public interest centering on her philosophy rather than on her love life was welcome indeed, as long as she felt there was a chance of being appreciated and understood.

In return, Parra received the encouragement of a new Creole audience to whom the definition of a modern feminine ideal was important. To them and to Parra at this time, the word *feminine* did not seem to need definition. They conceived of their sexual identitites in the classic sense determined by their capacity for motherhood, whether they fulfilled this capacity or not. To be nurturing of the human race and the earth in any way and to be gentle and loving may be an attitude adoptable by both man and woman, but these women publicly acknowledged it as their God-given mandate. However closely Parra's private dissatisfactions with patriarchal society might have resembled the ravings of Maria Eugenia, her public stance always adhered to a feminist viewpoint of seeming moderation. The ideal itself provided much more latitude for the progressive imagination. In an almost mind-boggling array of visions that strove to transcend the semantic net of ''masculine'' and ''feminine'' without ignoring the obvious delineations implied by biology, poets and politicians alike were trying to ring in the definitive woman of the future, whose previously untapped wisdom might even absolve the modern industrial age, characterized by the masculine excesses of scientific warfare, of its sins.

Lucila Perez-Diaz felt that Parra's two novels already contained the ingredients for the new feminine being. In her 1940 acceptance speech to the Venezuelan Academy of History as its first female member, she sought first to reassure her male colleagues that modern women had no intention of abandoning their ''sacred'' role in society. That role would simply be broadened now by each women's individual choice, but her approach to its execution would temper the competition with men thus entered. The perfect blend of character traits, by which this new approach should be spirited, resided inside Mama Blanca and Maria Eugenia—the old woman and the young. It consisted of the ''culture of the soul, more valuable than the intellect'' and the trained intelligence, eager to comprehend the material world. The modern woman's intellect would bring her out of obscurity and isolation, but her age-old instinctual wisdom and connection to natural processes would preserve her from selfishness and vanity. She would be, finally, a woman whose use of ''masculine'' skills to rebuild the family and ''feminine'' ones to bring love and understanding to larger structures affecting both sexes would ''save'' Venezuela from complete spiritual breakdown.[16]

Even the poet Rilke expounded as early as 1903 on the fact that the ''sexes are more related than we think, and the great renewal of the world will perhaps consist in this, that man and maid, freed of all false feelings and reluctances, will seek each other. . . .'' But then Rilke, who spent much time in the company of original and independent women such as Lou Andreas Salome, goes on to suggest that there was in fact some specially different category of nonmasculinity into which women could evolve:

> The girl and the woman, in their new, their own unfolding, will but in passing be imitators of masculine ways, good and bad, and repeaters of masculine professions. After the uncertainty of such transitions it will become apparent that women were only going through the profusion and the vicissitude of those (often ridiculous)

disguises in order to cleanse their own most characteristic nature of the distorting influences of the other sex. . . .

. . . This humanity of women, born its full time in suffering and humiliation, will come to light when she will have stripped off the conventions of mere femininity in the mutations of her outward status, and someday there will be girls and women whose name will no longer signify merely an opposite of the masculine, but something it itself, something that makes one think, not of any complement and limit, but only of life and existence: the feminine human being . . . and the love experience, which is now full of error, will alter it from the ground up. [17]

Parra did not enter this sticky debate directly. In the last two projects of her career, however, she called instead for retribution for woman in history. Rather than insisting on a "new woman," she insisted on the superiority of the already-existing, yet misinterpreted and maligned, influence of women whose personalities had found a wide variety of expression in the fringes of society. Delving into the dark memory of her ancestral genes, she resurfaced as the sole witness and minstrel to their heroism.

Teresa's own blend of masculine and feminine remains hidden at the core of her ever-shifting image. On the related subject of her sexuality, we find, not unexpectedly, no commentators save Lydia Cabrera, and from her we glean no insight save by implication. "Teresa was not without personal energies," she once stated, referring to her friend's supposed preference for platonic relationships, "but she did not care to express them. She did not believe in Freud's orgasmic theory. She was quite candid about this." [18] If this was indeed the case when Lydia knew Teresa, one cannot help wondering about the intense and repressed eroticism of *Ifigenia* and its author's professed belief in basing all opinion on personal experience: it is unlikely, but not impossible that Teresa did not experience some kind of physical love before relegating it to the inessential. The overall pattern, however, into which the pieces of indirect evidence finally settle, encourages belief in Lydia's terse analysis: Teresa was ruled first by passions of the mind. Once having despaired of finding the ideal soulmate and having then pronounced spinsterhood preferable to compromise, she placed her hope in the consummation of strictly ethereal unions, unspoilable by the failures and tyrannies of the flesh. Her emotions, too, fought their battles within the highly developed, private sphere of her self-analysis. Because she was easily offended and painfully judgmental at heart, that obsessive standard of perfection, in blocking the easy recourse of a sharp tongue, only strengthened her overall self-control. "I wanted passionately that my novel have a *disinterested* revolutionary protest," she once said, and therewith she betrayed in a single neat sentence the wide range of feeling she habitually relegated to the distancing place of her mind. Teresa's wasting demon was a kind of "tropical" indolence; she held it only tenuously in balance with the moral demands of what she considered were the higher aspirations of her soul. Platonic duality defined this curse of her physical quiescence and mental restlessness. The languid revenge of her body was sometimes so insistent that Lydia and she made it the object of a personal joke: Teresa once presented her friend with the perfect animal equivalent of herself—a sloth. It perplexed even Parra's own sister, Maria, that someone so comically absentminded and lazy could possess at the same time such universally renowned vitality of mind and grace in movement.[19]

As she was a personality riddled with contradiction, it is not surprising that Parra was obsessed with motions of transcendence, the ideal, or wholeness of experience. She was a woman born under the weighty dronings of fiercely asserted do's and don'ts, and it is equally unsurprising that she found herself compulsively testing both the open door of escape and the impregnability of her sanctuaries. Having achieved her fame prematurely, she considered it unearned, and she fled the spotlight in favor of obscurity. Wealthy and aristocratic, she rejected the prejudices and pretensions of the upper class, spending instead her favorite hours walking among the "grey multitudes"[20] and lending her sometimes extravagant aid to the unadorned and abandoned wherever she could. Admired in social circles as a great beauty and witty conversationalist, she preferred the conversation and company of people—either distant or long-since departed—with whom she communed through their books or their correspondence. She resisted all expectation with almost adolescent stubbornness: the familial pressure to be meek and married; the activists' pressure to be politically militant about her feminism; and the pressure from her art to commit her naked soul to print, at the cost of grueling labor and loss of privacy. It did not seem that Parra could submit to the authority of any one discipline, as much as she proved her capability to excel in whatever she did. The question of her vocation kept cropping up: "About my literary vocation," she would say in Colombia, "all I can say to you is that as much as I have hunted for it, to give it my studious concentration, it has happened the same as always—I cannot find it."[21] There appeared to be no channel that was consistently worthy of her considerable energies and talent, and the unequivocal success of *Mama Blanca* and *Ifigenia* notwithstanding, she seemed doomed to be a perennial visitor to her epoch, to literature, and to her own life. The universal prescription for female happiness so admirably achieved by her mother had never worked for Teresa; whereas she might possess the selflessness of heart required to serve her notions of justice and some true God, she could not envision a husband or biological children deserving of greater selflessness than she showed her close friends and readers. Selflessness, like the self, was to become another hard-won goal along the path to transcendence.

But Parra's soulful remarks about her vocation—or lack thereof—did not really express despair at being so blown about by the forces of biology, religiosity, art, and the intellect. In her first lecture, she implied a certain scorn for the very function of "having a vocation," and she emphasized her feeling of perverse pleasure in being able to periodically wave good-bye to her novelistic muse. Inherent in the following, typically ironic message is nothing less than an exact description of the creative process as expressed by many a male artist whose novelistic, poetic, or painterly vocation occasioned neither public challenge nor private doubt:

> [If they say] . . . I have lost my vocation, then I feel free of a great responsibility, having thereby lost the books as well. What is the nature of work, anyhow, that is accomplished with neither the protection from ourselves afforded by a vocation, nor the validation? That my books are no longer mine is true to a certain extent. Outside of the name that has remained as a distraction on the printed covers, I now recognize nothing of myself in my novels. The first was written by a contemporary girl whose whereabouts nobody even knows. The second was composed by a grandmother now dead, whose hospitable and caring life was just like so many others still perserved under the rooves in our good American cities. To me, these portraits or novels have no other authors save those two now absent. Located in the opposite extreme to life, they stayed with me for a while and told me, in the one, their anxieties about living, and in the other, their melancholy about having lived. Once having concluded their confessions they departed, discreetly, upon the books' publication.[22]

If there is a slight underachieving element in Parra's sparse literary product, if her irony is a little too agile, there is an overachieving, deadly serious one in her striving for personal wholeness—not to be all things to all people, but to be loyal to the warring factions of self, family, and God in one lifetime.

On April 1, Parra submitted to an interview in Lydia's villa. A "tranquil beauty," she entered the room with an air of aristocratic poise, or to translate literally the Spanish expression her interviewer used to describe her, "harmonious loathing" *(hastio harmonioso)*. "Always I am as if in another world, I almost never succeed at being present. My mind wanders," she instantly confessed. To the question about types of flattery, she denied without having been accused that she was either arrogant or haughty; the silence by which she rejected praise to her intellect was always misinterpreted. "I only fear they will find me bland. . . . Believe me, I am not arrogant—lazy, nothing more."[23] She was, of course, both arrogant as well as lazy, humble as well as ambitious. Her high standard of personal morality that set clearsightedness, humility, and modesty above all other virtues forbade the blinding "literary vanity" brought on by praise, and her overwhelming idealism made use of a sporadic laziness to anesthetize the dread of failure and the wound of censure. Her many statements on this subject—"I prefer censure to praise," for example, and "Try to be beautiful and keep your mouth shut [a French saying] is my actual rule of conduct"—merely proved that she was, above all, an ordinary human being trying her best to deal with an extraordinary gift. She was ordinary with a vengeance.

At heart, Parra wanted neither praise nor censure, but only acceptance as herself, and the fame that she felt inhibited her freedom of speech partially because she was so brilliantly matter-of-fact in expressing the onus of limitations on her being and so imperially graceful in bearing these limitations. The desire and capacity to have influence on her generation conflicted with a fear of being engulfed by her own vanity, as well as a suspicion of all "political evangelists' " motivation. Since she was passionately nonviolent, there was never any question of advocating the bloody overthrow of governments, and being personally dependent on her own familial ties, she could not in good conscience call for the abolition of marriage. A significant proportion of her friends were socialists, indicating a probable leaning to that ideology, but her family was archconservative. The role all ideology played in human affairs troubled her and lay at the foundation of her skepticism toward politicians. Even the "proponents of pacifism and socialism" were not exempt from hypocrisy and greed. Many of this sort "instead of loving piety and justice with their passion, loved the fire of their own eloquence more. . . ." In

1930 Parra told her Colombian audience that she considered politics as dirty as coal mining and that she was grateful that others were willing to do the job. "I am a born evangelee," she said to the interviewer, but refrained from naming her political priests.

If she felt it was part of her duty to stand up for the feminine principle, for which women both aggressive and passive, loving or indifferent, beautiful or ugly, are penalized, then she must have agonized over the means of this self-defense. Her Christian conscience balked at the apparent hypocrisy of fighting like with like. If being a warrior for peace, a hater of people who hate, an aggressor against aggression, was immoral, how should a woman exert her influence positively? The answer to Parra's calling lay first in the plotting of a morally acceptable course by which to steer attitudes of the mainstream, whose attention she already commanded, toward an enlightened rather than hypocritical acceptance of humanity's camouflaged outcasts. Perhaps, too, her hesitance arose out of a new sense of loyalty: should darkness and silence not be considered attributes purposefully imposed from above and therefore left untampered with by light and the word for fear of destroying the valuable secret they guarded? In *Mama Blanca* Parra showed a full-fledged mistrust of intellectuality as the path toward "clarity of soul." Deep down, Parra the mystic and stoic believed that only in the darkened corners of hardship and solitude could the eternal in her learn to spite and transcend its earthly limitations. But her only means to experiencing those corners rested in the acts of reading, thinking, and writing. Up until now, every time she succeeded in transforming her unspoken conclusions to spoken ones and every time she rendered dark corners light with the clarity of her prose, she considered it simultaneously an act of courage and an act of betrayal. When she finally spoke out a coherent defense of *Ifigenia* in her first lecture, there was no longer any doubt in her mind to which kind of act writing that novel had been. *Ifigenia* had brought to light a lamentable condition that society was attempting to cure by concealment. Parra said that an epidemic did not go away by hiding its victims, but through fresh air, light, and modern methods of cleanliness that neutralize the causes—which are sometimes even modern ones—of the sickness.[24]

Back in Cuba in 1928, the interviewer, assuring Parra he wished only to draw out a just and fair portrait of her, excessive neither in praise nor in criticism, ended up confirming her worst prejudices about interviews: he attempted to elicit her political opinion on the unpopular policies of Venezuela's dictator, President Gomez. Teresa, who had relatives working in the high echelons of this government and who was also receiving a desirable pension, responded with blatant diplomacy. She defended Gomez against the charges of excessive severity—"He is a friend of mine. He is severe because the country is in a permanent state of revolution"—and she praised his fraternal approach to other Latin American countries, stressing her own wish for greater cooperation among them all on the continent. If she did have any doubts about her country's president, this certainly was not the time to express them. Teresa confirmed in this interview that she planned to visit Caracas directly after finishing in Havana. Ending her five-year exile had now become her "sole preoccupation," she claimed, although it was as late as March 22 that she first expressed this desire, even to Carias.

Evidently the plan was a secret. The members of the Latin Congress expected her to return with them to France. Teresa owed her invitation to the congress at least partially to Maurice d'Waleffe, who was thought by some to be "enamored" of her besides, and she could understandably expect wounded feelings were she to simply announce that she preferred to separate herself from his party. This was a predicament from which only the fearless Lydia and Teresa's powerful new friend, the president of Cuba, could hope to rescue her. As she stood on the deck of the ship *Espagne* with the other passengers, awaiting departure to France, murmurs of impatience began to mount. For some mysterious reason, the ship was being detained. Suddenly, Lydia and a friend, Pepin Rivero, arrived on the dock, and "a sensational notice circulated that Teresa remain in Havana. The people present smiled with a complicitous air. . . . It concerned a brand-new invitation to prolong her visit to Cuba by those who by no means ever get turned down."[25] Thus Teresa disembarked at the bidding of none other than the president himself, and d'Waleffe was helpless to protest. Teresa, whom Lydia claimed was exhausted from her activites and badly in need of rest, remained in Havana only a few days, amidst an uproar of gossip about her romance with Machado. After such an uncharacteristically open display of her capriciousness, the "exhausted" Teresa then boarded a steamer for Caracas.

Very little news emerged from her subsequent travels across the Caribbean. One supposes that given the past, her Caracas homecoming was emotionally strenuous; it was also socially active, as an April 11 article in *El Universal* attests. The Venezuelan press greeted her cordially and questioned her amicably about her writing career; also, she finally had the opportunity to meet her godchild for the first time—the son of Rafael Carias and his wife, Guillermina. Teresa did not stay long, however. She returned promptly to Havana, to rest at Lydia's villa until the end of April. Then, instead of traveling directly back to France, she spent a week in New York City's Plaza Hotel with Lydia's sister, Seida de la Torre. From there the two friends completed the last leg of the journey across the Atlantic together. Teresa's first letter to Carias after her return dates from July and reports "nothing new to tell."

The summer of 1928 passed in the carefully chosen company of an old friend, Infanta Paz, and Teresa's sister Isabelita. The former, dowager aunt of the exiled king of Spain, was the one who had appreciated *Ifigenia* so heartily, who doted on Teresa to the point of bringing her breakfast in bed, and whose sister wrote a book in 1947—a feminist manifesto titled *For Woman*. She was also the same Infanta Paz to whom Teresa had addressed her famous "La Madre Espana" speech back in 1921. In July, the two women attended the Wagner Festival in Oberammergau, from where they ventured out to see the old-world churches and castles of Munich.

Teresa spent the remaining summer months in the Parisian suburb of Neuilly with her sister. *Ifigenia,* now in its second printing, continued to accrue new readership. An English translation, for which Parra had not yet signed any papers, promised "great success." But in the midst of these comings and goings, Teresa's happiness still eluded her, she told Carias, except for in "occasional short moments." New rumors were circulating concerning her financial affairs. The source of these rumors is not offered in her letter, but she denies having received any "large sums of money," complaining of the injustice by which she has not yet received her pension. "Injustice, of some and others, far from intimidating me, makes me reactionary. Today, I feel without obligations, entirely free and independent."[26]

In October she moved permanently into Isabelita's house in Neuilly. There a simple room and library in the back were to finally allow Teresa the much-needed peace and quiet that central Paris had prohibited. Since January she had been building this library with books sent to her from Venezuela; Carias, both guardian of her finances and procurer of her literary sources, administered both according to her specifications. For the remainder of the year and up until the summer of 1929, she would finally be able to indulge her appetite for reading, which was, like her friends, carefully tailored to further her along her "interior life." Her activities consisted of "books and a few friends whom we appreciate and who appreciate us," she wrote to Carias in June 1929.[27] Just like the Caracas teenager who used to bury herself obsessively in her private world of books, Parra at forty was a willing recluse. She expressed fresh complaints to Carias about the vulgarity of Parisian social life and how difficult and unnatural it was for her to lower herself to the people striving for "vulgar success." Her favorite books were religious and historical texts; during the spring, she had also enjoyed the works of Abel Bonnard, and she asked Carias if he was familiar with *Diary of Amiel.* Other books mentioned throughout her correspondence are largely unknown to English readers: works by Cecilio Acosta, Andres Bello, Juan Vicente Gonzales, and others.

A year after her Cuban experience and only months after *Mama Blanca* reached the public in Spanish, Teresa's life continued to follow some inwardly determined timetable. There is no evidence that she was eager either to make public appearances or to contribute further to the *"carnival de imprenta."* Around her *Mama Blanca* was creating a pleasant stir of reaction. "The French are very susceptible to the sweet exoticism of the tropics," Teresa wrote Carias. "The idea of saying in jest that their romanticism stemmed from there amused them."[28] This was a time of gathering new information, of indulging the whims of her intellectual appetite: "Each day I am less interested in the printed judgment and more in the word itself, not out of false modesty, but because I am entering the age to which only the interior life lends grace. When one has no hearth, no children, no cares and preoccupations necessary to material life, to live profoundly and not expansively is the only interesting way. Peace of soul and serenity is the only heaven of this kind of mysticism without faith nor hope in life beyond death."[29]

For years she had wanted to visit the relics of Christianity's past in Italy, and now, in the summer of 1929, the trip was finally materializing. Lydia, "very intelligent and artistic"[30] and with tastes most compatible to Teresa's own, would travel from Cuba to accompany her. Other friends, too, such as Seida de la Torre, were to join them in stretches of the itinerary. Teresa spent July and August with Maria in Switzerland, preparing herself by reading thirteenth-, fourteenth-, and fifteenth-century books—"'my favorites," she told Carias.[31] While her mind was thus immersed in the past and her "spirit presided over by St. Francis," she received the most heartening response yet to *Mama Blanca*—its value might even have approached that of Emilia Ibarra's responses to *Ifigenia* way back in 1922. Romain Rolland, writing her in Vevey from his house in Villeneuve on the opposite side of the lake, showed his appreciation for her novel with a flattering evocation of Blanca Nieves's fantasy world: "The six little girls are my friends and play in my garden while I work," he wrote. Teresa reported this letter to Carias excitedly—it had been he, after all, who first introduced her to Roland's *Jean Christophe*: "I think I will tell him I am his neighbor, that in my 2-year solitude I must have met him walking the shores of the lake." But unfortunately she missed the opportunity to meet him in person. His sister, "ugly, not young, but charming, exquisitely intelligent and full of enthusiasm for mystics, and her brother's collaborator," received Teresa that summer.They discussed Gandhi's nonviolent movement to liberate India from English colonial rule, which sparked further debate on white colonialism as it affected the American Indians. Teresa, at this time participating in ethnological classes in Paris, put in the last word by sending the Rolland house a book called *The Socialist Empire of the Incas*.[32]

When Teresa and Lydia arrived in Italy in September, they found themselves thoroughly unprepared for the spectacle of post-Renaissance art. All Teresa's reading had concentrated on the humble pre-Renaissance culture that had built churches with an ungilded and transcendental aesthetic. She resented the "river of colossal and muscular statues" inundating even the most venerable Gothic churches. "No sentiment or detail moved or spoke to my soul," she said of San Pedro; "how different are the small towns from Rome, triumphant and pompous, renovated and dressed by the Renaissance." She wrote Carias that the main lesson of her trip was, once again, affirmation of all that is restrained and discreet and negation of wealth and erudition, which prevent us from "living with ourselves, where everything comes from the soul and is impregnated with tenderness."[33] But in those small towns, in the cathedrals of the Middle Ages, whose workers "sculpted a stone and put it in an obscure place without engraving their names,"[34] Teresa found the gems of her "archeological exhibition"; in the end, the trip left her with great "tenderness and emotion" and a clear sense of where she felt most at home in history.

When Teresa returned to Paris in November and received an invitation to lecture from her many friends in Colombia, the woman outraged by injustice and repelled by hypocrisy would finally be able to meet the one whose expansive and democratic mind wished to "forgive everything by comprehending." In tracing the influence of heroines great and small on South American history, the seed for Teresa's last ambition would also begin to push forward. Her private correspondence would reveal that on the basis of her radical reinterpretation of Simon Bolívar through his love life, she hoped to incite nothing less than a spiritual regeneration of Venezuela. In these last two projects, she would achieve a fusion of her contradictions, which she, for lack of greater vitality in physique and for lack of fewer admonitions from the ghostly voices of an exacting heritage, had never before been able to orchestrate.

Notes

1. Rilke, Rainer Maria, *Letters to a Young Poet*, translated by M. D. Herter Norton (New York; W. W. Norton and Co.; Inc.; 1934), p. 104.
2. Teresa de la Parra. "*Ifigenia*, La Critica, Los Criticos, y los Criticones,"in *Obras Completas* (Caracas: Editorial Arte, 1965), pp. 499–500.
3. "Primera Conferencia," in *Obras Completas* p. 682.
4. Rafael Carias, *Teresa de la Parra, Cartas a Rafael Carias*, (Alcala de Henares, Spain: Talleres Penitenciarios, 1936), pp. 12–13.
5. Letter to Vicente Lecuna, in *Obras Completas*, p. 787.
6. *Briefe aus Muzot*, collected by Ruth Sieber-Rilke und Carl Silber (Leipzig: Dusel-Verlag, 1935) p. 337.
7. Commentary to Rainer Marie Rilke's *Duino Elegies* (W.W. Norton: New York, 1967), p.89.
8. *Cartas a Rafael Carias*, p. 67.
9. Ibid., January 17, 1928 (falsely dated 1927), p. 39.
10. De la Parra; "Primera Conferencia," p. 687.
11. "La lorita de Teresa de la Parra," Eduardo Avilez, *El Universal*, Caracas, December 16, 1953, p. 4.
12. Taped interview with Elena Mederos-Gonzalez, June 11, 1978.
13. Personal interview with Seida de la Torre, December 5, 1979.
14. *Cartas a Rafael Carias*, p. 37.
15. "Teresa de la Parra," *Diario de la Marina*, La Habana, April 1, 1929, p. 1.
16. Lucila Perez-Diaz, "Conceptos Sobre el Feminismo," in *Paginas Sueltas* (Caracas: Editorial Venegrafica, 1970), pp. 17–22.
17. Rilke, Rainer Maria, *Letters to a Young Poet*, pp. 58–59.
18. Letter received from Lydia Cabrera, February 6, 1980.
19. "La Vida Intima de Teresa de la Parra," *El Nacional*, Caracas, December 7, 1947.
20. *Cartas a Rafael Carias*, p. 40.
21. "Primera Conferenica," p. 683.
22. Ibid., See pages 683–684.
23. Teresa de la Parra, *Diario de la Marina*, Havana, April 1, 1928, p. 1.
24. "Primera Conferencia." pp. 684–685.
25. "La lorita Teresa de la Parra," Eduardo Avilés, *El Universal*, Caracas, December 16, 1953, p. 4.
26. *Cartas a Rafael Carias*, p. 86.
27. Ibid., p. 100.
28. Ibid.
29. Ibid., pp. 99–100.
30. Ibid., pp. 104–105.
31. Ibid., p. 104.
32. Ibid., p. 106.
33. Ibid., p. 105.
34. Letter to Zea-Uribe, in *Obras Completas*, pp. 812–15.

CHAPTER FIVE

Culmination of Ideas: The Lectures in Bogota

Colombia: A Mystical Fever

On May 30, 1930, in Colombia, Teresa began her first lecture on the history of the Conquest by stating that religion of the Creole Middle Ages consisted of an almost unconscious worship of Nature. Their Gothic cathedrals were boughs, raising musical and high a transparent arch (p. 692).* Queen Isabella of Spain, greatest of all the Spanish monarchs, sent out her barbaric adventurers to conquer the new land. In the style of the Venetians, they "came to discover gold, but instead they found ideals. Beginning with the brutal shock of the noble land, they began to discover the gold within themselves" (p. 693).

On April 23, 1930, Parra had given her second and last lecture in Havana to the women of the Lyceum and wrote to Carias that she was on her way to Colombia.[1] It was springtime, in the month of her namesake saint and on the very day she would die six years later. Colombia, the "healthiest land on the continent," (p. 688) as Mistral once said, promised Teresa a humbling stroke no less grand, relatively, then the one that met her predecessors four hundred years before. Under the benediction of the stars and at the invitation of a group of August friends—Guzman Esponda. Nieto Caballero, Alcides Arguedas (Bolivian ambassador to Colombia)—Parra answered the call of her native continent, in the belief that it was "almost a duty." The immutable specter of South America, opening once again its arms to her in the invitation, "Come to Colombia and lecture us in a serious vein about yourself, your literary talent, and your books," pulled her magnetically in the core of her being, causing

*All references to the lectures in this chapter are from *Obras Completas*, (Caracas: Editorial Arte, 1965).

her to add that it was not easy for her to explain to the Colombian audience what state of mind such a suggestive and dangerous vision produced in her (p. 682). More suggestive and dangerous than Italy it must certainly have been, because it lay so close to Caracas; there, she had confessed in 1925, was the "only public that truly interests me. All else is vanity."[2]

Nostalgia and adventure played side by side as Teresa made fast her itinerary and her lecture theme. The natural anxiety about these matters evaporated when through her window and between the golden leaves swept by the hazy Parisian autumn, the tropics called her. In the background she recognized the Colombia of the first romantic visions of her childhood—the Valley of Cauca and so on. Before the radiant dream of the voyage, the means of its realization and its immediate consequences ceased to exist for Teresa (p. 682). Often she would define her goals in terms of nostalgia: in 1926 she had announced facetiously to Don Lisandro Alvarado her new "revolutionary urge" to restore flowers and damp earth to mosaic patios—"the best restorations are presided over by nostalgia and sweet melancholy."[3] In her most expressive letter to Carias, of January 16, 1931, which has shed necessary light on the internal events of 1930, the word appears again. Teresa referred, in the context of her and Carias's mutual sensitivities, to the "nostalgia for the grand and beautiful, which we believe ourselves able to encounter more often over there, in other surroundings, in another kind of life, and which in reality was alone, without our knowing it, in the very foundation of ourselves." Likewise she spoke of the "nostalgia for sacrifice and commitment" that often is the price for independence from family obligations.[4]

Sacrifice and commitment, too, required faith in the ideal and faith in the self, but Teresa no longer had either. In losing hold of the one, she turned to find the other had slipped away. "I am a skeptic," she wrote Lecuna, "a great jaded one." She said the praise, the easy success, had done her much damage. Now she saw in her books nothing but defects, and this constant vision robbed her of all initiative, all faith in herself.[5] Ever since recoiling from *Ifigenia*'s fame, Parra had sought something that had been lost. The empty promises of old dogma and new glitter, one after the other, lay shriveled in her exacting hands. She was grounded for lack of wings: wings of love and mystical wings. The value of any regained faith in a mature self hinged now on the conditions of the very consciousness—endemic to her times—that had killed the instinctual and innocent faith of her youth. It was a time now in Europe when the search for the genuine and for the innocent—mourned by some two generations since the industrialization of the West—was changing direction. To progressively minded young writers, the landscape of the self no longer commanded credibility or relevance and the "tragic sense of life" was considered a luxury. In those serious writers able and willing to change, longings for religious faith once broken and the yearning to reestablish human civilization on respectful terms with nature transformed into a variety of concrete political and social activism, new religious affiliations, and the unearthing of solutions proven by time and visible in American Indian or African tribes, where the primitive origins of the human race were seen to reside unspoiled.

A writer's concern now had to deliberately relate to philosophical or moral issues of mass scope or national importance. Just as Parra had abandoned the saga of her developing personality by 1927 and *Mama Blanca*, so did Gabriela Mistral gravitate away from her confessional bent in the poems she wrote from 1922 to 1938 and published under the title *Felling*. Some of the following comments about Mistral's work help to put in greater context Parra's attempt to pull herself out of the world-weary negativity of her existence. Both public figures perceived an obligation as South Americans to address themselves to the issues raised within the turbulent climate of European intelligentsia as these affected, backhandedly, their own countries. That Mistral and Parra held one another in mutual admiration is plain. Whereas Mistral saw in Parra the magical South American blend of urban sophistication and rural ingenuousness, Parra saw Mistral's greater vitality as a source for a happier blend of the active with the contemplative life than she could never conjure up.[6] Thus the startling congruence of their beliefs was at least reinforced, if not created, by their gradual and finally wholehearted deference to each other's person. On Mistral's bond to nature, the South American landscape, and Bolivarian desire for continental unity, her biographer states that she [Mistral] saw the sun and the mountain range as unifying factors in the Americas and envisioned the United States of the South both as a political reality and a cultural unit based on the restoration of the indigenous past to the present.[7] On nostalgia, she also says that the theme of nostalgia, which Gabriela prefered to call by its more precise, richer Portuguese name *Saudade* (longing), is one of the most repeated and important themes in her work.[8] "Matter" is the title of a whole section of *Felling,* in which Mistral invokes the mystical quality of ordinary, material things: "[Matter] is a rediscovery filled with surprises, a kind of mystical union with reality. For a moment the poet senses the divine presence in things and loses herself in divine contemplation."[9] It is furthermore the result of a change in philosophical outlook:

139

"The poetic world of *Felling* differs radically from that of *Desolation*. Going from one to the other is like going from the Old Testament to the Gospels. Or it may be likened to entering the illuminating state of mysticism after leaving behind the asperities of asceticism."[10]

In 1930, when Teresa set forth to Colombia, the outside world still tugged against the world of the self in her conscience; there her stoic solutions and mystical reveries had not wholly calmed the restlessness. The personal and social triumph of her visit has been loquaciously and ubiquitously reported. But the fact that this visit would occur in a background of mystical fever, of supernatural omens and resonating coincidences, is known only to posthumous critics, privy to Parra's many letters written during this period. Both Parra's contemporaries and her biographers alike, however, seem to have glossed over the implications of her lectures as these reflected her literary and personal state of mind. Perhaps this was because, attentive to the speaker's duty to entertain, Parra addressed her Colombian audience so informally. Perhaps the usefulness of her stories as self-portraits went the way of her other, sometimes confounding rhetorical idiosyncrasies and thus her fascinating venture into the art of storytelling, as well as her challenge that history is a narrative told in bad faith, earned her that ambivalence behind the blank smiles. Having noted the central role books played in Teresa's life so far, both as rich experience on the one hand and as the medium of her talent and agent of her independence on the other, we are surprised these observers did not reflect on the irony of her attack on the printed word. Today, taking into account Teresa's affinity for the persecuted and her consequent—or even causal—sensitivity to the faults of dominant ideology, we recognize in her attack a consciousness of the power all recorded media possess to control cultural attitudes; as such, her perceptions sound extremely familiar to generations raised on television. Finally, in her decision to spotlight feminine achievement through the ages, we see her recognition of the ancient and inexorable need for example, for role models by which we consciously or unconsciously pattern our individual selves.

When Parra announced her lecture topic to the Colombian press, one reporter confined his comments to a single paragraph, lamenting that the lecture was to be on merely an isolated chapter of history, not a "global historical study."[11] The prologue to these lectures in *Complete Works,* in contrast, almost invalidates Parra's lectures completely with its intoxicated praise. It states that it is women who color and define the direction of human societies and societies are only as cheerful, sad, intelligent, valiant, frivolous, as are their women. She believed nothing resembles Venezuelan women as much as Venezuelan history (p. 694). Parra, so frequently in need of defense against charges of both feminine triviality and dangerous iconoclasm, did receive plenty of understanding, however, from the Colombian press for her attempt to define the "healthy feminist," and several listeners reported large audience appreciation for her choice of the 300-year incubation period of the South American spirit as vital to unsnarling the feminist controversy.

Those later, more seasoned critics dismissed Teresa's feminist message as tame and focused instead on her apparently far greater obsession: the biography of Simon Bolívar. It was no less than a consuming passion, occurring in synchronous and simultaneous rhythm with the lecture tour. Through Teresa's letters, her drum-sounding declaration that she had found the immediate answer to her questions of faith rose above the similarly impassioned voices of her favorite women in South American history. But the biography was an abortive dream. Like the last burst of energy in a child before he or she collapses in sleep, the uncustomary surge of energy filling the 1930 letters foreboded Teresa's slow collapse and subsequent death. She was later to call it her "fine fervor, which, like a sacred fever, attacked me in the tropics."[12] The one oral work and the other abandoned work lived undivided in Parra's mind; the first prepared an idological framework for the second, and in return, that second nourished Teresa's romantic hunger and strengthened her creative will. It was by the light of Simon Bolívar that she not only experienced Colombia, but also lived the next two years of her life, received the news of her disease, and envisioned a graceful death. Because this "sacred fever" bloomed into the full-fledged lung lesions of the white plague—tuberculosis—instead of into the grand opus it promised to be, Teresa's Colombian lectures stand abandoned and cut off, like a prologue without a text and burdened with representing the last valuable expression of Teresa as an artist: her last creative work.

Parra did not need to deliberate as long about this new invitation to the Americas as she had done two years earlier. The invitation arrived sometime in November; the Christmas and New Year holidays followed with their mandatory family ritual, and by early February she was already in Cuba, being welcomed by Lydia Cabrera into her villa and looking forward to several more months there before sailing on to Colombia.[13] Feeling at home in the company of Lydia, buoyed by the tropical Cuban air and the air of vitality surrounding Lydia's various artistic and social enterprises (she owned and operated an art gallery in Havana), Teresa plotted her Colombian tour. On May 6 she was due to sail there via Panama, and she had reserved the months of March and April for refining her lectures. It is not likely that she wrote them with the intent of later publication, especially since the Bolívar project would contain their underlying concepts. They did not appear in print until their inclusion in the 1965 edition of her collected works.

On March 31, a Havana newspaper reported the first evidence of Teresa's activities in Cuba, touching off a month of the usual press scrutiny that followed Teresa de la Parra everywhere. "The famous international novelist" had delivered a lecture to the Association of Friends of French Culture in Cuba, where she read fragments of French poetry and told the stories of their authors, who had all gone honorably to early graves. Parra's warm "clear and sonorous" reading in French made a good impression on the audience, to whom these poets, with the single exception of Guillaume Apollinaire, were totally unknown.[14] Teresa was to give a total of two lectures in Havana: the first one, on obscure French poets, was rapidly followed by an even greater success, mentioned before, at the Lyceum on April 23. Teresa was encouraged in this by Lydia, who realized the advantage in Teresa giving both her speaking skill and unorthodox lecture theme (the influence of Bolívar's lovers on his life and work) a dress rehearsal in Havana before presenting them to the general Colombian public.

In practical matters, Lydia claims to have exceeded her head-in-the-clouds friend. It was often Lydia who pushed a recalcitrant Teresa into fulfilling the harsh social obligations necessary to promote her career. They had enjoyed their mutual trust ever since the 1928 Latin Congress, and now Lydia was the one, as Emilia Ibarra once had been, to read Teresa's pages of writing and exert her own editing suggestions. In those days, said Lydia, Teresa was typically loath to burn any midnight oil. One of their regular habits was to rest after eating lunch, Teresa lying on a sofa and Lydia in the room also, listening with awe as the former, eyes closed in daydreams, would let loose an uncommonly eloquent and philosophical stream of thoughts. It was a time, also, of diminished finances for Teresa and her family, due to the devaluation of the bolivar during the great international depression; Lydia found herself frequently in the position of lending emergency funds to Teresa out of her own greater resources. The honorariums Teresa earned in Cuba and Colombia, instead of going to replenish her own dwindling savings account, went right back, in the first case, to the ever-needy Lyceum and, in the second case to her sister Maria, in whose husband was currently suffering fi-

HABANERAS

(Viene de la página CINCO)

TERESA DE LA PARRA

EN EL LYCEUM

Grata la noticia.

Y no demoraría en darla.

La señorita Teresa de la Parra, a quien el **Lyceum** tributó en días pasados un cálido homenaje de admiración, ha ofrecido a su directiva dar una conferencia.

Honrado el **Lyceum** con la determinación de la culta y talentosa novelista venezolana ha tenido que pensar en otro local mayor que el propio para la conferencia.

Ha escogido un teatro.

El Principal de la Comedia.

Con esto dará una ocasión de escuchar a la bellísima autora de **Ifigenia** al público de la Habana.

Teresa de la Parra corresponde al deseo del **Lyceum** autorizando hacer pública su conferencia y cediendo graciosamente el producto de la venta de las localidades.

Generoso rasgo.

Digno de señalarse.

De esa manera ayudará a la naciente institución a construir en su casa el pequeño teatro que proyecta.

La conferencia versará sobre la "influencia de las mujeres en la independencia del Continente y en la vida de Bolívar".

Entre esas mujeres figuran la esclava Matea, Teresa del Toro, Fanny de Villars, Manuelita Sanz...

Las localidades se pondrán a la venta en el **Lyceum**, Calzada 81, Vedado, teléfono F-1535.

También en los almacenes de **El Encanto** podrán adquirirse.

Los precios que se han fijado son 10 pesos los palcos platea y 6 pesos los palcos altos.

Peso y medio las lunetas.

Y un peso las butacas.

Diré ya, por último, que ha sido fijada la fecha de la conferencia de Teresa de la Parra.

El 23 del corriente.

Por la tarde.

Teresa de la Parra in Havana, April 1930

nancial hardship, as Lydia Cabrera expressed later to the author.[15]

At first Parra was very timid about declaring Bolivar the subject of her next book. She claimed that undertaking such a written project did not occur to her until the results of her Lyceum speech were in. When she wrote for advice to Vicente Lecuna, who remains today Bolívar's foremost biographical authority, she referred self-effacingly to herself as insolent to think she could add anything to the mass of Liberator literature already abounding. That she even found the courage to write to Lecuna was due to the enthusiastic applause she received at the Lyceum after presenting what later became the substance of her third Colombian lecture. The Cuban speech, compared to the Colombian one, contained a greater infusion of her concept that history had distorted Bolívar's true image and perverted his unifying message. "The 23rd of April . . . a success for which I would never have been so bold to hope—a true homage," she wrote to her sister Elia.[16]

May 18 was the ostensible date of Parra's first exploratory letter to Lecuna, and she was in Panama, bound for Bogota.* The urgent request for his counsel stemmed from her desire to make full use of her Colombian visit as a source of bibliography, which might even require a Venezuelan stopover for additional material. The ambition that she later invested in this project was currently either latent or unconfessed to both Lecuna and Carias, Parra's concurrent correspondents. She talks of an "easy, amenable biography, in the style of the novelized celebrated lives being published today in France." But then she begins to waver: ". . . The word 'novelized' is naturally relative. . . . I would want to touch more on the lover than on the hero, without dispensing entirely with the heroic life, so mixed up with the love life."[17] Only after she received Lecuna's generous approval, and after she had spent her month of lecturing and communing at Bolívar's last haunts, did she allow her aspirations to soar. She felt that to describe, to evoke everything surrounding Bolívar without painterly zeal, was what she wanted—but did not know how to liberate

---

*Dates of Teresa's itinerary retrieved from newspaper articles and letters present the usual contradictions. On May 27, she told a reporter she had been in Bogota for "fifteen or twenty days" already, making impossible her presence in Panama on the eighteenth. Since the boat passage from Cuba to Colombia lasted only four days and she supposedly left Cuba the sixth of May, it is more likely she mailed her letter on the eighth of May from Panama. Given that Teresa, the editors of her *Complete Works*, and newspaper reporters were flagrantly careless of numbers (ages, times, and dates), any of three schedules could be concocted from this information. Only the May 27 newspaper data is definite.

herself from all the literature of the past, of the time at which she writing, and of the futurists, minimalists, and others—that whole carnival that blinded and bewildered her and between whose clouds of error and vulgar pretension she suddenly discovered, in her disorientation, strong and great talents attracted her without succeeding entirely in converting her. It was this carnival of the printed word that had driven her to biography, to conform words to life, and to renounce without style all pretensions of personal success. It was the only thing that attracted her at the moment.[18]

This "everything" surrounding Bolívar that she wanted to describe was indeed inclusive. The "places and epochs through which he passed are in themselves, and even without him, very suggestive ones: the Colony in the 18th Century, life of the city and of the plantation; the court of Charles IV; Romanticism and the Paris of Napoleon, etc."[19] Between 1928 and 1936 alone, six biographies of Bolívar were published in English. Lecuna's editor, Harold A. Bierck, Jr., who wrote the introduction to Lecuna's *Selected Writings of Bolívar*, says, however, that "for the most part all of the biographies [written to date] . . . portray the man himself, while minimizing the powerful influences—social, economic, and political—of the time in which Bolívar fought and lived."[20] Teresa's as yet uncovered angle, then, was not unwisely chosen. How she would reconcile the Big Controversy—past versus present, colonialism versus independence, Catholic church versus positivism—would lie in her transcendence of the religious ideologies pitted against one another after the war; both of these she considered bankrupt. Neither the dogmas of church hierarchy, rendered indigestible once Bolívar and the Enlightenment hit the continent, nor positivism, shallow and destructive, had managed to eradicate the hypocrisies from their respective moral preaching.

Teresa called herself a "mystic without religion," a "mystic without belief in the afterlife," and always in search of the "mystical ideal." In September of 1930, she began making intonations about the occult and extra-sensory perception in letters to a new correspondent, Dr. Luis Zea-Uribe, physician and author of *Mirando al Misterio (Looking at Mystery)*, whom she had met in Bogota. Other, not so new allusions to Eastern religion permeate her letters to Lecuna, Carias, and Zea-Uribe alike. Ever since her very first story, "Buda Y La Leprosa," she had made evident her attraction to that stringently passive religious discipline and noted its similarity to the fundamental doctrines of Christ. Further traces of this awareness visible in *Mama Blanca* and *Ifigenia*, combined with the fervent drive for some pan-religious experience, amounted to an ostensibly personal yet (according to her third lecture) typically Creole approach to the universe: quasi-Catholic, slightly Oriental, and stubbornly pagan. By January of 1931, the religious mood had intensified to the point of her telling Carias: "I believe, dear friend, that alone we can be happy within mysticism." The current efforts of Romain Rolland supported her now unabashed desire to infuse the Bolívar biography with spiritual perspective. His new books were none other than biographies of "contemporary Indian apostles"[21] such as Mahatma Gandhi, a man of moral integrity who showed the world that nonviolence could wield revolutionary power.

Smatterings of Eastern terminology, familiar to us through *Ifigenia*, now began to punctuate the already eclectic religious vocabulary of Parra's letters. This habit of using religious imagery so loosely, sometimes even comically, was not just a peculiarity of Teresa's speech inherited from her mother, but one typical to all Caraquenans. Teresa's letters to Lecuna and Zea-Uribe characterize Bolívar as an "apostle and prophet, sacrificed to the individualism of the demagogues" and as "more than a hero—an apostle, messiah, and martyr." But also she refers to him as a "yogi." More than in Bolívar himself, she saw in his historical time a perfect backdrop in which to insert her views on morality and statesmanship. We can easily imagine that Teresa had been engaged actively for some time—alone there in her library—in a search for some lesser, more obscure historical figure around whom she could construct her philosophy of the South American problem before she decided to go for the center of controversy himself. Miranda, for instance, a revolutionary theorist who influenced the independence movement, crops up in a letter to Zea-Uribe as one whom Parra thought Europe finally damaged and proved mediocre. In the following passage from that letter to Zea-Uribe, written five months after her return to Europe, she reveals in her own words the wide range of her biographical concern, and we can detect in them the familiar bugbears of her post-*Ifigenia* intellectual and moral meditations. She said that the European influences, importunate, inadequate, and badly managed during the whole nineteenth century, had disoriented people and they walked around almost all crazy in search of power, money, and reputation. In the countries of the sun, however, Parra felt people had only to behold the sky to revive their spirits in the nights and dawns, in order to grasp the riches within themselves. Don't, she asked, you believe that the colony must have been impregnated, without knowing it, with the great mysticism of the Orient (Buddhism, or the primitive Christianity, that of the true "amor") and that independence, manifestation of this mysticism, opened the door to the Charlatanism of the past century? She saw Bolívar as a yogi: the consequence of 300 years in the valleys of Aragua.[22]

Parra's new obsession gained its intimate tone as the Colombian trip progressed. Intimacy with her subject matter had always been a prerequisite for firing up that talent ''so intermittent and fragile.'' When she should succeed in meeting the ''live'' Bolívar behind the ''stone wall of adjectives'' and behind the false legend of the ''superman hero that contributed to the awakening of caudillismo and an excessive national vanity that makes the present seem sad and decadent,'' she might also succeed in achieving union with a worthy man and master. This, she wrote Lecuna in the following July, was the answer to her desire. She stated that personal success interested her much less. That which left her passionate was searching, unearthing, and living for a time in intimate contact with the person of Bolívar when he was alive and describing this took second place. She believed, in spite of her inexperience, she knew the infinite pleasure of the historian.[23] In seeing Teresa's deepest impulses as mystic, writer, and lover so united, we are reminded of the infinite pleasure Maria Eugenia felt while bathing in the river, sending twigs sculpted into Indian barques to float down its stream as if down the Ganges, and writing a letter to Gabriel, who was absent yet vivid in her mind, as were the famous doomed lovers (Adam and Eve) of primitive Christian legend.

There is no telling how advanced Teresa's Bolívar project really was when she accepted the invitation to go to Colombia—that is, whether or not it significantly motivated her acceptance. Given that she went simply on the positive instinct of a woman living amidst Europe's lost generation, who after a hard-won fight for her right to be modern had then picked out of the myriad paths offered up by her times the one reverting to classic and essential truths, borne out by a now-broken tradition, she felt completely right about putting herself at the mercy of that so suggestive and dangerous Colombian public. As a mystic without religion, the idea of entering so close to the enemy territory of her origins, in professional armor, filled her with all the sensations of impending oneness, of consciousness at the interface of life and death—with or without Bolívar.

Ifigenia Raised to the Level of Tragedy

The chief question Parra's friends put to her, in hopes of receiving an answer, was the one of her identity. With a trace of slyness she wrote that when she went to Colombia in 1930, she sensed in a very immediate way a disappointment in certain people toward her lectures: they believed she would continue her confession and instead she spoke to them of historical evocations of dead people—Fany de Villars, Dona Marina, Manuelita, Inca Garcilaso's mother, and others.[24]

Disappointment by some at Parra's resolve for privacy was to turn, at the third lecture, to a fresh outrage by others at hearing her unmitigated praise of Bolívar's most colorful mistress, Manuela Saenz. The majority response, however, during her month-long visit, exceeded her wildest expectations. She behaved with her usual vague aplomb, confident (we imagine) at having arranged in her lecture material a good foil for her fleeting selves and a true, if sketchy, rendition of her lasting concerns.

"To be so at one with one's destiny that . . . the answer to the question Who are you? will be the Cardinal's answer, 'Allow me . . . to answer you in the classic manner and to tell you a story' "[25] is a quote by Hannah Arendt about Isak Dinesen that also serves to describe Teresa's approach to her lectures. On the one hand, it can be said that with these historical lectures she reached a new transitory level along her literary path, where the object had always been to inject the simple, concrete, and everyday—"that which always allows itself to be written"—with a compelling and uniquely personal interpretation. On the other hand, we know that Teresa always needed a cover for the truth that was not a lie. Her Colombian audience could not be counted on to respond as favorably to her ideas as the Cubans had. If callous judges were guaranteed to chew over her words, at least she could distract them with crust—leaving the finer-tasting implications of her alibis to be savored by people of corresponding sensibilities. But Teresa, like Maria Eugenia, did have a tendency to get carried away by her ideas, and Colombia's was still an old-world culture.[26] Amidst factions of extreme conservatism throve, nevertheless, a community of progressive intellectuals and philosophers unequaled on the rest of the continent. "Little Athens," Bogota was called, and while Parra was able to say, *Ifigenia* was better liked in France than in America, except for in Colombia, where its success has been absolute,[27] she was also aware that Colombia's Catholic clergy had been the most virulent of all her critics. The ensuing sensationalism had contributed significantly to *Ifigenia*'s popularity. Teresa's friend Nieto Caballero, one of the men behind her invitation to lecture and the author of a critical biography of her, commented on the difference Colombia's tradition of higher learning and Venezuela's more provincial authoritarianism made on their respective attitudes toward her work (p. 679): "In Colombia, land of intellectuals, a great writer is a caudillo. In Venezuela, where in those days Teresa de la Parra was spoken of with reticence and

148

even with contempt, General Gomez was acclaimed with enthusiasm.''

Once again Teresa stood on the Cuban island, pondering the oppressive and bewitching continent. Here she was free to talk to Negroes, carry chickens in public, and happily observe young middle-class women filing into the colleges alongside men. In Colombia, where many austere households remained closed even to friends, she would wake and sleep under constant public surveillance at a fancy hotel for visiting dignitaries.

The Colombian newspapers compared Parra's arrival at the Bogota train station to that of a conquering caudillo. Hundreds of schoolchildren greeted her and lined the road all the way into town. Some reports echoed Nieto-Caballero's 1929 declaration that she was a ''revolution on the march.''[28] Parra introduced her first lecture with a much meeker metaphor (p. 682). She said she knew her books were loved in Colombia, like a pet, flowers, birds in a cage, like everything that was both familiar and handicapped. As much as she despised the pompous image of the caudillo and disdained any such barrage of excessive praise, she did not in this instance express to anyone, not even to Carias, any displeasure. On the contrary: ''I enjoyed Colombia much more than I thought I would,''[29] she wrote him afterwards. Only occasionally did her modest composure bristle with her familiar warning: ''I fear . . . the discrepancy you will surely discover between the Teresa you have concocted and the real Teresa. I have a terrible rival in this idealized image of myself.''[30] Since the flattery was generally physical rather than intellectual, she made good her 1928 Cuban statement and accepted that flattery with grace. Never before had a whole city turned out to applaud her and strain to catch the sound of her every word and the sight of her every Parisian costume. It was a welcome that other countries gave only to boxers and football players, she exclaimed.[31] The lectures were sold out, yet they continued to draw such throngs of hopeful listeners that she had to repeat them seven times in the Teatro de Colon, a small auditorium in Bogota. At the Pension Augusta, a permanent queue of fans waited to ''shake the hand that wrote *Mama Blanca* and *Ifigenia*,'' some gaining admission by ruse—''I'm an old friend'' or ''I'm a distant relative.''[32] During the course of her visit, Parra was received by the president of Colombia himself and honored by a long string of events, including at least one bullfight. But far from relinquishing gladly her new sense of purpose to the din of adulation, she complained to Lecuna that she could not give as much attention to her bibliography as she wished. She had no free time. The two or three times she was in the libraries, she was distracted from concentrating on the search.[33] And to Zea-Uribe she even claimed that the homage produced an altogether inverse, humbling effect on her. Parra stated that among the many good things that she owed to her Colombian trip, she appreciated one above all others: that of not having sensed one moment's flattery to her self-esteem by that homage. Instead she sensed a very profound shame that it exceeded her. This reaction of spontaneous humility made her truly immense, because she awakened in herself the desire to deserve the methods of the mystics.[34]

The homage to Teresa de la Parra seemed a mass confluence of every Bogotan's personal and radically variant fantasy. She was one of their writers who had both conquered and survived the European literary scene. A majority of press reports concentrated on two themes that they felt interested their reading public the most: what was the name, in real life, of the Colombian poet who lost his glasses when Maria Eugenia rejected his clumsy kiss?, and "Teresa de la Parra is more woman than writer." That her first novel was a literal autobiography and that she was—thank heaven—not so unwomanly as to consider the cultivation of writing more important than that of physical charm, were presumptions the Colombians nevertheless conceived in an approving light. Teresa's beauty was so startling that it triggered an endless effusion of reactions.

Some discussion on the latter subject is fitting, if only because that divisive characterization occured so often in Teresa's life. Already we have heard the many allusions to her womanhood as it affected her writing. Some found her "feminities" a weakness, and others, such as Mistral, found them genuine and innovative. But here they were spoken of in context of her combined personality and calling. Habitual remarks Teresa made suggest that, indeed, being female and an author of books were mutually exclusive occupations and she had found it necessary to emphasize the one over the other,[35] either for the greater honesty of its more humble disguise, the greater peace its feigned ignorance conferred, or—a motivation she never confessed to—the simple efficacy of its mystical power over men. In her times, the apparently unnecessary and even derogatory reference to gender had many connotations. Some, like Maria and Nieto Caballero, stressed with marked vehemence that Teresa the woman and the personality was more interesting than Teresa the writer. The assessment is plausible, yet more than proving to us its veracity, her sister and friend were demonstrating their privilege of intimacy.

Others merely set out to differentiate Teresa from the terrifying image of the suffragette who followed in her wake as a result of *Ifigenia*'s notoriety. To Teresa, this differentiation was hardly undesirable. She advertised openly her professional reticence and profoundly loyal—if sometimes narcissistic—cultivation of feminine mystique. It seemed impossible to talk about her without taking her femininity into account. In the early days of feminism and in recent times, such taking into acount was a compliment the establishment felt was necessary to bestow on unmarried career women. The stereotypical suffragette had invalidated the cause in the eyes of many women by assuming a man-hating and Marxist pose, and it had become a public preconception that only an "unwomanly" woman—a freak—could wish to have social and legal equality. The suffragette was equally unpopular among many progressive men, because these feared that women, historically conditioned and controlled by the church, were likely to vote a conservative line. Indeed, this belief would motivate many of the South American governments under threat of legal leftist takeovers to belatedly grant the vote to women.

So, whether extolling her feminine virtues at the expense of or in addition to her writing talent, or placing the very masculine label of caudillo on her, many a journalist took the opportunity to expound on his or her pet peeve regarding feminism. One flowery and self-conscious article chose to inflate the importance of Parra's natural, girlish manner and seductive charms for the final purpose of chastising "the bluestocking . . . nothing more disagreeable. . . . The unfortunates forget that woman, when she is beautiful, is a living work of art, the best one of all. The poet, musician, and painter create beauty with great effort. . . . It is enough for woman to present herself, to look and smile, in order to produce the deepest aesthetic emotions."[36] Although to Parra the creation of just such aesthetic emotions was indeed important, there was a complexity of aesthetic imperatives behind her chosen appearance and manner flattering the reactionary reporter—so eager to advertise the seemingly effortless duty of all womankind to art—far less than he might have imagined. For instance, Parra defined *culture* in aesthetic terms: "It is moral elegance before one's self—the control of all feeling by integrity. It is harmony."[37] Aesthetics formed a major element of her crossdisciplinary creed. Also, Maria Eugenia's chief struggle seems to have gone unremembered: she had fought between just that old-world duty to be a pleasurable decoration for men and her modern inclination to write and enjoy the development of her personality. All the hours Teresa's alter ego had spent in front of the mirror contemplating her nude body had brought equal amounts of pleasure at recognizing its magnificence and bitterness at realizing its singular representation of her total temporal worth to society. The successful compromise Teresa finally reached, aided by the expertise of Emilia Ibarra and the cold supremacy of her own need for liberty, was probably costly in a way that only her intimates were able to observe. It was the typical experience, yes, of many writers torn between prohibitions inflicted by a narrow family world and the exigencies of free expression in literature, but here the added weight of the prejudicial charge carried by her femininity infected both worlds. If her family and her public felt betrayed, the first because she rejected its conventions and the second because she failed to live up to its fantastic expectations, Teresa, bound to both, was left with a narrow sliver of ground on which to tread. The professional reward would never be the highest and the family acceptance never the warmest. Ultimately, because the outside world persisted in pitting her gender against her calling, Teresa gained subtle revenge in her solitude, where she could function, as she did in the act of writing, undivided.

One of the more thoughtfully sympathetic critics to rise above the trivialities and blandishments said that Parra generated a vital message of spiritual emancipation for the women of her day. He recognized that one vital role for women like Parra was to deliver a message of hope for social progress. Not only was her message extremely important, but so was its effect on her audience. Parra encouraged them to have the self-control and inner strength so necessary for women embroiled in the conflicts of love and life.[38] Another reviewer summed up the first lecture by saying that after having discussed the ups and downs of the modern woman in an accurate and knowledgeable manner, Parra clearly and intelligently outlined the model of a healthy feminist. Informed by both observation and life experience, the reviewer added, she presented a masterful picture of the aware and well-balanced woman: a loving mother, a selfless wife, or a virtuous single woman who, refined and educated, needs to work and does work, ennobling what has been called penance, but is really salvation.[39]

The association with and repudiation of the embattled feminist image created a confusion that Parra did not waste much time in clarifying to her audience. First she played with the idea of her "lost" vocation, then teased them with the promise of revealing, finally, the real name of the Colombian poet some thirty years hence, when the danger of personal damage was past and she would be able to see "reflected in her listeners' eyes not the image of who I am but the divine vision of who I would have wished to be." Then she came around to the *Ifigenia* controversy. Her book, "not one of revolutionary propaganda but the exposition of a case of contemporary illness, that of a Spanish-American Bovary" (p. 684), was worthy of being treated as transcendental, as giving rise to discussion, and as urging a remedy: "I do not shun that." The remedy was work, not submissiveness, and she stressed that frivolity rather than healthy activity was the true enemy of feminine virtue (p. 685): Parra stated that for a woman to be strong, healthy, and really free of hypocrisy, she must not be suppressed with respect to the new way of life, but on the contrary, had to be free unto herself, conscious of both dangers and responsibilities. She should be useful to society even if she is not the mother of a family, Parra stated, and she should be financially independent by virtue of the work she performs in a spirit of collaboration with the opposite sex. In this she should be neither man's master nor his enemy, nor any candidate for exploitation by him, but should rather be his companion and friend. For Parra, work did not exclude possessing a mystique or sacred obligations. On the contrary, it was an additional discipline for purifying and strengthening the spirit. But when mystique, submissiveness, and passivity were imposed by force and even the inertia of habit or custom, it produced dangerous, silent reactions, awakened a hatred for imposed orderliness that in another time was good, and embittered spirits that took their revenge under the guise of peacefulness and that ended up by turning into entombed souls, she said (p. 685).

Parra went on to qualify both her notion of work and her brand of feminism. In no way did she mean to suggest that the shameless exploitation of poor women in menial jobs was a solution. As a contemporary example of a woman in whose life the "redemption and dignification" of womankind by financial independence and work is demonstrated and who, as a "fighter with regard to all her ideas, a socialist, Catholic, defender of liberty and the noble spirit of her people," had the skills to talk authoritatively on the "vibrant theme" of a "just and by now indispensable feminism," Parra invoked none other than her friend Gabriela Mistral. She reflected in this choice, and in an ensuing analysis of Cuban women from differing economic classes, once again her tendency to feel disadvantaged rather than privileged by her aristocratic upbringing, with its emphasis on past glory, on behavior limitation, and on shallow refinements (p. 688). She claimed not to understand the issues of suffrage, feeling, as she did, too much antagonism toward the loudness of the voice explaining why she should participate in politics—the "hardest and dirtiest" (p. 686) of jobs. Evolution, not revolution, was the approach of her moderate feminism. To demonstrate further how work and financial independence dignified women, Parra "took great pains" to draw a parallel between the lives of the two "best female American poets of our century," Gabriela Mistral and Delmira Augustini. To us,

this parallelism seems barely existent outside of their mutual poetic vocations, yet a certain parallel courage underlying their vastly different
personal destinies does emerge (p. 688):

> Delmira Agustini, young, beautiful, extraordinarily gifted, and
> born into a respectable middle-class family, is a case of a Maria
> Eugenia Alonso brought to the level of tragedy. By dint of the
> tradition that says "every woman ought to marry," she married a
> so-called "good match" at a very early age. A few days after the
> marriage saw the start of the drama involving the lack of under-
> standing. On the one side there was the silent disdain of the one
> who sees herself a thousand times superior and a slave. The results
> of this were mutual hate, still mixed with passion, divorce, and
> finally, on a day during the divorce proceedings, the husband kills
> her and himself—the only means of dominating her and of satiating
> his thirst for domination.
>
> Gabriela Mistral—poor, born into an honest and modest house
> free of worldly conventions—started to work while still merely a
> girl. Her work and good Christian faith reveal to her, as time goes
> on, new ideals that she will humanize and adapt to the real necessities
> of life as she goes through the world suffering and struggling in her
> mission. . . .

Teresa's answer to the "delicate" question of women's rights was
to provide a "historical glimpse" in three lectures of "feminine abnegation in our countries," a glimpse that would stimulate a noble evolution
by illuminating the strengths of the past. Despite great social odds and
despite the history books' omissions, women have had a "hidden and
happy" influence on the greater continent. By titling her lectures "The
Influence of Women on the Formation of the American Spirit," Teresa
furthermore wished to stress the common heritage of all Latin American
countries and to demonstrate her patriotism. She stopped short of modern
women. Parra would have liked to include them, but lacked the opportunity, and besides, she quite frankly preferred the "infinite poetry of
the voluntary and sincere sacrifice" of those women bearing out the
charm of the past" (p.687).

Parra on the History of South America

South America, haven of the romantic heart Parra considered so well guarded by her mother, Isabel, also harbored a tradition of super-women—not only the Amazons and Evitas of popular legend, but women of extraordinary intellects and passions who had lived unceremoniously up along the borders of the great bulk of human endeavor. Although Teresa made a point of including in her survey the general endeavor that was specifically feminine—that of the "obscure Sabinas, anonymous workers of concord, true founders of the cities for having settled the houses, their most effective work throughout the generations was their silent enterprise of fusion and love" (pp. 690–91), it was the individual heroine whom Parra sought to reinstate in popular legend and, more subtly, the female martyr whose theme had preoccupied Teresa since *Ifigenia*.

Her first lecture, once having dispensed with the formalities of her vocation and of redeeming *Ifigenia*, dealt chiefly with ways of telling history. One of these, she stressed, achieves a higher moral plane than any other, and this is the one that permits the individual woman to exist—to maybe even shine. Within her chronology of women's activities during the Spanish conquest, beginning with Queen Isabella—"She joined to her feminine grace masculine virtues, loved wisdom and books. . . . She was intrepid and sagacious. . . . The earth trembled when she died" (p. 691)—Parra focused in on the exemplary lives of two Indian women, as told by two sixteenth-century historians in order to lay the ideological foundation for Parra's own subjective narration. The first of these women was Dona Marina "Malinche,"* Hernan Cortes's Aztec lover and guide. Parra took her "glorified and happy" story from Bernal Diaz de Castillo's history of the Mexican conquest. The second was Ñusta** Isabel, melancholy Inca princess and bride of the conquistador Garcilaso de la Vega. Her mestizo son, the Inca Garcilaso de la Vega, accompanied her through her lonely sorrow and became South America's first native writer.

Parra ventured to imitate these early nonhistorians' "transparent," sense-impressionistic style in her speech. To let reality speak for itself was her objective, and reality, she conjectured, always manifested a

*In modern Mexico, the term "malinchista" is used to designate a person who rejects his or her national heritage and prefers a foreign one.
**Ñusta means noble daughter or a female member of the Inca empire.

disorderly state. No one, not even Plutarch, could narrate an event like Bernal Diaz or the anonymous authors of the Gospels, who wrote "as if they were talking, not writing." Their unofficial histories were "romances in prose," motivated by compassion and guided by a love for truth; they were therefore much truer to life than "official" histories, wherein nothing save the destructive feats of the military was glorified (p. 701). Striving consciously for the feel of unedited documentary, Parra strung her examples together. They consisted of the rambling, cinematographic sequences of Bernal Diaz and the lush prose of the Andalusian people's tale of Jesus' Seventh Fall: ". . . The impression was so intense it cannot be expressed in words. The sole witnesses to appreciate this are not men but the tenseness in the air and the soaring of birds across the sky. . . ." Like those anonymous authors and Bernal Diaz, who put "women and roosters in the forefront with the ups and downs of the drama," Parra wished to catch all the details. She felt that people might think she was speaking thus by habit of her trade and that in order to avoid talking nonsense, it would be better for her to remain within her novelistic restraints. But she saw it as a duty to proclaim the moral superiority of this kind of narration (p. 701).

Parra's tirade against "official history" was severe and her defensiveness toward possible charges of romantic insubstantiality therefore pronounced. She claimed not to be trying to "defame authority and respectability for its own sake (p. 704). Credibility was important to her. In the context of the Bolívar biography, she expressed disapproval of any author who embellished his subject's personal life without discretion: "I detest the historical novel," she wrote after the lectures to Lecuna. "The narration itself is superior to anything that could be imagined novelistically."[40] Parra's rejection of history was undoubtedly linked to her wholesale rejection of nineteenth-century culture and philosophy, about which she was well read. On the finer points of Venezuelan history itself, however, she was knowledgeable mainly through the oral tales of her relatives. In November, when the Bolívar preparations were well underway, she wrote Lecuna that her false interpretation of history was, until recently, very great. She was educated in Spain and did not know Venezuelan history in college. Tropical grandiloquence (regarding the glory of war), far from convincing her, affirmed her skepticism. She believed this oral hostility from Godo relatives towards Bolívar prepared her better for feeling close to Bolívar than any written eulogies. She said she knew by ear many things she encountered later in history and independence was a history of families.[41]

Teresa's defensiveness towards her oral education turned out to be not ill-advised. Although in the above letter she fails to place her undefined "false interpretation" of history in context of the lectures, in a succeeding letter she deferred to Lecuna's opinion that she had, perhaps, overemphasized the importance of Bolívar's lovers on his political achievements. (Other inaccuracies in her third lecture, as we shall later see, were due to the suppression of facts that were not discovered until after her death.) In the following comment by Hannah Arendt on the historical thinking process, we find a suggestion supportive of Teresa's feeling that she was tackling a major adversary: "The 19th century's obsession with history and commitment to ideology still looms so large in the political thinking of our times that we are inclined to regard entirely free-thinking, which employs neither history nor coercive logic as crutches, as having no authority over us."[42] Parra insisted that while "the truth of the historians is relative, the truth of tradition or the history of the nonhistorians is absolute, because it comes nearer to reality and approaches with more grace. Moreover, tradition goes. It is necessary to desire it doubly for its ideal usefulness and because it is condemned to die" (p. 704). Not only had official history—by means of the printed word—replaced the more flexible oral traditions of the past whereby men, women, and children each had an ever-changing story to tell one another, but it had entrenched racial animosities with its exclusive reporting of cruelty. It had even gone so far as to infect folk ballads with its distortions, because the mind, suffering from faulty memory and unwilling to let the story fade, naturally grasps at the printed word to fill its gaps. "Valiant champion," "Father of the Patria," "Glorious centaurs"—when Teresa once listened to a group of authentic native balladeers, she heard "in sum, a session of the Academy of History accompanied by guitar and maracas" (p. 704). Official history was nothing but a "banquet for men only," a "rumor of a fake fiesta. By excluding women they cut off one of the governing threads of life" (p. 701).

I believe that while politicans, the military, the journalists and historians go through life placing antagonizing rules of behavior on things—on the young, the populace, and above all on women, who are numerous and very disorderly—we charge ourselves with tangling up those rules, establishing once again an amiable confusion."

(p. 689)

When Teresa began to pore over Bernal Diaz's chronicle for traces of Malinche, she found that significant detail had escaped even the conscientious Diaz (p. 694). "Through the small bits provided much can be divined that has not been told." Malinche's role in Cortes's conquest was far more important than that of a simple translator and go-between. The ecstatic praise given universally to Cortes for his so-called political genius and his cleverness in making pacts with the Indians did not fool Teresa, who formulated her opinion on the basis of the two lovers' different personalities as they manifested themselves between the lines (p. 694). "I believe, ladies and gentlemen, that this mysterious cleverness of Cortes is called exclusively Dona Marina."

Dona Marina's story was a tumultuous one. Her own mother had sold her to an Aztec tribe in Tabasco, who in turn sold her as a slave to Cortes's party of conquistadors along with "four lizards, some blankets, five ducks, and two golden slippers" (p. 696). She owed nothing to the Indians—in fact, her sale to the great "white God" gave free rein to her talents, passions, and abilities (p. 697): "Upon allying herself with such ardor to Cortes and the cause of the whites against her own, Dona Marina, obeying revolutionary imperatives, initiated on the wings of love the future reconciliation of the races as well as, in very rudimentary form, the first feminist campaign."

Cortes immediately converted her to Catholicism and baptized her Dona Marina. Very rapidly she began to prove herself as highly intelligent as she was beautiful. Not only was she already fluent in her native Aztec and the Mayan languages, but she began to speak Spanish like a native from Seville. Her charismatic personality baffled Indian enemies scouting the Cortes camp, who would return home with awe-inspired tales of the "great mysterious force" with which she shielded the Spaniards' mission. Soon there was no message she did not personally transmit and no occasion of peacemaking when she did not stand by Cortes's side: "She sweetened the bitternesses when she translated for the negotiators. . . . This faith in her intervention as in an occult Providence leads us through the ups and downs of Diaz's chronicle. . . ."

Dona Marina's character was a forgiving one. When reunited with the mother who had once abandoned her and now kneeled trembling in anticipation of her powerful daughter's revenge, Dona Marina consoled her instead; discarded at the completion of the conquest by Cortes himself, she accepted her fate without resentment. Cortes, whose passions were "short and violent" and whose pre-Mexican youth was one of an opportunist, an adventurer, and a Don Juan, would have had little chance of success in Mexico had he relied solely on his own undisciplined arrogance to guide him. As soon as the war was over, he married a Spanish aristocrat and arranged for Dona Marina to marry one of his subordinate noblemen, to show his appreciation for her many years' loyalty. Drunk with the success of his conquest, he offended the people and profaned the sacred person of Montezuma, bringing about the sad night when Spaniards were sacrificed horribly to the god Huichilobos. Dona Marina, whose name Malinche has come to mean "one who prefers foreign ways," lived out her remaining years with a kind husband, "the memory of a great love, the rehabilitation of her power over the Indians, and her son by Cortes" (p. 699).

Parra characterized the women of the conquest—the "primitive founders"—as crucified by the "painful mixing of the races." Many a Spanish conquistador was tamed and made happy by an Indian woman; many an Indian woman suffered quietly the "Morganatic" marriage practices of the "white prince" (p. 704). Although these marriages were often superior to the slavery and hard labor of tribal life, they helped entrench the "chronic disease of Latin American society: woman's subservience to man's whim." The story of one such Indian woman, the Inca princess Nusta Isabel, has been told by her son Garcilaso de la Vega in a book titled *Los Commentarios Reales*. The sorrows of the Indian race he revealed in his mother's plight were testament to his creativity, and they earned him Parra's appellation: "The historian poet of America is a folkloric narrator" (p. 709).

Nusta Dona Isabel, a descendant of the last Inca kings, accepted in marriage the hand of Garcilaso de la Vega. Partaking liberally of her royal luxuries at the Cuzco palace, Garcilaso played at being a friend of the Indians and a prince to his princess until war broke out between Pizarro and the viceroy Nunez de Vela. With startling alacrity, Garcilaso betrayed the Indians backing the viceroy and abandoned Nusta Isabel to join Pizarro's forces. She held forth in the palace with great difficulty and mute sorrow. When Garcilaso finally returned after the hostilities were over accompanied by a Spanish noblewoman whom he planned to marry, Nusta Isabel's humiliation was complete.

Garcilaso, the mestizo poet, never forgot his mother's faithful endurance. He "seemed to go searching in the purest fountain of his mystical idealism for the compensation for such ingratitude." Parra finished her first lecture in sympathy with Garcilaso's lament (p. 709):

The *Commentaries*, said Prescott, the Anglo-American writer, are an emanation of the Indian spirit. In effect, if one listens well, under the transparency of the prose a plaint from beyond the grave appears to run with the murmur of tears. It is the echo of a maternal voice when, fixed on the stars, it told in the night the simple legends of Inca tradition. Trusting their voices for lack of writing, they became forever silenced as the last maternal accents subsided in the ears of the mestizó child. But the child, in old age and exile, had to regress to his infancy to pick up the voice of a millennium, with filial tenderness, and upon capturing it religiously in his crystalline prose he made a symbol of it. That fall of tears, like the distant rumor of the indigenous flute, is the meek cry that in the deepest of the race allows us to see our obscure and unrecognized ancestors. A sad note in minor key, it is the most genuine and delicate of all when vibrating in the tumult of our American soul. Like Garcilaso, we guard this note in Castilian without disowning anyone, blessing the harmony of union and faith in the future, and in forgiveness for the blood spilt and tears cried.

The Many Forms of Self-Abnegation during Three Hundred Years of Colonial Rule

In her second lecture, Teresa continued with her slow defusion of the charged word *feminism*. Her broad semantic application implied a refusal to accept the general notion that any feminine pursuit, whether self-confident or self-denigrating, submissive or domineering, was less consequential to the overall formation of the American spirit than masculine pursuit. Essential to women's "evolution—not revolution," then, was a heightened awareness of the impact of their actions on society and on self, without which the attainment of a feminine ideal had no chance.

For three hundred years, under Spanish rule, women were subject to the strict laws of silence and invisibility. This was a time of "old style, sentimental feminism," as Teresa said, coming to us not by way of history books, but through the oral tradition kept by every South American's grandparents. "It was a long vacation for men, and the reign, without documentation, over women" (p. 712). The colonial spirit was fraught with contradiction. In spite of independence, which "altered only exterior things, as does all revolution or brusque change, it continued to reign throughout the whole 19th Century to reach us." The revolutionary theories it nourished became its own practical enemies, and thus "it lived in contradiction with its own product." Women of this period spilled everywhere out of their narrow confines. Feigning religious vocations to escape matrimony and exhibiting fantastic displays of bravado—vengeful or idealistic—as the clubs of misfortune canceled their single chance of a full life, they were "mystics and dreamers": they were Sor Juana de la Cruz, Mother Teresa, Amarilis, Mama Panchita, and Teresa Soublette. Parra found it difficult to speak of the colony these women lived in without touching on politics. She wished to put politics rapidly aside, since the Godo and Liberal parties of the past were no longer the same, but her admiration for independence theory clearly stopped at its implementation into reality. In the stories of Mother Teresa, Mama Panchita, and Teresa Soublette, the villains were positivism, perfidy, and greed, administered to nuns, Godos, and Liberals in equal measure by the revolutionary government (p. 715): "The Federal party of the 19th Century lacked all poetic spirit, calling itself dynamic or progressive. Progress meant destruction."

This preindependence period was "full of enchantment" for Teresa. She took care to defend herself against the charge that she preferred the eighteenth century altogether, that she might even have preferred to have been born then: "No. My love for the colonial period is not nostalgic." Anyone who has followed her letters might raise an eyebrow at this declaration, knowing how often she expressed disparagement about the present and wistfulness about the past in them; this is yet another manifestation of the culture clash representing her greatest obstacle to personal integration. The alternately seductive and repellent "colonial spirit" generated a state of crippling betweenness, where she stood constantly in need of pronouncing the past either a condition of divine innocence or debilitating ignorance. This frustration, the lostness, was in itself what made Teresa such a prototype of her native culture in modern times. Claiming to feel "very good in my own epoch" and free to scan the horizons of the past as if from a "well-ventilated lookout," she admired its valiance, restlessness, intelligence, generosity, and above all, its tolerance (p. 712): "It knows how to erase from our passage the small sentimental tragedies and it has liberated us from many great terrors. . . ." Besides, "who among us has not lived a little in the Colony, thanks to that friend, relative or old servant miraculously unadapted to the present?"

Unfortunately, the breezes of the modern epoch had also brought with them whole new opportunities to shoulder guilt. Teresa's moral code predicated purity of intention and an idealistic motivation. Her self-criticism was the compulsive vigilance of those who practice what they preach—in her case, the obliteration of hypocrisy. Some terrible burden or memory of guilt surrounded the genesis of *Ifigenia* still, such that

Teresa was plagued with feelings of insubstantiality and the fear of having conned the world. Perhaps she called her demons the ghosts of her ancestors; to us they sound strikingly similar to the symptoms of contemporary stardom. Teresa stated with a frank confidence that all her childhood was colonial and the necessity of reacting against it in an age when all were revolutionaries, as much for a spirit of justice as for one of petulance, was the cause for her impulse to write (p. 713).

In the colony, women seeking a broader arena for talents unrelated to childbearing and housekeeping discovered it in the convents, which up until Guzman Blanco closed them down in 1872, had earned major influence and a central position in the daily life of the society. Gaiety and good humor in the indolent tropics (that "enemy of reserve") poured into and out of the convent walls in great style. Gifts and elaborate messages were exchanged between the Spanish nobility and nuns; there were discussions on theology and discussions on everything else affecting colonial life. This state of affairs troubled the more austere church officials from Spain, who finally drew the line when an investigation brought to light an apparently scandalous ratio of Negro slaves to nuns: five or six to one was average, and one convent even boasted a staggering 500 servants in all. But so popular a haven were the convents and so supportive was the population of nuns that the Spaniards lost the public dispute they had aroused: the slaves were allowed to stay. Parra learned the full story of convent life from an old nun named Mother Teresa, whom she had visited regularly as a child. Mother Teresa was a survivor of the positivists' "cruel dispersion," and "to visit her was like visiting another country and like passing from one century to another." When a nun took her vows, she presented her Negro slave with papers of liberty (p. 717): "The voluntary enslavement of the free one freed in turn the slave." Once in the custody of the convent, these ex-slaves were given educations and permitted to exercise their "jovial" African adaptations of Christianity. Mother Teresa, also seeking greater liberty, entered the convent mainly to live among books (p. 719):

> The woman who turned herself over to scholarship was a phenomenon who remained in the margin of life. This prejudice was fixed in the souls of men and is still strongly alive today. In order to excuse themselves for entering the world of books it was necessary to cajole them by writing about love themes. "A woman who knows Latin will have a bad end," it was said then and is still said today. Contempt for the loquacious woman changed to an excessive ad-

162

miration that contained more curiosity than affection. Incomprehension and condescension oppressed a delicate soul. In the convent, on the other hand, it was possible to live with impunity among silence and books.

The prototype of the intellectual mystic who abounded in the colonial convents was Sor Juana de la Cruz of Mexico. Had she been born in France instead of in Mexico, she could have been one of the most "brilliant literary geniuses and one of the most seductive women of the court of Louis XIV." Like Mother Teresa, Sor Juana did not appear to have a genuine religious calling. She probably fled society for the peace of the convents, where she could enjoy the greater part of her person: her "feminine intellect." By the age of twenty, she had proven herself the most "comprehensive female genius that ever existed."

> Pretty, ingenuous, passionate and full of life, she possessed every talent. Besides being a poetic genius, she was a musician, painter, grand humanitarian, and a scholar of the natural sciences.
>
> (p. 719)

Sor Juana's fame spread as far as Madrid when a tribunal of forty well-known theologians, doctors, and scholars answered the challenge of Juana's sponsor, the viceroy of Mexico, to outwit the nineteen-year-old prodigy with questions that would reveal whether her knowledge was "acquired or artificial." Teresa imagined that Sor Juana "must have used irony whenever her memory failed her" to defeat them, inspired as she must have been by the absurd spectacle of such a "waterfall of erudition" falling upon her. But she felt no joy in her triumph. Suddenly, Teresa speculated, because with "superior souls' victory harbors at times a sadness keener than the pain of defeat," Juana de Asbaje, as she was originally named, retired to the convent to become one of the colony's greatest poets. Surprisingly, Teresa left untold some of the most interesting and relevant aspects of Sor Juana's career in the convent. Far from living a quiet and humble life, she increased her reputation and activities in the convent to the extent that visitors arrived from all over the world to enjoy the benefits of her learning and talents. When her church superiors noticed the greater devotion she showed to these activities than to humble religious contemplation, they censured her. She became contrite and uncharacteristically quiet. Five years later, when only in her forties, she died.

Even more outcast than the nuns without vocations were the blue-blooded Mantuanas: "undefined mystics who lacked vocations for either the convent or marriage." These forebears of Teresa's race and class were known for their beauty, charm, and hospitality, yet they often were deceived by their first lovers and therefore stayed "at the margin of life" (p. 728). Donating themselves most fiercely to the service of their relatives' families, they spent the rest of their lives in dependent spinsterhood. As an example of this type of undefined mystic, Teresa presented the poet Amarilis, who was only assumed to have been a Mantuana. According to Amarilis's writings, her ancestors were "conquistadors and founders of the city in which she lived," but beyond that, nobody knew anything definite about her, neither her full name nor her origin. She "passed like a shadow through colonial literature" without leaving more than one letter for posterity; this she wrote to the great Spanish poet Lope de Vega. For that one feat she is studied as a major poet in all the Spanish-speaking countries. Perhaps she was born in Colombia or perhaps in Peru, at the beginning of the seventeenth century, and probably she was raised in Santa Fe y Bogota. Her letter contained a confession of her love for Lope de Vega in verse, infused with "her life, and the life surrounding her that she loved." Her verse, much of which Teresa quoted, betrayed her "lyrical soul," as well as the same thirst for self-abnegation and liability of which she spoke before, which represented such a denigration and incomprehension of the feminine ideal (p. 730). Amarilis knew there was no chance of being accepted by Lope de Vega. She had never been successful at love, and by choosing a man whom she would never see or touch, she could relish her love in the ideal: unrequited love was of all loves the most exalted and pure. All that she begged him to do was write her a poem about her beloved saint (p. 731). Lope de Vega, "charmed and moved" by her appeal, responded in kind. But there was no address to which he could mail his letter, and so he carefully placed both letters side by side in a book, where they were later discovered. The famous nineteenth-century Spaniard and literary critic Menendez-Pelayo brought the letters to popular academic attention when he noted with great surprise that Amaralis's poetry revealed greater skill and a fresher style than that of the great Lope de Vega. Such stunning proof of the folly of self-denigration made all the more lamentable the colonial women's custom of "giving themselves to men as a way out of their repression and boredom." "How many Amarilises have come and gone since then, watching life pass them by from behind Venetian blinds?"

These most obscure and unrecognized feminine ancestors, the undefined mystics, had a profound spokeswoman in the mysterious Amarilis, whose single letter mailed outward like an arrow shot in the dark carried their voice to its most plaintive note. By examining Amarilis's individual case, Teresa shone brilliant light on the whole of Latin American womanhood's approach to life, called mysticism. It was, as she had said through Pancho in *Ifigenia*, not a mysticism in the strict sense of the word, but an unshakable belief in submission to two gods: church and the male. From Sor Juana, the genius who approached God in a convent with her intellect, down to Amarilis, who approached God in the person of Lope de Vega with her love, Teresa continued to trace the outline of a powerful and pervasive doctrine in its various levels of interpretation. The message of *Ifigenia* still rings clear in this last example; it is the chilling paradox of a valid and humbly applied belief become invalid as it is pushed to hard ideology. The practice of "submission and universal fidelity, eternal law of the strongest," said Teresa in her first lecture, turns to a "certain chronic illness" when its tenets of self-sacrifice and renunciation of worldly things are translated to mean perverse self-flagellation, the willful narrowing of consciousness, and, ultimately, an unbreakable cycle of social and economic inferiority.

Teresa digressed a little to tell her last two stories. The women were her own relatives, they belonged in fact to the Independence era, and instead of being mystics, they were "dreamers." No doubt this part of the lecture enjoyed great popularity. General Soublette, the man who wanted to "rule Utopia," had been the very first president of Gran Colombia; Parra could count on raising plenty of hackles by discussing his spinster daughter Teresa, the "extreme patriot," and Dona Francisca de Tovar, the "hardened royalist," in the same breath. Although these two Mantuanas stood at opposite political poles, the colonial spirit infused their souls in equal measure: they both lived lives of dependence and frustration. All political labels became secondary as Parra told of how her great-great-aunt and her great-grandmother impressed the bitterness of their losses and unrealized dreams on her childhood experience. Mama Panchita lost her livelihood when her Spanish husband's fortune was expropriated, and Teresa Soublette lost her honor when her father was exiled and his name blacklisted. Neither woman was able to adapt to the changed world around her or to forget the injustice by which she felt she had been robbed. Mama Panchita raged defiantly until the very end, her life poisoned with hatred of poverty and hatred of Bolívar: "Poor princess persecuted by adversity, to her Bolívar was the ogre."[43] Teresa Soublette yearned still for that utopia where her father would never have suffered dishonor. Her deepest wounds had come at the hands of the Venezuelan government, which published a version of the O'Leary memoirs with all references to the bravery and loyalty of Carlos Soublette censored. From her Caracas home, Teresa Soublette cultivated a fantasy about the flawless superiority of all things Colombian and festered in permanent discontent with the perceived shortcomings of her own environment. To a certain extent, the fanaticism of both women was founded on a truth. Parra distilled from the examples of their "heroic," if somewhat self-induced, suffering the wisdom that one must live a life of modest means, dependent on no one and on nothing foreign. If one wishes to create a work of art or of usefulness, one must, from time to time, dine at one's own "Creole table, surrounded by the ambient air, tradition, and the countryside" (p. 739).

Love and Revolution in Idealistic Times

Teresa's imagination was totally alive with the colony. For a while, she transgressed into the postindependence period to demonstrate the tenaciousness of the colonial spirit dwelling in her own forebears. In Lecture Three, she backtracked again to the preindependence days, when the thirst for self-abnegation in some Mantuanas gave way to the thirst for revolution in others. A great schism in their faith had prepared their hearts to turn against the king and his instruments of power, the governors and the priests. The voluptuous tropical indolence that provided such an ideal background for Teresa's own sensual meditations, a colonial-style "need to dream that fed itself on distant ideals and hoped for the arrival of something uncertain in the swaying of a hammock" (p. 712), became troubled when that uncertain something slowly materialized. Mainstream women who had once been "tame idealists, mothers of families, molding the character of society from within their houses" (p. 716), owed their unconditional piety largely to the expert direction of the Jesuit priests. Those skillful "managers of the conscience . . . powerful by their wealth and influence, ruled absolutely in the realm of souls, especially in the realm of feminine souls" (p. 745). But Spain banished the Jesuit order from the South American continent in 1767, out of intolerance for its utopian experiments and general nonconformism. The outraged and loyal feminine population, in whom the Jesuits had inculcated the idea of an inseparable God, fatherland, and king, experienced an "anarchy from the discord spreading through their consciences" as the trinity dissolved and consequently the obligation to submit to the resented Spanish authority. The complicitous priests from other orders never succeeded in attracting the undivided loyalty of the Jesuits' abandoned flock. In place of the old rigid trinity, a new form of "complacent and half-pagan Catholicism" developed freely, a fact that, Teresa assured her listeners, "was not my invention."

> Cut off from its source, religion suffered the same transformation as had the race: it also became Creole. . . . The heat of flames from Hell diminished into a kind of tropical heat, oppressive but bearable with a little patience, rest and conversation. Mortal sin became a vague abstraction and the terrible God of the Inquisition changed into a kind of master of the plantation . . . even to the point of providing for and presiding over [the slaves'] dances. . . . During the Holy Week, the blessed images, the rosary and the mass continued to occupy their same positions but without councils, theology or Latin. The Creoles resolved on their own the arduous problems of casuistry and developed in a short time their personal creed. Into it entered—like Peter into his house—the protection and teaching of the works of Montesquieu, Voltaire, Rousseau, and other French encyclopedists.
>
> (p. 745)

The Mantuanas of the Independence period were "inspirers and performers." Whereas before they had martyred themselves to social harmony, now they unleashed their wrath against the representatives of Spanish rule who were disrupting that harmony with insults calculated to dishonor the proud Mantuan caste. "Flag-bearers of the resentment," the Mantuanas hid "souls of fire beneath languid manners," and they were ready for "all extremes, all sacrifices, and all feats of heroism." They encouraged and fomented and assisted the revolution in their own living rooms, where all the secret meetings took place. There, behind closed doors, they relinquished their customary silence in favor of expressing themselves vehemently to their menfolk.

Parra's third lecture differs measurably from the first two. The benefit of the extra attention she gave to it in Havana because of its importance as the seed of her future book can be seen in a more cohesive demonstration of her new approach to the art of writing. The prose is newly lean and creates dramatic tension through detail. Her general sketch of the predominant female psyche during independence emerges alongside the colony's gradual dissipation, within which course the star of Simon Bolívar rose and fell. It is an outline decided by Bolívar, product of Teresa's favorite era and embodiment of tragic idealism, and colored with the splashes of women enjoying the greater liberties of wartime (an underlying theme reminiscent of Uncle Pancho's much-contended dinner-table talk). This is how Teresa set the tone of her lecture:

> Before trying to locate the decisive and half-hidden influence that women came to have in the Revolution—or the War of Independence—I invite you to imagine the era. Let us watch it go by for a moment, as if on a cinematic screen. In this way the outward image will reflect more vividly the spirit of what is happening. Let us imagine any street in any one of our colonial cities—they are all so similar! The last years of the 18th Century are running their course. It is twilight. . . . Here comes a Mantuano. He is young. He approaches swiftly. His shoes click as the thick folds of his velvet coat sway with the motion of his steps. He, too, is going to have chocolate with Senor Marques. He is wearing a white wig, a silk jacket. . . . His pockets are stuffed with books. He keeps them hidden so the civil authorities, or the delegates of the Inquisition, should not discover them. One of the books, the most dangerous and therefore most anxiously awaited, is a pamphlet called "Declaration of the Rights of Man."
>
> (pp. 741–42)

Needless to say, Parra did not bother discussing any salient military details of the revolution itself. Lacking in time, neither was she able to discuss more extensively Bolívar's political vision. Briefly, her choice of historical trends touched on the following. The Creoles were betrayed and alienated from Spanish rule through continual offenses to their honor and their sovereignty over the land; these offenses were exacerbated in the women's minds by the expulsion of the Jesuits. The stronghold of feminine piety relaxed, and the motto became: "I believe in God, and the Saints, but not in the priests." French thinkers such as Montesquieu, avidly following the Jesuit sociological experiments, became more immediately identified with the liberation movement as a result of the expulsion. The infusion of Enlightenment philosophy increased as Creole students returned home from places of higher learning in Lima, Bogota, and Mexico, bearing news of current trends from France and the United States. The books were banned by Spanish authorities. It became an upper-class "sport to pass around these prohibited books." Teresa did not wish to attempt an "apology of the type of heroine such as Pola Salavarrieta who knew how to fight together with men and to die by bullets with bravery and dignity." History and a growing patriotism would continue to extol those well-known names. Since the dissemination and concealment of the books fell largely into women's hands, Teresa said, "To the anonymous women, those admirable women of indirect action, I would like to render my words of sympathy and love that their memory deserves" (p. 748). The women in Bolívar's life belonged also to this group. Teresa introduced the most picturesque of them as they entered his life in their turn. By influencing Bolívar they influenced —indirectly—the revolution.

Simon Bolívar together with his several guides and lovers were truly people after Teresa's own heart. Unconventional and passionate in the extreme, they lived willful lives guided by ideals; though they succeeded in penetrating mainstream society, their visits were short and inconsistently welcome. Teresa reflected longest, after Bolívar, on the lives of his soulmates Simon Rodriguez and Manuela Saenz. But also she gives due credit to Bolívar's governess, Matea; his first love and wife, Teresa del Toro; and his noble mentor Fany du Villars, for their timely influence at critical stages (p. 748): "A great lover as he himself confides, only the women for whom he felt passion were able to influence his taste, his character, and his decisions. . . . From his governess, the black woman Matea, to Manuelita Saenz, his last lover, Bolívar was not able to move through life without the image of a woman to inspire him, to console him in his great moments of melancholy, and to lend him her eyes with which he could recognize his genius."

Simon Rodriguez, unlike any of the individual women, exerted a lifelong influence on his onetime pupil. It was his "extravagant idealism" that lent the Liberator's genius "fire and wings" (p. 750).

> The portrayal of Rodriguez is always necessary insofar as it calls forth the group of women inspirers. It must preside over them. This Simon Rodriguez is the prototype of those men who fall just short of genius and remain merely crazy, to the torment of their supporters and the merriment of all those who know them both first-hand and from a distance. Wild philosophers in the manner of St. Simon, generous, paradoxical and original, these madmen nevertheless are the salt of life. They redeem humanity from its greed and egotism, which are the vices of sanity. His unquiet spirit knew

how to find new aspects to the most common things, and his presence was always accompanied by comic and unforeseen happenings. It was natural, then, that Bolívar; a level-headed genius, should fraternize so much with his namesake and professor, Rodriguez, who was the brilliant lunatic par excellence. . . ."

(p. 751)

Simon Rodriguez was born and raised in Caracas. At an early age, he caught a ship to Cadiz, Spain, and he wandered across Europe for the next five years. Finally, in Paris at the eve of the French Revolution, he discovered the teachings of Rousseau; these became his consuming and lifetime passion, such that he was infected with the desire to proselytize the "love and nature" philosophy in some distant land. He returned to Caracas, married, and had two daughters, whom he named Corn and Tulip. Then he wrote a book, which earned him the credential of respectability he needed to lure a disciple to parallel Rousseau's Emil. Into this niche walked the wealthy orphan Simon Bolívar.

Bolívar entered into Rodriguez's unorthodox tutelage fresh from the loving custody of his family governess, Matea (p. 750): "It is in the arms of Matea where Bolívar heard and saw for the first time the deep poetry of rural life which is the Fatherland." On Bolívar's family estate in the Venezuelan valley of Aragua, where Matea was one of the slaves, she would allow him to sit with her on the slaves' patio after a day's work and listen to old Negro tales of ghosts and mystery (p. 750):

The tales almost always used the horrible crimes of the tyrant Aguirre as their theme, that rebel conquerer and bandit whose penitent soul still roves around in the form of a light—small, yet flickering on and off more brightly even than the fireflies. It is a travelling light. At some times it appears in the valleys, at others it rises to the top of an immense tree visible in the distance from the plantation and called "El Saman de Guere." Thirty years later . . . in an historical night, Bolívar had to camp with his army under that legendary tree of his youth, which still harbors the soul of the conquistador, in penitence and in sin, in its foliage.

Rodriguez in his turn taught Bolívar the life of natural freedom, at the cost of any useful skills outside of physical endurance, so that Bolívar's earliest known letter was full of spelling errors. Together they left their families in Venezuela, when Bolívar was sixteen years old, to

170

live in Madrid. When Rodriguez's political involvements caused the Spaniards to expel him from the country, he was forced to abandon his disciple and his mission to convert humanity and turned his talents instead into being a "botanist, philosopher, physicist, teacher, and businessman as the occasion required." Bolívar continued to live with his guardian relatives at the royal court of Madrid, where he suffered all the abuses given to a provincial outsider and an adolescent. Friction began to grow between him—the solitary Creole—and his Spanish hosts; this was becoming unbearably abrasive just as Teresa del Toro entered his life. A major cause of this friction, and one that Teresa pointed out occurred frequently between Creole and Spaniard, was their conflicting taste in dress. She cited several historical examples of discrimination in which the Spanish court sentenced Creole defendants to unjust punishments because they wore their bright "plumage" during their trials. This offended the austere tastes of the king. Eventually, a law was created that condemned outright the wearing of fancy or colorful dress.

Simon Bolívar, at a tempestuous nineteen years of age, was deeply in love with the daughter of Bernardo del Toro, a wealthy caraqueno. At the same time, Bolívar stood in danger of imprisonment for resisting arrest by a policeman who had noticed lace on his wrist cuffs. His friends and relatives counseled him to leave: "He said goodbye to the black melancholy of Madrid. His sole preoccupation was Maria Teresa. All the fire of his genius and his radical temperament concentrated on she who was now his fiancée. It was great passion." Bolívar's single dream to live happily ever after with his new bride on the Venezuelan hacienda came true for only eight months after their wedding. Parra quoted (p. 757): "As the old song goes, 'dreams of love last a day; pains of love last a lifetime.'" Teresa del Toro died of a devastating fever; it was a "new explosion in Bolívar's soul."

> Teresa's death brought him such despair that where once he had wanted to fill the world with his passion, now he wanted to fill it with his anguish. In his frenzy he didn't know what to do. He returned to Spain, in hopes of reliving memories of Maria Teresa at her family's house.
>
> (p. 757)

There was no respite and no consolation for Bolívar's despair. Soon the image of his old "crazy mentor" Rodriguez began appearing in his mind. It spurred in him a glimmer of hope that he felt compelled to follow: "Yes, only Rodriguez, the sublime, the visionary, would be capable of understanding him." A long search throughout Europe unearthed Rodriguez in Vienna, living under the new name of Robinson, which he had assumed in honor of Robinson Crusoe. Wholly absorbed in his current laboratory activities, Rodriguez remained impassive at the spectacle of Bolívar in emotional, spiritual, and now physical misery. At Rodriguez's house Bolívar lay dying of consumption (p. 759):

> "One night," Bolívar wrote to Fany years later, "Rodriguez came to sit down at my bedside. He spoke to me with that affectionate goodness that he had always shown me in the gravest circumstances of my life. He reprimanded me tenderly and made me recognize that it was madness to abandon myself and to seek death only half-way into my life. He made me understand that in the life of a man other things besides the love of a woman exist and that I could be very happy dedicating myself to the sciences or turning myself over to ambition."

A divine stroke of luck befell Bolívar at this point. " 'Oh! Rodriguez! I prefer to die!' And I gave him my hand to beg him to allow me to die quietly. . . . 'I could doubtless return to life and throw myself into brilliant missions, but for this I would have to be rich. . . . I am poor, I am sick, I am worn out!' " Suddenly, "4 millions" of money appeared out of nowhere, supposedly inherited from an uncle and entrusted to Rodriguez. Thus encouraged in his willpower, Bolívar recovered from his illness and went straight to Paris, where his cousin Fany du Villars took him under her wing: "The time could not have been better for Bolívar, the prototype of the romantic hero par excellence."

Fany's love was "temperate and happy." It was the love of a "counselor and guide." Struck by his grandiloquence and his premature sadness, she went about banishing the torment of his lost dream. The "pain in his soul" from Teresa del Toro's death could not be touched, but the ambition of—maybe—having become the mayor of the town near his plantation could. Fany opened his eyes to his great potential; his imagination she made receptive to the best minds of the century (p. 761). "In Paris Fany had one of the most elegant salons of the Consulado era. It was the period of Chateaubriand, Eugene de Beauharnais, Madame Recamier of Talma, Madame de Stael, Humboldt and Talleyrand. All these people went to Fany's salon, she the lovely Creole Parisienne. They all encouraged and celebrated her.

"After he had been the Emil of Rousseau, thanks to Rodriguez, now he was going to become the Rene of Chateaubriand, thanks to Fany." On the surface, Bolívar was a changed man. He embraced Paris life totally, and Paris honored him in return. He gambled, loved, and engaged in discourse. But "success, admiration and honor" were not enough for him. His sadness continued. Luxury, praise, and pleasure left him profoundly bored. He made frequent journeys to distract himself, returned to Paris, and did nothing. Sounding almost like Teresa de la Parra, he wrote to Fany from London about his unsatisfied soul, about the vacuum of the present left by his beloved dead wife and the torment of a "vague uncertitude." Fany, with perfect instinct, steered him into a friendship with Baron von Humboldt. Fany had awakened the baron to Simon's charismatic genius; Humboldt now proceeded to rekindle in him the love for his native South America. Humboldt was a world geographer and natural scientist of revolutionary stature, who spoke with "indescribable enthusiasm" about the undiscovered wealth of the continent and the necessity of its gaining freedom from Spain: "I see the work ahead but I cannot see the man capable of accomplishing it." With the memory of Napoleon's Apotheosis still alive in his mind, Bolívar, terribly ambitious at twenty years of age, kept silent, but answered to himself, *I shall be that man* (p. 763). He decided to leave Paris and did so with Fany's blessing. Once again he looked up the elusive Rodriguez (p. 753): "In Rome, in 1805, one afternoon, one of those marvelous Roman afternoons before sundown, the two men reached a point of exultation as they spoke on the Sacre Monto, such that Bolívar was transfigured, and in a kind of romantic delirium he took the city of Rome and the sun as his witnesses and made his famous oath to liberate Spanish America."

This was the man Manuela Saenz fell in love with seventeen years later as he rode victorious into Quito, Ecuador. Ten years of fighting and many lovers had brought him to a peak in his fame and glory. Women especially "loved him as a God." At one point he had led a mass of forty thousand women and children on foot across Venezuela to escape the Spaniards. While he was attending a ball, a favorite Bolívar pastime, which usually succeeded a long hard day of battle, Dona Manuelita captured first his eye and then his heart. She may have been capable of the feats of Pola Salavarrieta's type of heroine, but she practiced her soldiery all in the name of love.

The figure of Dona Manuelita is extremely interesting, not only because of its picturesque side but because it represents—if we analyze it correctly—a violent protest against the traditional servitude of women to whom the only future is the not-always-open door of marriage. A woman of action, she would not suffer either the deceit or the comedy of false love. A daughter of the revolution, she had heard no language but that of the truth and that of everyone's right to self-defense. She was a woman *apres guerre* of Independence. She preached her crusade by example, without wasting time or leaving followers.

(p. 765)

Teresa's vision of Bolívar's staunch lover and soulmate Manuela gathered potency during the course of her lecture travels through Colombia, when she pointedly stopped at the locations where the fated lovers' lots were cast. The vision, first fired by admiration, became a natural extension of Teresa's own self in another place and age. On June 16, with the seventh rerun of her lectures now done, Teresa visited the Quinta Bolívar, the house on the outskirts of Bogota where Bolívar and Manuelita had lived during his tumultuous dictatorship of Gran Colombia before the forces of his enemy, Vice-president Santander, gained ascendancy. An accompanying reporter described Teresa—cheerful and clicking away shots of her friends with her Kodak—as suddenly made:

. . . visibly emotional and awed by the solemn austerity of the locations. Teresa walked from one room to the other followed by the distinguished entourage of ladies and gentlemen. Slowly she examined the old furniture and disused objects. . . . On the balcony and in the dried-up pond, the ghost of Manuelita Saenz came to greet us. . . . From that balcony the "lovable lunatic" must have explored many times the panorama of towers and rooves of the enemy city, whose popular pamphlets and jeering songs had wounded her. And in that pool she—accustomed to living freely—submerged many times her rosy body like a pagan goddess, dismissing as prejudices every moral and religious consideration. . . . On the balcony I heard Teresa voice her first comment: ". . . In Italy, where I have just come from, I visited many mansions of illustrious men of the past, but in none of these did I feel the impression I am feeling here. Here, in this house and its surroundings, there is a refined and fond . . . melancholy."[44]

From Bogota Teresa traveled to the city of Medellin, whose resemblance to Caracas infused her mind with powerful childhood memories. Farther north, in Cartagena, she requested a special airplane to take her to Bolívar's place of death, a villa called San Pedro Alejandrino just outside Santa Marta. Just before she boarded the plane, one of those startling little coincidences that crystallize our moments of existence happened to Teresa. Two separate communications from Vicente Lecuna that had been forwarded to her from Bogota and Medellin were placed simultaneously into her hands she stood on the runway. She wrote Lecuna the following paragraph, describing her thrill at the synchronous timing of these significant events and at the experience that ensued:

What they gave me there [San Pedro Alejandrino] was a touching demonstration, not of what might represent my personal triumph, which inhibits me a little, but because—it appeared to me and I believe it was so—they saw in me a live representation of the memory of Caracas at Independence and the memory of Bolívar: not the magnificent ruler but the other, the dispossessed invalid, sad and in pain of disillusionment, who was dying in the poor little house. I can say without exaggeration that I "saw" him enter the house in spite of the many people threatening to dispel the vision. I was touched by details like the following, which only I felt: at the entrance to the house an old woman with white hair offered me a bouquet of flowers and was introduced to me [*Doña Manuelita*, Teresa thought] . . . (I don't remember the surname, I didn't hear it well) ". . . Permit me, Señora, to embrace you in the name of Bolívar." It made me weep, but nobody took note of the coincidence, not even she. In the room hung the painting of his wedding with Teresa, which is the portrait of my sister Elia. Under the trees I read underfoot a fragment from one of my lectures. . . .[45]

Teresa had additional cause to feel aligned with Manuela Saenz now; a new tinge of scandal by association colored her departure from Bogota. Her friend the ambassador Alcides Arguedas speculated about the "wide gulf" between reactions to her arrival and her departure; "Where were all the people who had come to greet her?"[46] Anonymous fliers had been circulating the city. Some people attributed them to the Jesuits; others blamed a "diligent writer" whom the public called Ifigenio. Arguedas felt that thanks to her timely departure, she had avoided the blow of a much larger public disenchantment as the substance of her lecture sank in, without giving due consideration to the possibility that many Bogotans were simply not aware of the time of her departure. According to *El Tiempo*, there had been a misunderstanding about whether she would merely attend or speak at a cultural function at the Teatro Colon and invitations to another speech had been sent out. Teresa, who had agreed only to attend the former function, was absent from both events and—the newspaper reported—had already left town the day before. Furthermore, Teresa herself registered neither comment nor complaint about the lack of fans present to wave her good-bye, thus allowing the deduction that it could just as well have been her own desire to slip away quietly. Arguedas reflected on another peculiarity of Teresa's visit, which—if accurate—might have called forth images to her mind of Manuela's life in Bogota. While the Colombian men were plying Teresa with compliments and flowers, the women were cool and observed her with a critical eye. Two remarkable photographs appeared in *El Tiempo* showing Teresa completely surrounded—in the one—by a group of all men and—in the other—by a group of all women. Did they attend her lectures in segregated groups as well? Arguedas claimed that only once the women heard her speak did they allow themselves to be won over by Teresa's charm and erudition. Manuela, whom Teresa tells us was revered by Colombian society as Bolívar's legitimate wife, also experienced a wariness on the part of Colombian women (p. 767). "But this did not alarm her. She believed women's conversation to be less interesting on the whole than men's."

The last part of Lecture Three focuses exclusively on Manuela Saenz and singles out her most extravagant capers for praise. Through these anecdotes, Teresa reveals the degree to which Manuela was willing to go to protect her lover—the revealed capacity for both feeling and action placing her soundly in Teresa's gallery of ardent souls. At the age of twenty-five, when she first met a Bolívar nearing forty, Manuelita cut an engaging figure. Brave and adept with both sword and pistol, she would ride her horse "dressed like a man with red trousers fringed with black velvet and her curly hair falling to her shoulders, above it a small hat with feathers" (p. 766). Always her two wild black servant women, Natan and Jonatas, rode by her side. Manuelita's eyes were black and brilliant, her skin milky white, her figure shapely, and her height moderate, and "she was always right."

Bolívar had many enemies, of whom he could not possibly keep track. Manuela in her passion enlarged her role to include that of being his chief protectress. "The Liberator's Liberator," Bolívar called her proudly, and she saved his life two separate times. During his many necessary absences from the Quinta Bolívar, she would hold down the fort to the point of aggressively seeking out his enemies. Some of her uninhibited acts of revenge went so far as to cause Bolívar damage to his reputation. Once, in order to publicize the treachery of Vice-President Santander, currently governing in Bolívar's absence, she staged a huge party to which she invited many guests from high society. The scandal began when Manuela raised a clownlike effigy of Santander she had made herself and had it shot to pieces: "After the shooting they danced until early morning." Bolívar was forced to placate the public with a letter criticizing Manuela and shrugging off her act as that of a "silly but charming madwoman." By the same post, he then condoned the affair and reaffirmed his love by telling her she was the "most gracious and sympathetic woman I have ever known."

On another occasion for revenge, Manuela charged at night with Natan and Jonatas into a public plaza where grotesque effigies of herself and Bolívar—tagged Mr. Despotism and Mrs. Tyranny—were to be celebrated with fireworks. Attacking the soldiers in charge of the light display, the three women brought an embarrassing darkness to the plaza. It was a public-relations triumph. When Bolívar died, the Colombian government sought once and for all to be rid of her:

> They told her they would use force and gave her a deadline. When the day came, Dona Manuelita declared herself ill and went to bed with two pistols while Natan and Jonatas, armed to the teeth, guarded the doors. When the law arrived and saw them ready to resist, they feared bloodshed and went back to deliberate with the minister and the president. After many secret conferences and much coming and going, they decided to take the two black women by surprise and to exile Dona Manuelita bed and all. Stretched out like a dead woman with her feet in front of her she left her house in bed, never to return. She always remembered the symbolic image and it brought her much honor.

(p. 769)

Manuela exiled herself in the town of Paita, Peru, where she lived out her life in poverty, "proudly bearing the title of Libertadora" and making medicinal syrups that her still-faithful servants sold to the public. "By chance," Paita was the very town that Simon Rodriguez also chose as his last home. He arrived there after Manuela, destitute after the last of his many failed ventures. In 1824, Bolívar had given him the money to found an institution in Upper Peru (now Bolivia) where he could teach "freedom, equality and happiness." On opening day, he shocked his students by introducing himself stark naked "to show the proper example of the return of man to nature," managing therewith to destroy his much-advertised school before it had even begun and to ruin his reputation forever by the immorality litigation that followed. Together in Paita, "what didn't these two old originals tell one another in their decline?" When Rodriguez died in 1854, it was Manuela who collected the funds with which to give him a decent burial.

According to Parra, Manuela remained poor by choice. She was born probably in Ecuador and supposedly of upper-class parents, and she married while very young a much older and very drab Englishman, Mr. James Thorne. It was love on his part alone. When Manuela first laid eyes on Bolívar, she fell in love with him instantly and declared it openly (p. 765): "At that time divorce did not exist. Therefore there were no lawyers, no trials, no matrimonial displays, but neither were there deceptions and games of hide-and-seek." Mr. Thorne was resigned, though society was scandalized. Even after Manuela's long dedication to Bolívar and her subsequent lonely exile, James found it in his heart to forgive her. When he died, he willed her the whole of his fortune (p. 769): "With Anglo-Saxon generosity he had absolved her, because maybe he understood her." To the people who—according to current opinion—found Parra's eulogy that Manuela "fashioned her own code of morality to which she was true and faithful until her death," paradoxical or even shocking, Parra declared, "Let him who, living in poverty, is able to give up a heritage in homage to a memory, let him throw the first stone at Dona Manuelita." This is how Teresa interpreted Manuelita's moral code:

> Born and raised in full wartime, she thought, not without certain logic, that if the Fifth Commandment "Thou Shalt Not Kill," was being attacked with impunity, then well could the indissolubility of marriage be attacked in a case such as hers. And she attacked it alone, head-on and ready for action, pistols at her belt as she used to wear them whenever someone schemed deadly plots against Bolívar or herself. Some say Dona Manuelita behaved this way because she was an atheist or a freethinker. I believe, to the contrary, that when on horseback and dressed as a man, escorted by two valiant Negresses who served also as aides-de-camp, over there in the depths of her conscience remembering the Englishman, she

defied death at the same time as she defied hell, and that is the height of heroism.

(pp. 765–66)

Teresa's portrayal of La Saenz was among the first to interpret her extramarital love for Bolívar in the context of feminine integrity, courage, and idealism.

Up until as late as 1945, "the actual factual material gleaned from her [Manuela's] known letters would not have covered two sheets of foolscap."[47] Like Teresa, Manuela died of a contagious disease (a plague of diptheria swept Paita, Peru, in 1856), and all her precious mementos, including correspondence with Bolívar that she had not yet turned over to O'Leary, were burned. The tales that carried over from the indelible impression she made on her contemporaries conformed to one of two schools: the Quito school, which gave her a "saintly nimbus," and the Caracas school, which interpreted her willful nonconformity as a sin against God. Whereas both these opposing schools and Teresa interpreted the same available legends to suit their own ends, Teresa's point of view stands closer to the truth today, in spirit if not always in fact. She credited her information to Ricardo Palma, a raconteur of the Quito school who, however well intentioned, was chiefly responsible for propagating the false legends. But those chiefly responsible for the wholesale absence of documentation on Manuela were none other than the Venezuelan authorities. After making their decision to reinstate Bolívar's image as sanctimonious patriarch and "liberator" of the people whose allegiance they sought to garner for themselves, they accordingly purged all available reading material of references to his illicit relationship with La Saenz; therefore, just as Carlos Soublette had done, so Manuela disappeared from the pages of the principal source of information about the War of Independence, the *Memoirs* of Daniel O'Leary.

Although the documentation contained in an appendix detailing Manuela's love for Bolívar was discovered and returned to the *Memoirs* in 1914, a second document known to have existed was not destined to enjoy the same fate. It was a large folio of papers titled *Correspondence and Documents Relating to Senora Manuela Saenz, Which Demonstrates the Esteem in Which She Was Held by Various People of Importance*, which disappeared mysteriously from the shelves of the National Archives.[48] Luckily, the intriguing ghost of Manuela survived her blacklisting and persisted until her tireless biographers, Vicente Lecuna and Victor Von Hagen, finally published material in 1945 and 1952 respec-

179

tively that was "rich, so varied . . . that no biography can again be written on the Liberator without using it; it dispels the legends without making new ones; it shows a Bolívar shorn of the chiton of an immortal and makes of him, as he was, a passionate human being striving after an ideal, a man of complex attitudes and, like a vast country, of vast climates and vast contradictions."[49]

This material unveiled a Manuelita of still extraordinary power and integrity. Unfortunately, Teresa had made her most defiant stand on the basis of one of the false legends: Manuelita's English husband was hardly a longsuffering, kindly cuckold, but rather a possessive and shady shipping merchant who was murdered by a gang while walking down the street with one of his two mistresses. Far from leaving Manuela his vast fortune, he left her only the exact sum of her original dowry plus interest. In spite of this, however, Manuela was not so hard as to be untouched by her husband's murder. Parra's claim that deep in her conscience, Manuela always remembered the Englishman appears to have had basis in fact. "I am very upset with the notice, which has just come to me, of the horrible assassination of my husband; while it is true that I did not live with him, I cannot take indifferently his lamentable demise."[50] But Manuelita was hardly a saint either when it came to asserting her rights. At the time she heard of the small inheritance, she was suffering from a dislocated hip in addition to severe poverty; out of Paita she made every move in her power to secure the money, but Thorne's family contested the will and thwarted her desire.

This flesh-and-blood Manuelita, with all her egocentric excesses, enjoyed nevertheless the esteem of important persons, not only that of Bolívar's best friend O'Leary, who wrote her faithfully and had her to thank for valuable portions of his Bolívar material that she had buried in Bogota before her exile, but also of Bolívar's great mentor Rodriguez, who came to Paita not "by chance" but deliberately to seek her out. Passing individuals, too, such as the Italian revolutionary Giuseppe Garibaldi, whom she nursed in a fever, and author Herman Melville, were compelled to record their short encounters with her. Melville, then an unknown sailor twenty-two years old, remembered her riding through Paita on a small gray burro, "eyeing the joint workings of the beast's armorial cross," and wrote a eulogy with which Parra would have been in accord: "Humanity, thou strong thing, I worship thee not in the laurelled victor but in the vanquished one."[51]

Notes

1. *Cartas a Rafael Carias,* April 25, 1930 (falsely dated 1927), in (Alcala de Henares, Spain), p. 52.
2. Ibid., July 14, 1925, p. 23.
3. Teresa de la Parra, *Obras Completas,* p. 897.
4. Ibid., pp. 866–69.
5. Ibid., p. 786.
6. Ibid., p. 911.
7. *Gabriela Mistral: The Poet And Her Work,* trans. Helene Masslo Anderson (New York: New York University Press, 1964), p. 54.
8. Ibid., p. 108.
9. Ibid., p. 54.
10. Ibid., p. 52.
11. "Teresa de la Parra no descifro ayer el enigma de L'accolade," *El Espectador,* May 27, 1930.
12. Teresa de la Parra, *Obras Completas,* p. 814.
13. Coral Gable, Florida, December 10, 1979.
14. "Teresa de la Parra," *Diario de la Marina,* La Habana, March 31, 1930, p. 1.
15. Coral Gable, Florida, December 10, 1979.
16. *Cartas a Rafael Carias,* p. 53.
17. Teresa de la Parra, *Obras Completas,* p. 781.
18. Ibid., p. 786.
19. Ibid., p. 782.
20. *Selected Writings of Bolívar* (New York: The Colonial Press, Inc., 1951).
21. Teresa de la Parra, *Obras Completas,* p. 868.
22. Ibid., p. 814.
23. Ibid., p. 786.
24. Ibid., p. 930.
25. *Men in Dark Times* (New York: Harcourt Brace Jovanovich, 1968), p. 105.
26. Interview with Professor Rafael Maya, who knew Parra and was among the audience during her lectures in 1930, Bogota, July 6, 1977.
27. Letter to Carias, December 3, 1927, in *Teresa de la Parra, Cartas a Rafael Carias* (Alcala de Henares, Spain: Talleres Penticarios, 1936), p. 82.
28. "Teresa de la Parra,"*El Tiempo,* Bogota, May 26, 1930, p. 5.
29. *Obras Completas,* pp. 864-865.
30. "Unos Minutos Con Teresa."
31. *El Espectador,* May 27, 1930.
32. "Unos Minutos Con Teresa," *Cromos,* May 31, 1930.
33. Teresa de la Parra, *Obras Completas,* p. 789.
34. *Obras Completas,* p. 815.
35. Carias, *Teresa de la Parra, Cartas a Rafael Carias,* p. 24.
36. "Unos Minutos Con Teresa."
37. *Obras Completas,* p. 812.
38. Guillermo Manrique-Teran, "La Conferencia de Teresa de la Parra," *El Tiempo,* Bogota, June 1, 1930.
39. Georgina Flechner, "Teresa de la Parra en el Colon," *El Tiempo,* Bogota, June 2, 1930.

40. Teresa de la Parra, *Obras Completas*, p. 788.
41. Ibid., November 29, 1930, p. 794.
42. "Thoughts about Lessing," in *Men in Dark Times*, p. 8.
43. Teresa de la Parra, *Obras Completas*, pp. 794–95.
44. "Unos Minutos Con Teresa."
45. Teresa de la Parra, *Obras Completas*, pp. 783–784.
46. *Obras Completas* (Mexico: Aguilar, Impresiones Modernas, S.A., 1959) Vol. I, p. 854.
47. Victor Von Hagen, *The Four Seasons of Manuela Saenz* (New York: Duel, Sloan and Pearce, 1952), p. 303.
48. Ibid., p. 302.
49. Ibid., p. 301.
50. Ibid., p. 289.
51. Ibid., p. 287.

CHAPTER SIX

Cruel God of Perfection
and God of Friendly Disorder

The Thirties: Parra and the World on Borrowed Time

First Teresa had aspired to shape her words to print and then to let them play before a live audience. As a craftswoman, Teresa de la Parra had always found her chief preoccupation the hypnotic cadence of the human voice trapped within sensuality of language. Before she would pick up her writing tools again, however, she would demand silence of herself, that thought and action—the idea and its realization—might bond beneath the commanding image of reality pure and simple, unshielded by pretty corpses of vain design and thus shamed into obedience to the dictates of purity. Unbeknownst to herself, she slid into the ineffable realm of consciousness where good and evil do battle in the individual—the preverbal coming to awareness by which one's material world gains utterance and in whose grip many a brave soul has become paralyzed.

Still a questioner in her serious-minded maturity and an embracer of life to the heart, Teresa discovered her precarious stand against the conventions of her upbringing required a doubling of her energies. Had she been complacent in her iconoclasm, she could have relaxed to the repetitive beat of her self-hewn dogmas, just as many people happy within convention do time and time again, if only—and one must say this with due respect—for the pleasures of surrendering themselves to the exhausting yet blissfully automatic rigors of reproducing and maintaining the corporal species. Isolated from the group yet desperate for fellowship, Teresa gained only partial sustenance from the tradition of unconventionalism itself. In her time, the term ''modern alienation''—now become a cliché—was capable of extracting fresh tears like salt on an open wound.

These were tears for the loss of the golden images that words such as *honor, home,* and *work* used to conjure up without effort. Whereas Teresa had once displayed the effects of this separation on a society refusing to admit to the hypocrisies they represented, now she wanted retribution. When the vast distance between her conscious and unconscious selves would close up, then so might the distance between meaning and words. A "wretched" philosophizer and a "great jaded one" had only one goal worth seeking: divine truth. Teresa called it the mystical ideal.

As the thirties swung into being, the simple act of getting up in the morning after listening to the news of world events on the radio required the defiant cheer of sailors heaving to on the umpteenth dawn of foul weather. Accompanying the fall of the Western economy and the rise to power of Stalin were the small yet emotionally provocative outbreaks of the Spanish revolution and the border clash between Colombia and Peru; meanwhile, the deep growl of Hitler's awakening mutation swelled up on plentiful cries of fallen honor and the dynamic fuel of fear. It had not yet dawned upon those folk, little and big, who thought they had chosen life and racial salvation by calling for order, that they were being tricked. From the pulpits of leadership were thrown slippery chains composed of the words *logic, truth,* and even *godliness,* designed to lasso into collaboration what was still wordless and shameful in its baseness, what was only half-awake in a crowd of needed followers. Fascist and communist tyrants alike made clever use of elementary dogma to tighten their grip, especially the one declaring *order* and *chaos* to be synonymous with *good* and *evil*; never before in the known history of mankind did disorder become so subservient to the forces of evil and chaos remain so pathetic a haven for the forces of good. By middecade, the end of civilization, willed halfheartedly as in a dream, seemed to be at hand and stunned lips everywhere began to broadcast, hoarsely, the coming of the antichrist.

To the war-and-ideology–saturated society of 1930, Teresa seemed a sentimental revolutionary indeed. There was more than a trace of the reactionary in her growing horror at the state of the world, for which she—as a former proponent of nonconformism and modernity—even felt partially responsible. To her it was the final, suicidal completion of positivism's course that had polluted a still fragrant, yet fragile and changing old organism, just like the oil upon which it depended, for the purpose of exalting individual greed, "egotism, and limitation." She had come so far as to relegate not only the revolutionary call of Bolshevism, but also her own youthful craving for worldly success to that lowest denomination of behavior called pompous hypocrisy. She now firmly believed that there was no hope for the alleviation of human suffering—of any kind—outside a stringent and costly adherence to the mystical ideal of universal amor or that of "postponing avarice of the moment for an eternal ideal" (p. 792).* The path of hatred and violence was easy, she told Carias. On the opposite side of the revolutionary leaf, however, she saw in veined silhouette the face of her hero, Mahatma Gandhi, the recent subject of Romain Rolland's biography (p. 868): "How beautiful and true is this doctrine of redeeming the world with love and not with violence or hate. Only because violence prosetylizes more than love, because it exalts easy and recurring emotions such as envy, bolshevism grows and no one believes in Gandhi."

Rather than to take sides in any of the conflicts, Teresa grieved over the world's accelerating insanity; though the threat of communism was doubtless one of those topics embittering the dinner talk of such a conservative family as hers, her personal sympathies found as little quarter in the Fascist rationale supporting racism as they did in communist solutions for economic parity. In 1931 she personally wrote to President Gomez "at her own risk," asking him to allow Professor Rivet—"a top ethnologist of our era"—to conduct an "urgent and noble" archaeological mission among certain Indian tribes in the Venezuelan mountains in hopes that it would hasten her countrymen's conversion from the "apathy and disdain" in which they held the Indians (p. 806). To her elation, permission was granted. This motion to help the Indians stemmed from her newly enlarged view of their cultural influence, which along with that of the blacks permeated the intimate life of the colony. She had come to realize it was indispensable to study their folklore.

Teresa enrolled in more classes at the Paris School of Ethnology and wrote every friend conceivable who might help to unearth the detail and nuance of South America's varied racial inheritance. In seeking thus to embrace her country's realities, she went so far as to express an idle wish that the Mexican philosopher Vasconcelos's theory—that a mestizo superrace might eventually arise on the continent would come true—improbable as she thought that was. In 1933 she had been trying to instruct herself on the recent ideological developments in Germany. To this effect, she read Gobineau's theories on Aryan supremacy and found them unacceptable to her as a South American. She told Zea-Uribe how she recalled the ungovernable Cochocho's fairness, immense charity,

*All page numbers in parentheses in this chapter refer to *Obras Completas*, by Teresa de la Parra (Caracas: Editorial Art, 1965).

185

and lyricism and remembered how "full of generosity, true love and caring in the purest sense" were the poor peasant Negroes of Venezuela who filled her childhood and youth (p. 838): "The Aryans are good in their role of organizing sanatoriums, armies and cities where progress reigns, but over there among those races without conscious direction, one can apprehend very profoundly the sweetness of being alive." It was ironic that her own race had played such a large role in forging those valuable character traits; to bring a comparable humility and bittersweetness to her personal life would prove a similarly cruel and relentless task.

Solitary and unencumbered, cushioned by the Virginia Woolf ideal of "500 pounds a year and a room of one's own," Teresa should have found it easy to execute her so-frequent threat to block out those myriad prickling guilts along with all the other intrusive stabs of modernity by making a fortress of her library, her friends, and the fairy-tale past. Certainly she tried to do this; her most recent and radical dream, born when she was soaking in the luxurious Colombian landscape, was to buy a small country house outside Caracas (one without the slightest pretension of calling itself a villa, as she would later describe it with the intensified imagination of the invalid) and spend the rest of her life there in peaceful communion with nature, "knowing nothing about politics" (p. 868). But the disruptions to her peace of mind had roots growing deeper than in the unstable political situation; they belonged to the face-on abrasion with society that had determined her existence from the very beginning and that would remain uncushionable and inescapable for as long as she kept true to herself. It was the full brunt of the centuries-old psyche hitting her squarely in the fourth dimension where mostly she lived.

As Teresa confronted the mountainous territory—physical, intellectual, and spiritual—yet to chart for her Bolívar project, she began to sense the inadequacy of her "unofficial," patchwork education. There was an anarchy reigning in her compulsive intellect; humble before the assemblage of ideas multiplying uncontrollably and ranging all the way from the primitive to the classical to the Oriental, Teresa was also smarting, still, from the last cries of Don Quixote. The clarity of her instinct had guided her thus far into the world of letters, but would instinct be enough for a major work of the following proportions?

In Venezuela we have lost the faith and we must all try and awaken it anew. If I bring a grain of sand to this work of regeneration I would feel satisfied thinking I will not have passed through life entirely uselessly. Up until today, I confess, I've occupied myself solely with advertising the skepticism of my generation by means of irony—in the long run, it was a destructive occupation, motivated by my desire for personal satisfaction. How vain! I want, furthermore, without changing my medium, to try and make a work of transcendent ethics, to reunite instead of disperse. I have now entered the age in which I stop being revolutionary and begin to find some mystical ideal.

(p. 792)

But was such an ambition any less vain? Deep down, she could not decide whether her project was a more pompous arrogance than she had ever dared or the deliberately chosen wheel on which to break her accursed pride.

To feel equal to her task, Teresa needed time to prepare, to be ready, to know as much as possible. The "easy success" was not her goal (p. 791): "I prefer the difficulties and the work up to destruction, but following an end that I consider a state of mystical conscience." In the ideal process of writing a book, vanity must be purged and motivations made pure; what then emerges is the perfectly logical by-product of the self's re-orientation to self, reflecting in the angle a brilliant wedge of the comprehensible universe. Teresa's work of art had become her own life. No more could she be heard defending Maria Eugenia's bitter acquiescence to social mores against the angry demands of her critics that such acquiescence be deliberate and graceful; nor could Teresa be heard decrying the "killing of thought by the herculean effort of thinking," as she had done in *Mama Blanca*. Now it was time to enforce virtue upon the character and knowledge upon the intellect. For the first time since *Ifigenia*'s publication, Teresa was "frightened and humbled" (p. 731) by something other than her fame, and her project carried extra weight now that her first forty years were spent and the second season loomed ahead, asking for direction. Maria Eugenia's dissonant song of brutal surrender was, after all, merely a variation on the symphonic theme of sacrifice and the nightmare corresponding to Teresa's dream of sweet sublimation.

Between Colombia and Cuba, the shadow of doubt seemed to fall as Teresa abruptly announced her decision to forego the necessary research in Venezuela for the meantime and to sail to Europe without delay. Somewhere between Santa Marta and Havana, an immense fatigue had beset her, caused by the blinding tropical sun and the deafening voices instructing her next book. Urgency itself, arriving from disturbing and shadowy points of origin, percolated underneath her phrases: perhaps, however, such thoughts were typical of a Teresa in the grip of indecision. A restlessness, a desire for spontaneous and drastic action, and then self-recriminations for abandoning other responsibilities dominated the letters she wrote as she waited in Havana, at least ten days longer than she had planned, until Lydia recovered from an illness that was keeping them from traveling immediately to Europe via New York. There would have been plenty of time after all to go to Venezuela—"I who did not go to Caracas out of my eagerness to get to Europe and reach the waters!" she wrote to Lecuna (p. 790). "The waters" was a health spa where Teresa and her mother were slated to have their respective liver ailments cured; these spas closed in September. Supposedly it was her only obligation in Europe, this overriding desire to "reach the waters" with Mama, and the only apparent obstacle to remaining in the Western hemisphere. She had discovered that Cuba was not a bad substitute for Venezuela: more than Venezuelan Negroes, the Cuban ones had retained an essentially colonial spirit in their cultural fabric. The seemingly logical solution of using Havana as her base of operations, maybe even Lydia's comfortable villa, from where Teresa could gain access to the "living atmosphere" as well as research materials from the continent, did not even enter into her formal debate. Having declared herself unprepared and lacking in energy to benefit from the scheduled short visit, she postponed it until "next year," subjected it to the eventuality of another major ocean crossing, and even imagined that when she finally returned, she might stay forever.

Teresa was not one to dwell on her infirmities to her friends, but she had confessed to feeling weak in Colombia in one Lecuna letter, excusing herself for a general state of mind made dissolute and frantic by the "implacable" heat of the tropical sun and the pressing of crowds around her (p. 784). An eyewitness to her Colombian lectures, Professor Rafael Maya—reported to this author that she looked pale as she spoke at the podium of the Teatro Colon in Bogota, and he remembered noticing that she coughed frequently. It is entirely possible that she was already suffering from the first mild symptoms of tuberculosis: fatigue, a slight fever, and nausea. A general if slightly heightened sense of malaise would have been easy for her to shrug off; as far back as 1929, Seida de la Torre also reported to the author that Teresa tired noticeably quickly while sightseeing in Italy, suggesting thereby that some chronic fatigue plagued her either as the result of a sedentary life or of a "bad liver." Worth noting here is that the French are often known to consider liver

Teresa de la Parra in Bogota, 1930

malfunction the cause of digestive imbalance per se, for which they universally prescribe the mineral-water cure. Contradicting this notion are the words of Maria Bunimovitch: always quick to deny anything negative said about her sister, she said that Teresa had never been the slightest bit sickly before the onset of her disease in 1932.[1]

Now more than ever, Teresa appreciated the value that evocation of place could bring to the biographer's understanding of her subject. Writing to Lecuna on July 12 from Havana, she told of her near despair at not having made the so-necessary pilgrimage to Venezuela, without which she could not even begin to write, "thinking I would return in time, not to live in the city but to make a life in the country" (p. 785). Not only did she feel too exhausted to visit Bolívar's places of historical moment in Venezuela, but she didn't feel she knew enough to do these locations justice. All the preliminary facts of official history had to be absorbed before she would feel capable of divining the true past out of the immediate detail of the present. Thus, she begged Carias to find three books for her—"as always, it is urgent for lack of time" (p. 866)—and departed the Western hemisphere for the last time, holding an image of Venezuela in her fantasies that was much changed from the real memory; now it had become the passage to the fulfillment of her most important book and the idyllic final refuge from the "vertigo, velocity and work that has invaded and rendered ugly the entire world."[2]

In the short period before her departure from Havana, Teresa kept herself busy by observing and conversing with the black servants at the villa while Lydia recuperated. Their shamanistic cosmogeny dovetailed most smoothly with the sequence of invisible phenomena linking Teresa to Bolívar and Bolívar back to them again through his slave-governess Matea, and the following incident added even more proof of Teresa's sensitivity to things invisible. She and Lydia had recently made another attempt to reach Emilia Ibarra via seance. It was, Lydia said, cryptically, "not without some results."[3] Then, late one night, Teresa woke up to a small green light at the foot of her bed. American Indians most commonly belonging to the peyote cults, as well as African immigrants, believed in the immanence of the spirit world in such lights, whose color is determined by individual perception. That Teresa's color was green—emerald-green eyes, an emerald ring to match, and the close attachment to nature symbolized by green—must have strengthened the effect of this light on her. Only a month before, she had told her Colombian audience about the spirit light of Aguirre haunting the Tree of Saman just off the land where Bolívar was raised. A person well versed in matters of the occult might tell us that the spirit world does not manifest itself on our plane for idle or frivolous reasons. At the time, Teresa drew no definite conclusions about her experience; she felt herself in the presence of Emilia, yet could not determine the message. Two years later, as Teresa lay in a sanatorium bed writing to Zea-Uribe, she elaborated on the mystery that had clearly been the subject of discussion in some previous letter (p. 820): "The luminous manifestation of which you spoke has moved me. In Beaulieu [where she first felt truly sick] I saw the light come to visit me several times. Here in my month of solitude I have searched for it often but have not seen anything. Perhaps I carry it in my soul and it consists of this infinite and sweet peace that accompanies me without cessation." But as her illness gathered momentum and she began searching her past and present for clues to her fate, the small green light must have taken on the role of a premonition. If such things can be said to exist, the spirit light was Emilia come to warn Teresa of her impending death.

Searching for the Perfect Tone

Teresa's return to Europe in early August was attended by rain and cloud. She spent the remaining weeks of summer with her family, at Mama's side in Switzerland and made no further mention of her health, sinking relieved into a life of "rest and tranquillity." By September she had begun the first book on her reading list: the much-contended, abused, and then rehabilitated *Memoirs* of her distant relative, Daniel Florencio O'Leary. Through them her devotion to Bolívar accelerated to its highest pitch, such that despite her feelings of inadequacy, she also could feel the "mystic fever that pushes us to superior enterprises . . . holding hours of happiness and enthusiasm" (p 791): She embarked on her study of official history as if beginning her second childhood, taking notes on chronology like a schoolgirl and rejoicing in the magnificent world of the colony, brimming with anecdote and detail. She had enlisted Carias as her collaborator in the only "probable" work and now awaited his shipment of books like a "child awaiting toys" (p. 793). But she had no urgency to write as yet; in November, not without a certain defensiveness, she stressed her priorities to Lecuna (p. 796): "I'm not in a hurry, and instead of reading I want to travel so that the live image will obliterate the printed word. In order to work in this way one must fight people who don't know how to respect time. I am going to defend myself however I can and, good or bad, continue to the end."

The present, the past, Venezuela and Bolívar, Teresa and the whole universe, became indistinguishable in her intertwining thoughts. As a mestizo not of race but of culture, it was as if, lassoed by antiquity and its charmed absences, she was being roped into a veritable dream—the elusive dream of divine grace that had infused the colonials in such opulent measure with their oneness, "their gilded mediocrity, and assurance of God" (p. 868). Teresa's European vantage point had conspired to drive her to this stage in the Bolívar search, both by power of its repulsions and its artistic expectations. She had always considered this awakened appreciation of Venezuela Europe's sole gift to her. Yet now, perceiving the physical distance as a barrier and the analytical coolness as a blinder to live, sensory participation, she allowed Europe the land to shelter her without giving it the slighest concession of gratitude in return. All things Creole, "that do not travel nor turn European, attract me extraordinarily these days. In them rests everything that I value,"[4] she told Carias. For as long as she actually pursued the "live" Bolívar, until around August of 1931, Teresa anticipated eagerly, yet postponed regularly, her journey homeward:

In February:
I wish, circumstances permitting, to make the Bolívar voyage as slowly as possible—that is, to go through the interior of all five republics.

(p. 798)

In April:
I have . . . almost a hunger to travel very slowly through the tropics, by horse, on foot. . . . I want to travel like the pilgrims and the soldiers.

(p. 802)

To "reconstruct the environment" of the colony, Teresa strained to retrieve her grandmother's tales from her memory,[5] and in February she decided that courses in Indian folklore would bring the reconstruction around more effectively. So intent did she become on restoring this ambient life to all six senses that intrusions by her immediate environment angered and distracted her (p. 814). What her perfectionism demanded of immersion her capriciousness too lightly dispersed. All things external that tempted the impulsive Teresa became enemies to Teresa the deadly absolutist, who resented chiefly their representation of the very materialistic bustle that had so despoiled her mystically saturated colony. It was a mechanical present whose repetitive surges had become passé as soon as the second stroke was done; moreover, its fate had been decided long ago by the eighteenth-century twist of idea and event. Like a time-machine traveler hoping to reverse the course of that fate, she was punched into the pivotal hour of Bolívar, determined to redress him and thus redress Venezuela in the modest cloak of his idealistic virtues for all future generations to emulate: truth without glory, virtues that "anyone can attain—abnegation, the spirit of sacrifice, rectitude, purity of soul" (p. 795).

It was just as great a boldness that Teresa had entered into direct debate with her ancestors as that she now competed with the academic community for those intellectual honors she had formerly shirked and shunned. But she considered herself well motivated for this task by her goodwill and caring (p. 797) and well guided by the faith whose first roots had taken hold in Colombia like antennae pushing downward into the earth-sounds of history. She hoped her long and luxurious bath in the waters of gilded mediocrity would transmute the dry exercise of recording the colonial biography to an impassioned exercise of remembering, such that biography turns to autobiography or even—in the case of remembering an entire heritage—to meta-autobiography, more accurate than the tale of dates and facts and more honest than the observance of impartiality. Teresa's plan to elevate Bolívar the idealist without endorsing independence itself, contrasting her feeling that had she to choose between those two "savage fanatics, the Catholic and the Materialist" (p. 814), she would prefer the first, bespoke the difficulty she would face in brooking her argument, for both Catholic and positivist had been responsible for creating Bolívar the legendary ogre-hero. Perhaps by way of her irony she would find the just tone that could rise above the romantic biographer's "sugar and perfume" (p. 802) as well as the vengeful Godos' hellfire and damnation. Was Teresa really prepared to sacrifice of her intimacy—as she felt Zea-Uribe had done in his book *Mirando al Misterio*—in order to effectively challenge these two? And beyond the political argument, what would her studies reveal to her about Bolívar's true personality, upon which these perhaps not-so-false legends were based? In spite of Vicente Lecuna's advice and assurance, which fell like "water on dry soil," she carried with her from Havana the persistent fear that "not one weed will appear" (785), and the dark suspicion not only that her goodwill needed assistance (i.e., from intellectual training) in the writing of such a spiritual work, but also that it lacked sufficient

193

quantity and purity. This fear, the offspring of her new resolve to control mind and motive, became a hindrance that she appeared to recognize sometimes, yet other times to blame on the outside world for its lack of unmitigated complicity. Wanting a desert, a mountain peak, or the ocean shore to gratify the demands of her solitude, Teresa strained under the forced compromise of Neuilly. So the material world, which loves to lavish revenge on those who use anything to tame it but the courteous exertions of a Zen master, became the scapegoat for her failure. By December she had "not exactly lost faith," but her eyes could no longer "see way over there" for their contamination by "external things" (814) or, since she failed to name a concrete offender, by the still irresistible specter of Paris and the incongruous life she led at her sister Isabelita's house.

Teresa spent the better part of 1930–31 in her rooms at Neuilly. Burrowing deeper into the secrets of preindependence bliss, she increased the flow of letters outward. To Carias she remained loyal and like-minded, his polite confidante and adviser; to Lecuna she played a charming yet argumentative historian-apprentice; and under Zea-Uribe's guidance, she blossomed into a vulnerable and trusting disciple, speaking with a distinct—precapitulation—Maria Eugenian flavor. In her unique style blending spontaneity and self-control, she poured out to all three her vision of the need for both national and individual redemption. Suspecting that the flesh-and-blood Teresa was prone to be all the things against which she railed, we can imagine that much of her insistent and repetitive moralizing functioned as self-discipline: not only must Venezuela be steered away from its "tropical vanity and narcissism," but she herself must strive for "inner perfection." Like one trying to squeeze her feet into a pair of shoes too small, she castigated herself for her imperfections and bound her excesses in the eccentric practice of the many disciplines and healing techniques that science and medicine brought to the 1920s. It was a private restructuring that kept her inactive on the surface and avid in her correspondence, through which she gained company in her solitude. In addition to the above-mentioned three, Zaldumbide was known to be a steady recipient of Teresa's letters, as was Mistral after 1930. The latter claimed to know Teresa better through her letters than through the off-and-on contact they enjoyed in Paris and later in Spain.[6] Lydia, too, holds onto a considerable stack of Teresa's letters from those occasions when they were separated. Thus Teresa claimed to live "happily in the shadows, with some good friends, books, life itself, and the interior world of the spirit that gives so much" (p. 804), and subtly, the magnetic pull of Bolívar became a pretense for the more diffuse and all-engulfing pull back into the shadows, not only of her privacy and of the past, but the shadows of lands, friends, and evidence of higher being, made more real by their existence uncompromised by space or time. In January 1931, Teresa reported she was ". . . continuing my tranquil life, shut up with the dead of Caracas from the last century. What agreeable company and how it moves me at times to hear them, see them, yet not speak a word for its certain devaluation of who they were."[7]

As the Parisian winter gained force, so did Teresa's doubts. She attributed her perplexing manic-depressiveness to her dwindling faith in self and seemed almost apologetic that not one weed had yet appeared. By February, the work was "still in the studying stage. . . . I have moments of enthusiasm but so many of discouragement, or lack of faith in myself" (p. 797). The material she had collected was already too voluminous for a single book, she felt, and so she had pared down her immediate task to that of writing an initial volume on Bolívar's childhood and youth; successive volumes to complete the chronological series would come "only if the project does not abandon me" (p. 799). Part of her spreading paralysis was due to the simple fact that she had always disdained mechanical working habits, a category under which her compulsive reading had never fallen. This failure to derive pleasure from regular discipline became a major drawback once she fell prey to the vicissitudes of terminal illness; it stood in the way of her muse, which needed such constancy to fulfill itself. Clearly the learning of official history had turned to a tedious exercise and her goodwill had become skittish under the dark and superior surveillance of the dead. It was during these first two months that she began to lose weight dramatically. ". . . without apparent reason. I felt an infinite moral fatigue, a great lack of appetite for life, but nothing affected me physically. Liver and stomach specialist diagnosed appendicitis and put me on a diet. I felt better" (p. 818).

By March of '31, Teresa was having trouble facing the expectancy her eager apprenticeship had fostered in Lecuna. As delicately as possible, she confessed (p. 801): "Your letters, dear Lecuna, animate me, yet they fill me with a certain dread. You expect too much of me. In any case your sincere and generous friendship, companionship, council, give me great inner joy. Your understanding of my so-called goodwill compensates for many misunderstandings and accompanies me like the presence of something noble and strong: it looks like faith." At this stage, the tuberculosis was indistinguishable from the spiritual disorder. Despite the physical odds now corralled and primed to trample her, Teresa struggled to hold onto her sense of purpose. She plodded along with her Bolívar reading and wrote Lecuna dutifully, about her latest achievements in and plans for the accumulation of her research material. On the larger points of historical causality, she voiced her characteristic themes, familiar to us and unchanged in essence from those of the lectures. Between March and April, the range and variety of her references multiplied, bearing evidence of a more extroverted search for stimulation. There were the lectures by Count Keyserling in which he not only predicted the "advent of a new mystical era" in Spanish America, but also reasoned, encouragingly, that the people's nonintellectual and emotional gift would be the agent. "Would that the prophecy come true!" Teresa wrote (p. 801).

Teresa's nationalist sentiments had never been higher, but then neither had the political situation in prewar Europe ever bode worse for foreigners. Not even a recent Caracas article she felt was designed to slight her reputation appeared to dampen her patriotic optimism; once again, it was but the tiresome and tireless hound of small-town mentality yapping at her heels. Her patriotism, though not immune to the stimulus of current political trends, was still rooted in the dubious sentiment of the exile at war with an inalienable attachment to the fatherland. The native country, so ideal yet so maddeningly uninhabitable, so beloved yet so cruel, has a conscience in its exiles; intolerant and untolerated by their compatriots, their only hope for return is the eventuality of grand-scale national reform.

By June, Teresa was fully engrossed in the study of Indian folklore as well as in the procurement of political favor for the worthy cause of the French ethnologist Dr. Rivet. She assured Lecuna that she continued to follow his direction obstinately—"though not in a straight line." Even when not reading directly about Bolívar and the colony, she felt surrounded and encompassed by its themes: "When we seek something with love we meet it everywhere, as with God." She announced her desire to read the mystics and "some poets." A biography of Tolstoy had served to console her that her discouraging battles with herself were—like his—the natural pain "inherent to every spiritual work," even though her battles were small compared to those of so great a writer. Also, she was reading "some authors who have influenced me in order to be stimulated, since at times I feel I have lost the ability to tell a story" (p. 805). Was Teresa getting ready to begin writing, or had she made a discouraging first attempt?

At the beginning of August, from La Baule, Brittany, she wrote her last letter to Lecuna that pertained to their collaboration. She was exhausted by Paris to the point of feeling "rheumatic, very prone to states of moral and physical depression," due to something she now called her "tropical heritage and the years passed there." She hinted at her fear of cancer. "Condensed D. . . ." 'a drug stimulant in vogue, which Parra recommended to Lecuna as a source of "great vitality," also was "assured" to give protection from cancer. About Bolívar she spoke these final parting words (p. 808): "Other biographies I have been reading have a bad or frivolous tone. These animate me to continue my study and try to seek the amenable and serene tone with which to write my biography of Bolívar."

The Mystery of Disease

Distance from books, proximity to nature, the green countryside of Brittany, and the beaches of southern France—Teresa's notebooks lay fallow, yet Teresa the revolutionary for restoring humid earth to mosaic patios sowed the seeds of devotion into furrows that—as always—traced the prerogatives of elegance. The striving for moral elegance before herself had become a too-graceless struggle, foundering as she was inside the schism of faith-in-self, looking as she did like a runner in quicksand; by her summer vacation 1931, she appeared to have called a halt to being dragged into any deeper depths. Rather than agonizing over her spiritual work, she turned to work directly on her spirit and called it a rebirth of faith. Not that she didn't still see the ideals of Bolívar's independence lurking in all her diversions: the colony gaining in complexity had led her to places where Bolívar's martyred personality subsisted in Christ-like echoes and where the shape and the sound of her reconstruction was emerging as the totality of the Godhead.

To this rebirth of faith, which did not as yet encompass either the Catholic church or total self-acceptance, the Colombian doctor Zea-Uribe was the "voice on the road to Damascus" (p. 816). He was a doctor, inspector of health at Baranquilla, and author and known largely for his progressive scientific experiments with telepathy, helium, and astronomy. When the figure of Vicente Lecuna faded out as Teresa's "priest of the worship of an illustrious dead person" (p. 793), that of Zea faded in as high-priest in the search for the invisible. Jesus Christ, who had made the "true Christian revolution not so much by displaying miracles as by having been born in a manger and having died together with assassins and thieves" (p. 795), outstripped Bolívar as master of the modest virtues. Transposing her needs to these figures with the ease of a butterfly alighting on sweeter flowers, Teresa revealed an unabashed craving for the nectar of her own salvation. Such a move did not make her any less a woman of her times. T.S. Eliot himself, poet of *The Waste Land*, had turned his disconsolate following upside down in the 1920s by announcing his conversion to Catholicism; Lydia and Teresa had both been greatly impressed.[8] Nor was Teresa's desire to have a guide, someone to look up to in the here and now, surprising. Her towering loneliness, made all the more striking for the crowd of family and friends surrounding her, found respite in her friendship with Zea.

The first two letters written to him were spaced widely apart: one was dated December 1930 and the other September 1931. Much unpublishable communication between the two must have gone by in the interim, upon which the intensified religiosity Teresa accredited to Zea's influence had to have been based. For Zea entered her life in the whirl of Bogota's high-society homage to her, hardly a time for soul-searching conversations, and did not win her confidence until months later, when he took it upon himself to write a public letter in defense of Teresa; once again a subject of the press, she had been publicly accused by a Colombian journalist for making some broad comment about culture that the woman, with "typical Spanish oversensitivity," took as a personal insult (p. 813). "I don't believe C.E. is of bad character. . . . Her reaction to me will pass; but her [letter], published for the purpose of misrepresentation, of spreading lies, is a vulgarity I cannot pardon." Zea's unwarranted and unsolicited show of loyalty was a rare occurrence in Teresa's life; ever since *Ifigenia*'s success, the threat of envy, deceit, and derision such as hovers over any woman blessed triply with beauty, wealth, and talent, had been fulfilled largely by her own countrymen. The ecstasy of her welcome to Zea bespeaks the pathos of the successful in their heightened vulnerability (p. 812). "I did not know that the incident with Concha Espina, so unjust as it was sad and vulgar, would bring me the pleasure of receiving such a noble sign of friendship. If you had the material certainty of my innocence in this affair, your letter would have been an act of loyalty and affection; having nothing more than moral certainty, your attitude moved and strengthened me with another necessary faith: the faith of friendship, that 'communion of saints' as the Church says, that neither time, distance, nor death can undo."

Aside from Lydia, whose function for Teresa was also predicated by loyalty and devotion, there was probably no other friend or family member who received this level of intimacy in return. Lydia, the wizened younger sister, smoothed out as much of the obstructive and the treach-

198

erous from Teresa's physical path as she could, and their shared interests were many. But Zea filled the special place that Teresa always seemed to hold for the older, eccentric, and highly refined man; maybe her Uncle Antonio Parra, the model for Uncle Juancho/Pancho, had originally forged this leading place in her heart. It was the apostolic side of *Mirando al Misterio* and its "spiritual love for our fellow man" (p. 813) that moved Teresa, and later, after a particularly nasty tubercular relapse, she told Zea his book awaited her at the "other crossing" (p. 837). Then there was his description of the "importance of Helium" (unexplained), which made her feel "impregnated with the infinite for several hours" (p. 816). All these factors flowed into one like tributaries to a river. More than anything, Teresa was fascinated with Zea's study of telepathy; she felt linked to him in this way and referred to it often, with frank pleasure (p. 816). "How much more intimate and sincere is the spiritual presence of an absent friend! Of these visits, my dear Zea, you give me plenty, and I always receive you 'dashing through the house to the open window!' "

If this rebirth of faith had its roots in Catholicism, its branches flowered in the occult—not with the conscious embrace of sham, as positivists viewed it, or of devil worship, as the Christian churches viewed it, but as many respectable intellects of the 1920s practiced it in their search for truth beyond the jealously guarded boundaries of convention. Telepathy, only one of many natural tools used by practitioners of the ancient occult arts, was considered equally untrustworthy; despite the spurious reputation brought upon it by charlatans, nowadays dissipating as scientists and even governments (the so-pragmatic Soviets, for example) raise telepathic phenomena to the blessed status of fact, truth-seekers of all vocations in Teresa's time adopted a welcoming approach to the newly popularized antimaterialistic disciplines. French and English poets and writers especially did so, among them William Butler Yeats, who joined the Order of the Golden Dawn and committed himself to defend the authenticity of automatic writing, communicating with the dead, and clairvoyance. For Teresa these promises must have been irresistible; distrustful of volubility and in love with the very word *occult*—shadowy, sheltered, true by virtue of concealment, and concealed by virtue of truth—she was powered by her legendary fear of deception to seek honesty there. Once settled into the sanatorium, she would describe her room in detail so that the "reverberations of his travelling thought" would not mistake it for another (p. 837). In September 1931, on the beach at Beaulieu where she walked and contemplated after Lydia had gone home, he accompanied her more than once (p.817). "I heard you converse with your slow and gentle voice of a master as I heard it in the house of F. R. . . ." In 1933 she described the reasons for her special attachment to him (p. 825): "I wish to tell you about my health. I'm not afraid to bother you with this because you are a doctor and moreover my best friend. I believe that in you are conjoined the attributes of a perfect spiritual friend: you have lived, you are a doctor—what I want to say is you have lived more humanely than others, and you are, moreover, knowledgeable not only in science but in feeling."

Thus it was to Zea that Teresa related the chronology of her tubercular symptoms as they became conspicuous in the summer of 1931. During the first part of her vacation taken with family members in Brittany, "I spent morning and evening riding a bicycle in the sun, despite the disapproval of my poor mother. Then I smoked" (p. 818). Political turmoil reported over the airwaves undercut the peacefulness granted by the countryside. She wrote a short and despondent letter to Carias at the time: "The pessimists are predicting general bankruptcy followed by European Bolshevism caused by Germany, war, horrors."⁹ Then she traveled down to the Cote d'Azur to be with "a Cuban friend whom I like very much and who likes you very much for having been her collaborator in the new direction of my spirit." Finally she was left alone, reading the German philosopher Messer and trying to "remember so many things badly learned and forgotten." Returning to Paris afterwards, she:

> . . . embarked on a hygienic program in accord with the inner life, and against the wind and seas (invitations, telephones, etc.) I arose early and walked 3/4 of an hour while doing breathing exercises. But I continued to lose weight. I began to feel circulatory disturbances. One day I became conscious that on my left hand many small warts were in the initial stages of growth. I returned to the Professor's house, who found all my organs in good health. As time passed, the warts grew and increased in number. One day, when casually visiting a skin specialist with a friend, I showed him my hand. . . . His experience told him these [rare] warts were generally a reaction of the organism against tuberculosis. I returned to my professor with this diagnosis and he again told me I had nothing. But my poor organism, no noble, continued to warn me. I began to get boils, things I had never seen before. I then checked my temperature and saw I had fever. I attributed the fever to the boils

and the cough, which was worsening, to cigarettes. Time passed; I had already lost 30 kilos since my arrival from Colombia; now it was February, three months after the first symptoms, but since my general condition was good (despite worries—I have always been terrified of the phantasm of cancer) I continued my active life until one day I felt pain in the back. I returned alarmed to my doctor and demanded an X ray. I ordered him to do it just to "placate me." If you could have seen the anguish of the poor man when he had to show it to me! Five days later I was on the train to Leysin . . . and in Leysin I am, dear Zea, living as I have described: bed, bed, bed, solitude, clean air, snow, azure mountains, books, a radio, serenity, resignation, and something I've never known: a great friendship with myself!

(pp. 819–20)

* * *

The tubercule bacilli can reproduce as fast as every 20 hours and in just 10 days they can produce a colony of 5,000 organisms, enough to create a nodule in the lung. In less than a month a tubercule bacillus can produce one billion organisms, enough to create a cavity in the lung.[10]

Teresa's sanatorium letters say everything and say nothing. Signposts, they point toward all we don't know, and sometimes they even block our view. Then, too, the dictates of privacy kept Teresa's censors busy snipping out names in too personal a context, complaints that might have been unseemly, praise too effusive, or thoughts too eccentric. She who skirted the fringes of dishonor, who with every move designed to join her to the group wedged herself further apart, had contracted a disease so common it was the leading cause of death worldwide; ironically, tuberculosis was also the just fate of the melancholic, the artistic, and the chronically maladjusted; it was the brand of the pariah by which those sound of mind and body could be forewarned. And how aesthetically satisfying a picture of death is promised! The slow expiration of life's very breath and the flushed glow of an ethereal face, betraying the state of euphoria "that sometimes frightened" Teresa, comprised the illusion of complete dematerialization that so often sucked artists and poets—she felt—into its twilight waiting room, to be plucked away as the early chosen of God (p. 842). Until the discovery by Koch in 1882 of the tubercule bacillus, these at once charmed and accursed consumptives submitted meekly to a barbarous array of treatments that ultimately elicited nothing but a "meditation on death." But in the interval between Koch's discovery and the discovery of antibiotics after the Second World War, the treatment stimulated plenty of meditation still, by the medical profession whose accomplished logic and method had located the enemy but was stalled before further mystery: the mystery of bacillus logic.

The Swiss town of Leysin, built one mile up into the Alps, was renowned for its sparkling weather and the longevity of its inhabitants, since both rain and viruses were condemned to blow beneath the layers of cloud at its feet. It did not become a healing center until 1903, however, when Dr. August Rollier arrived with his plans to cure tuberculosis of the bones and joints by means of regimented sun and exercise therapy. The "sun doctor," as he became known, achieved good results, and soon the terminally afflicted came from all over the globe to place their despairing hopes under his care,[11] as well as to flee their neighbors' wrath. Parra was to speak often of the "Black Legend" of tuberculosis, which she felt caused more suffering than the actual disease, due to the mistaken notion that it was as wildly contagious as the plague. Poor Chopin, for instance, was chased out of Spain and Portugal, turned out of houses as a "pest breeder," and eventually threatened with prosecution for having infected others. Thus there existed just as great a demand for mutual protection as for a cure. More doctors were recruited to answer the demand, and within several years sanatoriums were cropping up one by one to receive the tuberculars and their money. There were expensive ones and inexpensive ones, but they all had the same methods of treatment: bed rest, then the pneumothorax, and finally thoracoplasty (rib extraction). Patients were forewarned that none of these guaranteed a cure. They were released and sent home either when their blood tested negative (a condition leading easily to a relapse because of the ensuing change in climate and increase in activity), when their money ran out, or when their cases were judged incurable. Of all the diseases Teresa could have contracted, she had been afflicted with the prime—the tenacious—deceiver. For although in many cases the treatment achieved a modest success, in just as many others the most virtuous doctors were transformed into incompetent liars, their calculated bedside cheer souring into a malevolent joke. For tuberculosis in its angelic bloom was an unhappy experience made miserable by the barrage of X rays, chest punctures with long needles, operations to cut lung tissue, endless blood samples, and experimental drug therapy, all of which had to be weathered under the paralyzing fear of the bacillus' caprice, the delirious seesaw of fever, the devastating cough and demoralizing blood-filled sputum, and finally in the last stages, the pain and often the hemorrhage. Many was the time, too, that a doctor misdiagnosed a recovery on the basis of healthy-looking X-ray plates that for some reason had not revealed the extensive damage found later, after a sudden fatal relapse, in the postmortem. Teresa's case was beset from beginning to end by bad luck in doctors and in the rarity of her symptoms: the warts, the boils, and later the bronchitis and asthma each delayed her cure by their obscure connection to the disease.

Teresa's sister Isabelita accompanied her to Leysin and stayed for several days until she was settled in. Carias ("you who have never deceived me" [p. 872]), was the first of Teresa's three correspondents to hear the news, and her mother was the last: "Take care that this prolonged bronchial malady doesn't degenerate into TB!" (p. 834), she pathetically warned her daughter a full year after the diagnosis. The doctors assured Teresa her case was favorable and only in its beginning stages; the right lung was affected by a lesion, the left lung looked healthy, and as yet there were no cavities. She exclaimed to Carias that she had lost four months due to her ignorant doctor, yet she told Zea it had all started a year ago with the weight loss. Perhaps she told herself an even worse truth, that it had pursued her like some low-grade infection for much longer* until first the Colombian sun, then the sun of the French beaches, released it in full force. For direct sunlight was contraindicated in lung tuberculosis by medical experience accumulated up to World War II; in Teresa's time, however, everyone had a theory about the ideal climate for cure, whether it should be mountainous, arid, or close to the sea. Often doctors recommended an ocean voyage. Teresa was never to find her ideal climate, and we cannot know either how sick she was in 1932 or to what degree she was helped or hurt by her treatment at Leysin. Maria, claiming that Teresa's illness began with a simple cold during that winter in Paris, was to later exclaim, "Two years in the best sanatorium in Switzerland, with the best doctors, could not cure her. When someone is going to die, it's a matter of destiny!"[12] Teresa placed her complete trust in her Swiss doctors. Since a major component of their therapy, according to Lydia, was optimism, it is most likely Teresa's reports on

*Through either parent Teresa could have also incurred her initial infection: in 1898 when Rafael Parra died, or around 1910 in Spain, where Luis de Llano-Sanojo reports to the author that Teresa mother also suffered a minor bout, which was "cured" by the ocean voyage back to Venezuela. Teresa was ignorant of these facts.

her health to her friends erred on the positive side, even though she would always take care to voice the double-edged reminder (p. 871): "Some arrive on a stretcher and leave cured, while others come in very lively and after two or three months do not go out again." She called it a "game of geese" (p. 841).

The whiteness of the snow-covered mountains and the hush of in-activity framed Teresa as she lay in absolute bed rest, with the French doors to her balcony opened to allow the crackling thirty-seven–degree air into her lungs. Gone was the romantic heroine who had once pondered the illusions of love and success by the shores of Lake Geneva in 1926. Today "I act the life of the grand invalid" (p. 805). Leysin was far from being a lonely place; on the contrary, the other inmates would seek one another out in their rooms almost too often to relieve themselves of the monotony of keeping death at bay. But Teresa had not accepted any permanent membership in this group; rather, she revelled in that precious solitude of which Paris had so persistently robbed her (p. 873). "I must be famous for my savagery. I don't want them to tarnish my pure sad-ness." Moreover, this was finally the "place and time to feel what I want," without guilt, to rest without prodding from others, and to read without obligation. "Time passes with an absurd slowness, absurd for our times" (p. 871), she wrote Carias, and it was a relief to be so ensconced in the "country of poets," where one could believe oneself "no longer living on earth" (p. 871). She wondered how Bolívar could have repressed his energy had he been sent to Leysin in 1830, musing that the great poet within his complex personality might have become unravelled (p. 810). Venezuela flooded her mind with uninterrupted mem-ories, scenting the flavorless chill of her Alpine view with its tropical intoxicants. Endless itineraries and plans for travel composed from travel-ogues kept her in a "Buddhist paradise," in which she claimed to have renounced all will and desire (p. 871): "I feel resigned, almost contented with my luck; I see these months or years of cure like a white road, all full of spiritual life, something like the moonlight over the snow. It is the state of grace. May it never abandon me."

Yet dramatic moods—death depressions and the gushing heights of that imagined state of grace—took their turns with her, and the truth was that in spite of her pragmatic self-advice, she had invested inordinate hopes in being well and free again within as little time as three months (p. 830). Indeed, by June she was seven kilos heavier and convinced that her nature "was hostile to TB" (p. 873), despite the fact that she remained test-positive. The month before had introduced her to her first flu as a tubercular—a minor-enough bout, though one whose like she would never again experience without feeling an onrush of the darkest premonitions of unchecked doom. In May her saddest letter to date had revealed a Teresa admiring her youthful achievements in the shadow of her total "resignation to the approach of death," and as the spring snows fell heavily and the hours passed in clumps marked by the nursing routine, she thought, *What an extraordinary opportunity this could be to write a book, if I could only find even a small crumb of faith in myself! Of the kind I had in Macuto in 1922. You had faith and I had even more, and how faith moves mountains! But these 10 years have taken everything and I do not complain about my orphanhood.*[13]

Come July and the illusion of strength gained during the previous month and a half when first Isabelita and then Lydia came to visit, to read to her and to join her in listening to the radio, Teresa did not feel she needed the sanatorium anymore. A wave of impenetrably gray weather had descended upon the peaks of Leysin. Fog blanketing the rails of her balcony felt to her bronchial tubes just as it looked to her eyes: thick, irritating and distasteful. It was hard, too, to take orders from "assembly-line" nurses and authoritarian doctors, to stifle the restlessness that was sole betrayer to the disturbingly natural calm observed by friends and enemies alike. Calamitously, Teresa made a decision to defy medical advice, to flee the rain and cold, and to descend to the Plaine, as the lowlands were called, where Maria lived. There in Vevey, the second and more regrettable stage of tubercular revenge awaited Teresa in the form of a severe bronchial attack that reversed the course of her six-month recovery. She would later look back on the month of August as a major turning point in her comprehension of the disease and its implications. Four months of remorseful pondering afterwards would produce the confession to Zea that "up until August everything went well. I lived in peace thanks to the puffery and fanfare I exhibited from the first day I knew I had tuberculosis" (p. 825).

Thus humbled, Teresa modified her hallowed pose and looked out with newly apprehensive eyes to the future—blurred and mute, the only clue it provided was that of long distance. "I don't know what will become of me, " she wrote Carias in October. "Now I'm not so optimistic." She tried to call forth her old fighting spirit. Recasting herself in the role of a soldier, she envisioned the sanatorium as a stage for war; "In the trenches, where some fall, others help . . . knowing tomorrow they might also fall. . . ." Cowardice and escapism in face of illness and death became her new bane. She wanted to embrace her fate, to "know the disease and to have a philosophical attitude. One must always be prepared to receive a disagreeable surprise with cheerfulness, without falling, and with elegance'' (p. 874).

To this end she attempted for the first time to read Thomas Mann's *Magic Mountain*. The relevance of this book to her present condition seems either to have escaped her or scared her; possibly she even reacted in opposition to the unqualified praise the book had received worldwide. All the qualities of her Leysin experience—the distortion of time, learning to cope with death, struggling with the needs of the spirit—had been thoroughly implicated in Mann's Nobel Prize–winning novel. Yet in a short and preemptive derision of Mann's wordiness and what she saw as his fixation on the "external—the ordinary manifestations of the ordinary," (p. 875) Teresa told Carias she had not been able to finish reading as much as the first volume. Her contrasting enthusiasm six months later for a discourse by Maeterlinck on the life of bees, termites, and ants proved what she would admit at that time: she had truly lost her taste for literature (p. 877). "Meditating on these things [Maeterlinck] makes me aware of how poor is the intelligence of which we humans are so proud, when compared to the marvellous harmony of the laws that govern the world: that divine energy penetrating all beings and awakening them to the mystery of life. I believe in fact there is no better reading for children than this kind. It awakens poetic sentiment and mysticism." Poetic sentiments came to Teresa often at Leysin. (Was she still thinking of Bolívar, the hidden poet?) "How a single word, a single silent look can reveal a suppressed and heart-rending drama!" (p. 875) she exclaimed by way of criticizing Mann.

After September, Teresa finally opened herself up to the suffering of her fellow invalids, who more than she had been shunned by their relatives. She wanted to listen to all the death fears and death wishes that sanatorium policy suppressed; she wanted to transform their pain to pleasure and their loneliness to fellowship. Patients, however, who visited her compulsively to chatter away their death sentences, who had no inner lives from which to draw strength, and who became indignant when reference was made to their illness earned Teresa's condescending pity. The most touching incident she reported, which oddly enough occurred back in May, when she claimed to have had no contact with other patients, concerned the death of a young girl occupying an adjacent room. Teresa never saw her—"she knew me by my footsteps and I by her cough" (p. 823)—yet she sent the maid to the girl with flowers and words of consolation so that the girl would not feel alone on the very evening of her unexpected relapse. Teresa did not learn of the death until two days later, although she sensed it as soon as the coughing ceased. When she asked the maid if it had happened, she received a curt denial; surreptitiously the body had been taken from the room in the middle of the night "as if dying were a crime." The image of her unseen friend lying there holding the flowers she had sent, with the light snow falling outdoors and the thought of going home in the eighteen-year-old girl's mind, left Teresa crying all day. "I didn't think it possible that death could leave so great a poetic, so light an impression," she wrote Zea. Also in September, a letter of Zea's had brought Teresa to this straightfaced meditation on death's disencumbered aspect; her marveling at its discovery is not surprising if we remember the pain and guilt she ascribed to Maria Eugenia's perception of the death of Uncle Pancho, as well as her own lasting grief over the death of Emilia. Zea, approaching a major operation whose outcome was uncertain, had sent Teresa a letter of farewell, moving her to think of him daily without cessation and to "help with the little flame of my desire to save your life" until the good news of his survival finally arrived (pp. 821–22). "Now I do not fear death. The monotony of the days, exacting in this prison, has augmented the velocity of life: I have the impression of flying in a train towards a point, at whose attainment I am not able to rest. Sometimes I question if it might be some presentiment, this sensation of travelling, but because of the progress I have made it is not likely that this is the train to my final destination."

It was a guessing game, like pulling petals off a daisy. Today, death is nigh; tomorrow, death is not nigh. In October Teresa's spirits had sunk to those of an exhausted soldier. The so-celebrated mountain weather was not living up to its reputation, and she reacted badly to the abuse. Seeking change, she packed her bags once again to descend the mountains, to spend the "gentle autumn months" at Vevey, where she could reassess her flagging morale and finances. A Teresa feeling physically and spiritually shattered spoke of her mysticism in sad and simple terms: "I have reached the age in which the soul is more mature for sacrifice and mysticism. Among other things, because it now knows its treasures are not as great as it believd at 20 years old. Therefore I observe, admire, and absorb."

Both pocketbook and conscience were feeling pinched by the sybaritic Grand Hotel—Teresa had originally justified the expense as insurance against the flagging morale so easily brought on by bad food and tacky furnishings. But now declaring it bad taste to be cushioned and surrounded by the rich and vacant, Teresa called forth Keyserling once again to denounce material wealth as the breeding ground for decadence. She resolved to return to Leysin in November refreshed and willing to put in her time with the less fortunate tuberculars at Richmond House, a smaller and less expensive sanatorium. Three months passed without a printable letter from Teresa. Then her first one of the new year went out, and it was to Zea-Uribe. She yearned for the open countryside of Colombia and the stars that he could reveal to her through his telescope. Emerging from her plunge into total isolation at Richmond House, Teresa seemed to bear the marks of an encounter with her demons, the "infirmities of the soul, root of all weakness and error," and confession was on her lips. Zea, unlike the Catholic priests, could be as trusted with such secrets of the soul. Teresa had been "encircling" her illness with silence and solitude out of rebellion, "as if I wanted to avenge myself by negating expansion, and that is a big evil to those who must confess." Her confession began with the tale of her first seven months at Leysin, in which she regretted her vain display of "fanfaronia" since first hearing the news of her tuberculosis. The rest of this confession was censored, although the following abstracted glimpse into her private nightmare, which she allowed her more formal friend Carias, was spared: "I experienced a relapse in December that depressed me greatly. In spite of having inured myself to dealing courageously with 'whatever may come,' this courage doesn't last 12 hours a day, and above all not through the night. There is a wakefulness in which the subconscious world invades with all its terrors and egotisms to make us suffer."[14] Leaving the Grand Hotel proved to be an impulsive mistake. Although part of Teresa's motivation, besides the financial one, had been to extricate herself from the social obligations she had all too rapidly managed to accrue, she reversed her mood completely once solitude and threadbare furnishings were hers. These were the shortest days of winter, and her case of the "blues" made her so disconsolate that her friends from the Grand Hotel almost took her by force away from the Richmond House back to the old sanatorium, so rich in splendor and gaiety. All Teresa wanted was to write again, to have a room that bore no trace of the hospital, to be able to hang up a "No Visitors" sign on her door during the day, and in the evening to "descend to see the world: one or two hours socializing would suffice" (p. 826). She would even prefer to spend her active hours visiting the poor and the sick than to while them away in the incestuous and shallow dramas of high-society invalids.

One whole year had gone by. The infiltrations in the upper portion of Teresa's damaged lung could no longer be detected on the X rays.

The "ghost of chronic illness" that had haunted her in autumn had departed, and she was "almost alarmed" at the healthy color of her cheeks (p. 830). "No one would suspect I am ill and I feel accordingly: divine." Her days flew by, the intervals between 7:45 and midnight, when the nurse checked in, seemed like seconds, and Kant's phrase "Time does not exist," which Teresa had never before truly grasped, took on the significance of dogma, a "true metaphysics." She stated she was perhaps happier than she had ever been before, "but it is a sad and negative happiness."

> I speak frequently of nirvana to define this, but I give it the pessimistic sense of Schopenhauer which is, I believe, the pure and orthodox one: the absence of desire to the point just before life is negated. Neither pleasure nor suffering. A continuous well-being in limbo where nothing comes to disturb us in the soul or the feelings, not one disagreeable noise; impeccable service, a white and warm bed, the books, the pretty view, the radio (almost static-less) that carries us like invisible winged ghosts to theaters and conference rooms. . . .
> . . . But all this well-being is silent and negative like the snow covering the trees and ground.

Teresa was never idle. In the mornings, after dressing, she would practice Coué, a form of autosuggestion by which she hoped to improve her memory and her willpower and to awaken her lust for life as well as interest in study (p. 832). She had been using this self-hypnotic technique for over a year, she wrote Zea, despite the mockery of "vulgar people." Then she would pray for Emilia Ibarra and visualize her in different places. The state of nonbeing continued to hold Teresa in a time-warping trance until one day, when a minor incident seared through to the quick of Teresa's forgotten life. Clemencia Miro, Gabriel's daughter and a victim of bone tuberculosis, had asked Teresa if she could pick up any items for her while shopping in town. Teresa, shocked, could not think of a single request to make. The longed-for moment of liberation from the coarse demands of the material world had finally arrived, yet she found herself regretting, painfully, that she must now be the "woman who needs nothing."

> Do you think it should cheer one up or sadden one to discover in oneself such a lack of ambition? Could it not be, Zea, a sign of

impending death? Life that feels or knows it must let go?

(p. 833)

Teresa endured the next relapse with courage. Like clockwork, it came in April, and in May her doctors decided the bed-rest therapy had failed: it was time to induce a pneumothorax as the next stage of treatment. A long, hollow needle would be inserted into her pleural cavity, through which air would pass to collect in a pocket over the damaged lung, collapsing it to a fraction of its original size. Since the lung's activity would be greatly restricted, the tissues could then be free to rest and heal. This short and minor operation would have to be repeated every two weeks when the air had become absorbed into the bloodstream. Both May letters to Carias and Zea were cheerful: "My general health is magnificent but for one spot that won't heal. I resolved to get a pneumothorax."[15]

Once Teresa got an idea into her head, it rarely went away. For all her flaws of self-indulgence and of flightiness, she still trod stubbornly along a path that she had decided long ago would lead her to something novelist Hermann Broch described as "the unity of thought and being that can be realized within the most modest limits."[16] Her Bolívar project, born of her need to both heal and be healed, had backfired in that the huge body of knowledge to which the biography had to refer condemned her—a mere novice—to even less authenticity as a historian than as the novelist above whose personality she had hoped to rise. Although she had apparently judged herself "abandoned" by her Bolívar mission, if only because her illness had robbed her of all tenacity and made the Venezuelan pilgrimage impossible, her mind still hungered for background knowledge: the spiritual meat of civilization's official history. "How I miss the petulance of my youth!"[17] she confessed to Carias in one of those now-frequent moments bereft of fire. After a full year of reading travelogues and adjusting to the furtive pace of her cure, she seemed to be looking for the strength of youth to continue the flight from literature she had begun at *Mama Blanca*'s writing. To Teresa's delight, the sanatorium library contained no less than 18,000 volumes:

> Since I arrived at Leysin I have learned the simple reading of easy things—mere literature, that is—could not suffice to fulfill life and that to endure this prisoner's and pariah's existence with resignation one must put the spirit to work, like the Carthusian and Benedictine monks. I think I told you I have embarked for my pleasure on the

210

study of Greece and Rome and everything related to it: history of art, literacy, philosophy, religion, etc. In your erudition you [Zea] know how extensive these things and the years required to learn them are. One must begin with the two languages, of which I know only a little Latin, yet without expecting to ever know them thoroughly I have already traveled as if by automobile across these distant epochs and given my spirit thereby an equilibrium and comprehension of life that it was greatly lacking and that I hope to continue cultivating. . . .

(p. 837)

Teresa still wanted to live, to learn, and to travel. Two months later, she picked up another of the threads dropped at the time of her incarceration at Leysin (p. 308): "If I followed my instinct, I would go to a dry country, to Spain for instance, to live as I do here, which I find enchanting only when it doesn't rain. But in spite of my general improvement I am far from cured, and the hecatomb of this wintery Grand Hotel has cut my wings of independence. . . . I continue to dream of very slow journeys through Spain and South America. I think I've told you several times of my thirst to live in Spanish-speaking countries. . . ." There was symbolism in the steady mental march toward sun, any Hispanic sun, and knowledge, all knowledge. That a homecoming was implicated was certain, yet whether its curve would land her flatly back in the swaying hammock of her tropical childhood, so absent of strife and confusion, or in the arms of a death whose character and certainty she could not grasp, was a ciphered matter of fate. Another story of a tragic relapse haunted her: A young woman, only nineteen years old, had returned to Paris after being pronounced cured. Instead of convalescing quietly as she had been advised to do, she danced, drove around, and stayed up all night, "etc." After twenty-five days she was dead. "All this was the consequence of bad education, and failure of moral discipline," ventured Teresa (p. 838).

Four months after the induction of her pneumothorax, in September, Teresa announced to her doctors a plan she had been hatching since May to return to Paris and live with her mother; the advantages would be both sentimental and economic. The doctors turned her request down unanimously, warning that she was too susceptible to pleurisy in the first months of pneumo-therapy. Teresa obeyed, but not without the sulky retort that her health and morale were good and that since the treatment had already shown results, her lung was on the way to certain recovery

(p. 910). Ultimately, since only the incurables were allowed to come and go freely, she accepted the doctors judgment as a sign of their optimism, and in lieu of major travel, she changed hotels again the first time to the sanatorium Mont Blanc, which maintained stricter discipline than the Grand Hotel, but at only half the price of the Belvedere Hotel. Thus autumn of 1933 found her positive in outlook, despite the cough and the presence of bacilli. Her doctors assured her the pneumo was a good one; only "one or two adhesions" too small to be cut prevented its total effectiveness: "Meanwhile, be it death or chronic illness, I always retain hope." She reassured herself that her cure would eventually be perfect ("knock on wood"), an event that still lay a minimum of two years ahead. But "when time is locked in fog and rain and the angel of conformity abandons me, how long and eternal these remaining 20 months seem!" (pp. 841–42).

Teresa began to focus some of her newfound energy on the "monstrously stupid" injustice of tuberculophobia, which caused wild fears of automatic contagion, adding insult to the already grievous injury of tuberculosis itself. She never complained of rejection by her own family and friends; one or the other would spend as long as three weeks with her at least twice a year. In Teresa's proposal to Zea that together they wage a "war against tuberculophobia" in their countries by writing a book, he the scientific part and she the descriptive, lay the beginnings of a new attitude toward illness itself. Tired of seeing her fellow tuberculars suffer from the fear and avoidance of their loved ones, she was beginning to work on transforming the stigma of illness in her own mind to "the opposite, into the euphoria of the privileged who are able, by mysticism or art, to experience states of soul that the majority of those who have material happiness in the world can never know" (p. 844).

If Parra ever felt self-pity at Leysin before, or more likely the shame described by Thomas Mann of "the living creature that slips away into a corner to die, convinced that he may not expect from outward nature any reverence or regard for his death,"[18] then such a transformation of self-image had its personal value. For Teresa, superstitious though she was, had every rational reason not to blame her disease completely on the infirmities of her soul. Thanks either to the equilibrium brought about by disciplined reading or to the "dematerialization" (p. 843) promised by the tuberculosis, Teresa's new tone suggested that she had come to terms with some of her subconscious terrors. The thought of growing old no longer hurt. This was the homily she offered to a young tubercular friend of Zea's (p. 845): "Life is like a voyage. Each step has its weather, landscape, and charms. The important thing is to know how to adapt to each step and not to dress up for summer when entering fall or winter." She even ventured to declare—"call me positivist or heretic"—that it had been illness by which Saint Teresa had acquired her "perfume of sanctity" (p. 843). Thus Teresa de la Parra's inner soldier, even torn between guilt and her mission, had devised an elegant strategy to fight her illness: active, wholehearted surrender. Writing Clemencia about a critique by Mauriac "of a book treating precisely those cases of long illness requiring detachment from the world," she enumerated the points that had impressed her (p. 911):

> Those who suffer an isolated and extended illness are the crucible, the altar of sacrifice by which all of humanity is purified and brought closer to perfection. It is the renewed sacrifice of Christ. The chosen one must comprehend his mission and make himself worthy of the privilege; the flow of pain will then be a fountain of otherworldly bliss; and of that bliss life will be the beneficiary. This passive soldier not only refrains from attack but does not even defend himself from the great enemy of pain. He is transformed and blossoms into a new existence where the pure spirit predominates. You already know this existence, since the day you took leave of me; I won't forget it even if the turbulent joy of falling again allures me with its nostalgia. . . . How far is this from the natural (but vulgar!) aversion of those who curse Leysin, because they will never appreciate how its sacred environment resembles the exhalations of empty churches."

Sliding into the Land of Absence

If there is truly something worth the telling in Teresa de la Parra's life, it lies in her personality, to whose independent flowering she first sacrificed her social respectability and which, in the end and with vengeance, she sacrificed to the mystical ideal. Out of the emblematic, admirable, pitiable, and fleeting manifestations of this personality, a cohesiveness takes shape, a two-sided portrait of the artist as woman and the Christian martyr as woman, sacrificed to art and to God instead of to the male. Call it the classic story of the modern Catholic woman in the throes of guilt over her sexual and intellectual awakening or simply, like her own story *Ifigenia*, the "pure depiction of the female soul at this

The Grand Hotel

Mont Blanc Hotel

Hotel Belvedere

Richmond House

Sanatoria of Leysin in Switzerland

place and time, without transcendental pretensions.'' It was the timing of Parra's modest achievement, her quality of dream, taken in the context of her gender and nationality, that lent her the rare glow of great loneliness and responsibility. Buckling under its weight, she fell, and the sound of the fall still resonates today. As went her personal conscience, so too went the first decades of the twentieth century, to which the peace of mind of ensuing generations became martyred. Her nostalgia for an idyllic childhood was the flight from its bad second, the hypocrisies and egotisms of the semiconscious adult; it was a tiny memory of innocence within the memory of the modern age's haunting, euphoric infancy, both running parallel as digging began on the oil wells in Venezuela. In the time between two world wars, she launched her private army against social mores, caring secretly about the divine; then turning upward toward the divine, she lashed out against the laxness of her spirit, caring about correctness of expression, correctness of motivation, correctness of internal government, to finally expire in slow march with some shrouded regiment of the soul just at the onset of Spain's last futile burst of idealism, the Civil War of 1936.

There was something about Teresa's death that perfectly illustrates the Rilkean theme: each of us carries within us the seed of our own death, which we nurture, lovingly, to its full expression. Teresa's self-destruct mechanism lay in the hollows of her lungs, where some world-weary grief, opposing every breath, took its revenge on a weakened organism. To grant the force of disease even greater cause and cunning, one can hint at the perverse fulfillment of an emphatic wish—three wishes, to be exact—granted from above and prepared by her, word by painstaking word. Did she have just cause to complain when, upon delivery, their reality proved quite different from what she had in mind, nevertheless complying faithfully to the letter of her request? When speaking of her search for the right tone, she had perhaps voiced too often her desire to obliterate the printed word in favor of the ''live'' communication. What better way to experience the real suffering of Bolívar the tubercular invalid, the thwarted grand-scale planner, than to die this death, that he had experienced at forty-seven and she would at forty-six? And what better deliverance from the material world than indefinitely prolonged bed rest in the Swiss stratosphere! It is the final wish, the end goal of the first two wishes, whose answer we can only encircle; did she catch a personal glimpse of that mystical ideal? Did she make amends with her ancestors? Was the seed of her death her book *Ifigenia*, branching bronchially into its ideal denouement of self-abnegation by the only means at its disposal, the humbling, crushing, promise of physical annihilation—literally, the killing of her ability to ever write again? Lest our readers begin to think we are imposing meaning where some impersonal stroke of bad luck would be more fitting, we must emphasize the likelihood that Teresa viewed her illness in this light. She understood the power of individual will just as she believed in the power of otherworldly forces; and simple occurrences, void of significance to many, to her would resonate with metaphor and hint at larger, more universal connections. This was what made up the substance of her world and her writing.

Just like Teresa's beauty, which Mistral described as the optimal, almost supernatural, sum of imperfect parts, the mystical grace she sought—after all the stubborn contradictions, ultimatums, and resignations—appeared on the surface to be a totally achieved reality by the time Mistral welcomed her to Spain in 1935. Because they shared no truly intimate friendship, however, Gabriela's impressions fall into a category neighboring on those of people who believed the image Teresa projected. Taking this into account, along with the Chilean poet's grave eccentricities (such as her bizarre habit of feeling cheekbones to establish the presence of Indian blood in one so obviously Spanish as Teresa or the "unexpected festiveness" in her combination of words and ideas that Teresa called positively St. Teresian [p. 911]), we venture to say that Gabriela was nevertheless one of the few people to express an affinity for Teresa the person, woman, and writer from a shared poetic center. Therefore when Gabriela wrote in her (1936) *recado* that "a second Teresa de la Parra was born to us in the Swiss Alps, whom none of her friends from either shore knew. . . . She searched for a life free of the senses and she did it in a special and secretive way . . ."[19] we go back to her last year at Leysin to decipher, out of its confounding ups and downs, signs that Teresa succeeded in taming her pride to become of unified will with her Creole God.

At Christmastime of 1933, Teresa had returned to the Grand Hotel, having once again failed to overcome the hardships of a lesser-endowed sanatorium, the Mont Blanc Hotel. Her bacillus count had reached an ecstatic zero, leaving her positive only in the "agenization" [culture tests?], and despite the ominous vacancy rate of the Grand Hotel, the unsubtle "tomb-like" message of each empty chair, Teresa had never before and never would again express such unqualified happiness in the understanding and universal love she had acquired through her reading (p. 846). Even the predictable plunge during times of fog and rain was softened by the solace of a Schopenhaueristic nirvana, wrenched from her solitude to glow darkly until the sun returned. A clarity of vision, untangled from emotion, infused her last letter to Zea, on December 25; it gave substance to her announcement earlier in the month to Carias that solitude, formerly a self-inflicted therapy for disciplining her frivolous impulses, had now become her natural calling and socializing with others had assumed the disciplinary role by which peace of mind, engendered in lofty isolation, becomes genuine: "I feel at times that I am on the road to [inner perfection] but afterwards I discover there is no merit in having the meekness of the blessed when one lives distant from the world, without the great and small obstacles of the 'inevitable neighbor,' spoken of by Keyserling, that each instant rations out to us."[20] Thus balanced within the grip of her illness, Teresa mused only casually to Zea about her persistent desire for the cottage in Los Teques (not that far from Caracas) that awaited her, its surroundings a little too beautiful in her imagination to ever be real, the peasants filled nevertheless with infinite wisdom and profundity, and the "sweet insistence" of the longing itself that made her ask (p. 847): "Could it be a foreknowledge of death, Zea?" She pictured herself returning within several years, when released from the short tether of her pneumothorax, with:

> bomb-proof lungs and maybe even a new book written or in preparation. . . . I would like to write a book that will raise some of this hope and happiness I am feeling today in the souls of others and that also will communicate something of my fanatic love of nature and the tropical Creole atmosphere. I believe, Zea, over there we are poisoned by non-conformism, we have been injected with false European and North American culture, assimilated it badly, and adopted therefore a dangerous kind of barbarism. *Ifigenia*, my novel, is filled with that spirit. I would like to write the anti-thesis of *Ifigenia*, but I lack faith, the temporal faith that engenders action, and above all the ardor and enthusiasm of those days when I wrote.
> (pp. 847–48)

With this letter's closing, the chaper of Zea-Uribe was over. How many letters Teresa must have written in desperate confusion at his silence until the news of his death arrived—not by the telepathic link she had felt grow stronger back in September, but by post! Clemencia Miro was able to partially fill Zea's vacuum as one who understood the ways of tuberculosis, but she, like Carias, did not receive any letters from Teresa until June of 1934. March had been bad, bringing with it the worst case of bronchitis and asthma that she had yet suffered. She believed so strongly that the month-long attack, with its concomitant "black ideas" and fever, represented the fruit of too much isolation, a "saturation of the spirit" with introversion, that one foggy day in May she lurched toward some precipice above what she called "worst disasters," feeling for the first time "truly sad and disheartened," imagining her doctors were hiding some serious complication and envisioning, "without resignation, the slow decline in confinement, bereft of all hope, towards the end accompanied by who knows what suffering!" (p. 880). Her doctors begrudgingly acceded to her demand for leave down in the Plaine; she must make the move "at her own risk" only. On May 10, the willful Teresa was in Lausanne, trembling with an excitement she hadn't felt since riding in her mother's coach to the hacienda at the age of six or seven. The most trivial things filled her with rapture: the sensual flow of everyday life itself, the cinema, the steamboats on the lake, the gardens outside the house where she stayed. Lydia had arrived to meet her, and together they socialized and made plans. Teresa was treated to a spectacular vindication of her theory on the relationship of sun to her morale and her morale to bronchitis: her health wasted no time following the lead of her rejuvenated spirit. Just before the onset of July's summer heat, she returned to present herself triumphantly before her doctors at Leysin, who agreed that she had never been closer to cured. X rays showed the continued improvement of the lung, and her bronchial tubes were "almost" back to normal. But superstition prevented her from announcing, yet, a definite victory (p. 881).

During the last year and a half of Teresa's life, her ambitious letter writing was drastically curtailed; a daily journal, however, covering the last three months of her life, betrays the therapeutic value that writing still had for her. Her last professional work consisted of two articles taken directly from her lectures on Malinche and Ñusta Isabel, which were published in a New York City magazine in 1935.[21] Aside from one last letter written to Carias in January 1935 from Paris, when Teresa was organizing her final departure to Madrid after her three-year absence (and succumbed to an overwhelming emotion of nostalgia for Macuto, 1922), no others emerged between the two old friends. His personal problems had also increased, and the pension that he had been administering for her was losing value in the foreign exchange.

What remains for us to peruse is a picture of frantic travel toward point after point that still offered no rest. Dates, border crossings between France and Spain, some comments by Lydia, and a moving description by Gabriela of Teresa in her last months are all wedged within the grim progression of bronchial and asthmatic complications that Teresa watched microscopically and reported to Clemencia. Clemencia, who had come to know Teresa at Leysin, now wrote faithfully from Madrid with a standing invitation to settle there as her neighbor. It was in on this semblance of true family, like-minded and receptive, that Teresa and Lydia homed, albeit indirectly, and it was the image that life promised to draw for her down there that spurred Teresa to plunge into direct encounter with her fate, uncushioned by the expensive privilege of Leysin.

When Teresa returned from a short vacation with Lydia in low-lying Sierre, to organize her final departure from the Grand Hotel, she was acting under the influence of certain misapprehensions fed to her by her doctors. It was evident that her state of grace, no matter how honestly attained and truthfully experienced, was fragile, and one can imagine the doctors' distaste for frankness in explaining to someone so temperamental the seriousness of her condition. Teresa's dark suspicions that "they were hiding complications" (p. 880) were not mere fantasies of a morbid imagination. Her X-ray plates showed a complete healing of her lung, true, and her last five analyses had all been negative, but what about the adhesions, and what about the bronchitis and the asthma? Was the suppression of symptoms in her lung forcing the bacillus to live in other mucous membranes? Lydia explained that the Swiss doctors never pronounced her cured, only "better," and that they refused to make official pronouncements to Teresa on the odds of her recovery. To Lydia and to her family, however, the doctors were more openly discouraging,[22] and the ease with which they released her from the sanatorium had implications that could hardly have escaped her notice. How sad it is to read her letter from Barcelona to Clemencia in Madrid only six months later, in which she referred to the incongruity between her doctors' continually favorable prognosis and her true condition (p. 916): ". . . When I think about this, Clemencia, it seems like a lie. During my last year at Leysin, viewing the inefficacy of the pneumothorax, I had the fixed idea of chronic illness, which depressed me greatly in spite of my attempts to adjust to it. The cure came when I least expected it. Now it may have brought me this most horribly oppressive asthma which makes me regret, sometimes, leaving that euphoria at Leysin where everything was all serenity and wellbeing, physical and moral, and even the thought of death was sweet and beautiful." But back in September, as she packed her bags for Paris and planned her itinerary to Spain come January, she must also have made some internal decision about chronic illness: what was life worth when one was isolated, locked in a manic-depressive cycle, haunted by the inevitable future rather than determined to face it, and when—this was the final straw—all this was supported by monies that no longer existed? Another dreadful winter lay ahead, and sunny Spain had yet to be traveled. In Madrid she could bolster her morale with the sun, friendship, and the sound of Spanish being spoken everywhere, and surely her health, maybe would follow. Furthermore, just next door she could discuss even an initial Bolívar volume, politics, life and death, the lessons of good and evil, with Gabriela—Teresa the ex–society lady and Gabriela the ex-schoolteacher—above all grasping at their memories and hope for South America and for the Land of Absence, Gabriela's vision of some skyward homeland.

And in land without name
I am going to die
And my land is where
I live and die

Lighter than angel
And of feature vague
Color of dead algae
The color of hawk
The age of forever
Without happy age

It bears no pomegranates
It yields no jasmine
And it has no heavens
Nor indigo seas.

Its name, its name
Never have I heard it

It seems a fable
That I have learned
A dream of taking
And letting go

I lost mountain ranges
Where I once did sleep
I lost golden orchards
With living sweet
I lost the islands
Of cane and azure deep
And as their shadows merge
I did see
Them together and loving
Form a land for me.

221

Long locks of mist
Disembodied and free
Sleeping breaths following
I did see
And through wandering years
Formed a land for me.

And in land without name
I am going to die
And my land is where
I live and die.[23]

Between October and January of 1934, Teresa lived again in the environs of Paris. But the pleasure she expected to find in her convalescence near Mama was not forthcoming. During the short week at Leysin following Teresa's beneficial vacation in the lowlands of Sierre—that week of September 23 when she put clinic life behind her—a sudden asthmatic seizure dealt her its parting blow, augmenting when she descended the mountains for the last time. "I am again perplexed at my bronchial condition," (p. 916) she wrote Clemencia in October. She felt this was further proof that high altitudes and cold climates were harmful to her. All that remained to try was the "sunny and warm Mediterranean coast, be it in France or in Spain." Already she was struggling to be tolerant of the distractions of city life and therefore looking forward to her upcoming trip with eagerness, but first she would have to establish the medical connections, before deciding which Spanish city was the ideal destination.

From now on Lydia became her steady companion. She had visited Teresa many times at Leysin, leaving the latter at least once feeling lonelier than ever for her good company and pondering the unbreakable friendship they shared. But it was not until Lydia's mother died that she assumed responsibility for Teresa's health; both mother and older sister—Seida de la Torre—had been extremely fond of Teresa (Lydia herself had never been accepted by Teresa's family, and if so with some reserves though her credentials of wealth and blood were spotless), and in June of 1933, just before the old woman who had helped to inspire *Mama Blanca* died, she extracted from Lydia her promise to care for their Venezuelan friend until the end should come. Lydia claims to have acquired her empathy with tuberculars the hard way: at the age of fifteen or sixteen, she had suffered a short bout herself, and her older brother, the favorite of the family, died an agonizing death from the disease when she was only three years old: "I will always carry with me the memory of my brother lying between the bottles of oxygen, suffering." The simultaneous passing away of her mother and the slow demise of her best friend, Teresa, who, at ten years her senior, had always been like a "second mother," did not weigh Lydia down with self-pity, however. She provided for Teresa's comfort in every way possible, although Teresa's Madrid diary confirms that she was a proud invalid and found it difficult to accept her burdensome dependence on her friend's time. Thus Lydia's efforts often met with criticism: "Many people think I sacrificed myself greatly in taking care of Teresa, especially considering the danger to myself of contagion. I always reply to the contrary: living with her in the sanatorium and the other locations was marvelous. Of course it was a sad period because of her suffering, but I felt comfortable and happy just being close to her."[24]

Because of Lydia's proximity to Teresa she might not have been able to perceive the gradual physical deterioration that so shocked Mistral in the early months of 1935, after a five-year interval without seeing Parra. According to Lydia, Teresa did not look very sick at all, and at her October 1934 reentry into the world at large her worst symptom was a persistent, hacking cough. Her lungs, as seen in the X ray, were scarred, and the adhesions stretched initially by air pressure had been further lengthened by the cough and might be cut in the near future. In late January Lydia and Teresa traveled to Barcelona to live; by mid-March they were eager to leave. Although Teresa loved the city, the weather was hot and humid, and she felt the same or even worse than she had in Paris. For some reason, they could not find suitable accommodations. Fatigued, they "renounced the project of finding a peaceful, semi-sanatorial life," and declared themselves tourists (p. 919): "There is no other remedy!" Teresa told Clemencia she would next try her fortune in Madrid. Gabriela, who still retained in her memory an image of Teresa at the height of her Parisian popularity,

> could not believe the misery in which I found her in the hotel in Barcelona. . . .
>
> I had to be tranquil and smiling in front of her, very subtle in order that my concern did not reflect her lamentable fatigue. The Teresa of before, the deer of our sierra, walked slowly now; the heavy breathing was lodged in her throat; her back was slightly deformed; the gathered gray hairs gave her a sudden maturity, although lending greater sweetness to the face that was both pious and beautiful.[25]

Teresa appeared to have lost all faith in the medical profession. She rejected the warning of her Barcelona doctors about spring in Madrid and proceeded toward the rest she hoped the special attention of her friends Clemencia and Gabriela would afford. Once she had arrived she was given an apartment in the Mario Roso de Luna complex, where, indeed, everything seemed to improve. She even received as a visitor Romulo Gallegos, the celebrated Creole author and future president of Venezuela. The sequence of events that occurred during this first Madrid sojourn, lasting approximately between the months of March and July 1935, is not clear; at some point, Teresa took the advice of her Barcelona doctor, Luis Sayé, to have her adhesions cut and went with Lydia up to Fuenfria, a sanatorium situated on the outskirts of Madrid, to undergo the operation.

Lydia says they spent "several months" up there and "several months" at the Mario Roso apartment. The operation brought Teresa instant relief; she considered the results a "marvelous cure." But instead of heeding the lessons she had reiterated time and time again, that convalescents must curtail their desire to live normal, active lives, she relentlessly pursued her whims. Everything was easier said than done up at the ivory tower of Leysin—how could she have understood then what Lydia called the "inquietude of the tubercular"? The heat of summer was approaching Madrid, and it had always been Teresa's custom to flee it, even when healthy; besides, she had not yet been able to indulge in that "sweet insistent" yearning to travel slowly through a hot Spanish countryside. For the ostensibly simple purpose of tourism—the "only remedy," as she had called it in Barcelona—they left Madrid in a chauffeur-driven car to ride through the ancient towns of Castile toward, ultimately, Paris. Thus hope itself had become handmaiden to death, as Teresa looked toward future destinations, the better climate, the more inviting family. Thinking to defy death by outrunning the weather, she saw life-giving power in the landscape rolling by and carried on, as Mistral pictured her, "in her maturity, embittered by illness, with perfect decorum, knowing how to live stoically and without surliness." By the end of the year, Parra would know "how to suffer her end, swollen in some realities of the spirit that anyone with eyes to see could have seen."[26]

In the face-to-face grapple with death, a kind of objectivity must set in if one cares for dignity; only a distant cousin of indifference (no one can be totally indifferent about their own death), such an attitude requires a passion for discipline and for dissolution of the transient bonds of the ego. For every outward clue to Teresa given us by a letter, a comment, an action, there lies buried the bones of a moral battle that was not necessarily resolved, and like the tuberculosis bacillus, it could resurge at any moment. The notion that a barter was taking place, a deal going down between the disorderly Teresa and her God of Perfection, did not escape Mistral either: " 'To whom, and in what type of transaction?' I asked her this, knowing she would not answer, that this time an answer would not avail me, nor even this courtesy of hers. . . ." Her beauty had been replaced by "something of equal fascination and force."[27]

Teresa did not seem to talk about death anymore or, rather, not about her own personal death. Her reading had turned to exclusively religious subjects, such as *Life of Jesus*, by Bailly, and *La Reponse du Seigneur*, by Chateaubriand, recommended to her by Carias in his last letter of 1935. Lydia confirms that in this last part of her life, Teresa was studying the theme of life after death, metempsychosis, and the notion of karma: "She discussed this a lot. We all discussed it. She strongly believed in immortality and keeping the soul alive. She was an extraordinary woman above all nonsense. She never accepted Hell, Purgatory, or Paradise."[28]

As soon as the chauffeur-driven car began to ascend the Castilian mountains, Teresa received the full brunt of her punishment in the form of an asthmatic "hurricane." Miserable and contrite, she wrote back to Clemencia en route that "in the hours in which I feel well I am full of melancholy for having left you and Madrid so soon" (p. 918). They made it back to Paris by August only to find the whole medical profession on vacation. What bad luck for "anyone absurd enough to get sick!" (p. 922.) Poor Teresa spent the months of August and September hunting down the doctor who would save her and ended up with several opinions, none of which brought much comfort. One doctor, a celebrity, incited her rage by refusing to even try his miracle techniques on her, claiming that it would be "useless." Antother doctor ran her through the usual tests and declared her lung in perfect condition, except for one little surprise: the Spanish doctors had somehow missed cutting one adhesion. A third visit to the offices of the nephew of Louis Pasteur ended the confusion by eliciting from him, finally, a detailed explanation of the cause of her unrelenting asthma: of all things, the healing process of the lung itself was producing fibrous scar tissue that aggravated the breathing function, and the resultant stress on the lung had in turn reactivated the lesion. Her operation may have temporarily relieved the asthma, but until the lesion had completely healed, the destructive cycle would continue. In the end, even this doctor had to shrug his shoulders, not at the mystery of tuberculosis, but (Teresa seems to have abandoned altogether the word *tuberculosis* when referring to her health) at the mystery of asthma, and he could only reassure her that her condition was stable and that yes, she could be cured if she could find the climate perfectly suited to her. Teresa reported this last bit of advice not without a tinge of sarcasm. But when the doctor recommended Madrid as his first choice in seeking such a climate, Teresa sighed with relief; this was the location upon which, once again, she had set her sights.

Teresa and Lydia remained in Paris through October, the former staying as usual with Isabelita and the latter at a hotel with her sister Seida. On this, Teresa's last visit to Paris, site of her personal and professional disheartenment, she viewed the city with newly unprejudiced eyes. She took slow walks in the park, recognizing for the first time a harmonious quality in the city air, and feeling distant, as if she were traveling through by coach. Her asthma had slowly released its grip—she even felt so close to being a "normal" person that she had not one complaint—yet the beauties of autumn would soon pass, and Madrid had to offer better, infinitely better, weather in the coming months (p. 318): "Teresa went with me to the sanatorium of Fuenfria, in Cercedilla near Madrid, in November 1935. We came down from Fuenfria in Janaury 1936, to live in the area 'Cuatro Caminos' in Madrid. At the beginning of January, Teresa's condition became very bad. I notified her sister Maria, who came with her mother around the end of February or the beginning of March."[29]

According to Lydia, Teresa's bronchitis had returned full force at the beginning of this second visit to Fuenfria. A French doctor by the name of Soulage, whom Teresa called a charlatan, was suspected of having infected her healthy lung with a bronchial wash. There was no longer any attempt by her Spanish doctors to conceal from her the hopelessness of her case. The tuberculosis was "generalized" in her whole system. She suffered chronic pain now, which Lydia alleviated with regular spoonfuls of codeine and, during sharp attacks, with an injection of morphine or camphorated oil. Portions of Teresa's journal written at this time and released by the daughter of her sister Maria demonstrate her valiant attempts to control her mercurial moods and to discipline herself with the act of describing each passing moment: the movements of Lydia to and fro, the latest quote Teresa had read concerning the path to spiritual perfection (the renunciation of all possessions, including the self), and the necessity of loving the earthbound and the ordinary, no matter how imperfect. They were all the things, in short, that served the letter of that "rarest" technique she had learned from Emilia, which was to "forgive by understanding everything."

In Madrid, a constant stream of visitors would come around, hoping to cheer Teresa up or distract her, and sometimes Gabriela would stop by to be served bread and coffee:

> Teresa spoke of great successes, and of domestic trivialities from a special center or axis, such that the theme whether serious or trivial did not matter: her accent, posture and intonation had changed. They made me want to ask what experience she had had in those days and nights in the foreign sanatorium. Her responses were sometimes elusive, other times trusting; I count them among the priceless things I have come to know of the ineffable of this world, where nothing mattered . . . except that silent and certain industry of bartering Teresa of the world for Teresa under divine, mute management.[30]

The Madrid winter was bad, the worst in years; on the political front, preparations for civil war were underway. The saintly composure of Teresa gave way to vexation and boredom once again (*aburrimiento!*) as each new morning outdid the last in bringing pain, annoyances, and frustrations. She was obsessed with the word *disorder*, the very idea of disorder, and its perceived presence in the arrangement of furniture around her. The maid was incompetent, every meal was a greasy trial, and Lydia's friends, who, one can imagine, had been prompted to help distract and entertain Teresa, were judged superficial.

Teresa still spoke of the book she wanted "so badly" and the disciplined, goal-oriented reading that she felt was so necessary to a "slow and orderly" spirit such as hers. At times she felt that her mind was going. Maria and Mama arrived as February turned to March, and the three women most devoted to Teresa stifled their differences to await her end. The winter was late in giving way to spring. April came, the month Teresa had chosen for Mama Blanca to die, and she still held on to life. Then, on the twenty-second, she took a turn for the worse. It was a long, hard night for Lydia. A bit before 6:00 A.M., she decided to make herself some coffee and asked Teresa if she would not like to try a little. In a perfectly natural voice, Teresa replied, "I am going to eat a little earth." Lydia, too exhausted to respond, availed herself of the ensuing calm to lie down and rest, only to awaken at around 11:00 to an uneasy feeling. She thought she sensed the proximity of death. Running to Teresa's room, she discovered her flat on her back and staring at the ceiling, with her mother standing over her saying, "My daughter, prepare yourself to meet God."

"Don't say that, Señora; she'll hear you!" Lydia chastised her, and thinking that Teresa was in the grip of pain, Lydia went to find the needle to give her an injection.

The sun was radiant, the first rays of the year almost scorching their way through the window; when Lydia returned, Teresa was already gone.[31]

Notes

1. "La Vida Intima de Teresa de la Parra," *El Nacional*, Caracas, December 7, 1947.
2. Rafael Carias, *Teresa de la Parra, Cartas a Rafael Carias* (Alcala de Henares, Spain: Talleres Penitenciaros, 1957), p. 115.
3. Interview with Lydia Cabrera, June 3, 1977.
4. *Cartas a Rafael Carias*, p. 120.
5. Ibid., p. 117
6. Gabriela Mistral's 1936 letter to Zaldumbide, in *Obras Completas*, p. 935.
7. *Cartas a Rafael Carias*, p. 120.
8. Interview with Lydia Cabrera, August 28, 1981.
9. *Cartas a Rafael Carias*, p. 130.
10. "Tuberculosis: Medicine Conquers an Ancient Disease," by Lawrence K. Altman, M.D., the *New York Times*, Tuesday, March 30, 1982.
11. Dr. A. Rollier, *Quarante Ans D'Heliotherapie* (Lausanne: F. Rouge and Cie S A., Librairie de l'Universite, 1944).
12. "La Vida Intima de Teresa de la Parra," *El Nacional*, Caracas, December 7, 1947.
13. *Cartas a Rafael Carias*, p. 137.
14. Ibid., p. 148.
15. Ibid., p. 151.
16. *The Sleepwalkers* (New York; The Universal Library, Grosset and Dunlap, 1964), p. 575.
17. *Cartas a Rafael Carias*, p. 151.
18. *The Magic Mountain* (New York: The Modern Library, 1934), p. 533.
19. Gabriela Mistral, "Recado Sobre Teresa de la Parra," in *El Nacional*, Pagina Literaria No. 9, Caracas, December 7, 1947.
20. *Cartas a Rafael Carias*, pp. 158–95.
21. "Dona Marina," May 1935, pp. 28–30, and "La Nusta Isabel," September 1935, pp. 15 and 30, in *La Nueva Democracia*.
22. Interview with Lydia Cabrera, July 3, 1982.
23. Gabriela Mistral, "Land of Absence," translated by Relene Masslo Anderson, in *Gabriela Mistral: The Poet and Her Work*, (New York: New York University Press 1964), by Margot Arce de Vazquez pp. 109–12.
24. Interview with Lydia Cabrera, August 25, 1978.
25. Mistral, "Recado sobre Teresa de la Parra."
26. Ibid.
27. Ibid.
28. Interview with Lydia Cabrera, December 16, 1978.

29. Interview with Lydia Cabrera, June 3, 1977.
30. Gabriela Mistral, in *Gabriela Mistral: The Poet and Her Work* (New York: New York University Press, 1964).
31. As told by Lydia to the author, Coral Gable, Florida, August 28, 1981.

BETWEEN FLIGHT AND LONGING
The Journey of Teresa de la Parra

by Louis Antoine Lemaître

Like a brilliant tropical butterfly, Ana Teresa Parra emerged from the chrysalis of the reactionary aristocracy of Venezuela in the early years of the century. As beautiful as she was intelligent, she saw many opportunities before her. However, Parra was not one to choose the easiest path. Against the wishes of her family, she chose to become a writer.

Between Flight and Longing: The Journey of Teresa de la Parra is the story of this woman, who, from the time she began writing, under the name Teresa de la Parra, renounced all the easy comforts her position in society might have offered. The results were two books that, while currently unavailable in the English language, were quite influential in European and American literary circles in their day. *Ifigenia* and *Las Memorias de Mama Blanca* established Teresa de la Parra as the foremost woman of letters in Venezuela in the twenties, a writer who achieved wide readership through her courage in addressing the issues of women and their role in society.

An early death cut short Parra's career, and time has erased her memory to a great extent. In this volume, author Louis Antoine Lemaître has once again evoked the jewel-like brilliance of this talented and courageous writer, who in her novels dared to take on many of the problem of her own land, class, and sex.